STEPHEN SONDHEIM AND THE REINVENTION OF THE AMERICAN MUSICAL

Stephen Sondheim and the Reinvention of the American Musical

Robert L. McLaughlin

University Press of Mississippi   Jackson

www.upress.state.ms.us

The University Press of Mississippi is a member of the Association of
American University Presses.

First printing 2016
Library of Congress Cataloging-in-Publication Data

Names: McLaughlin, Robert L., 1957– author.
Title: Stephen Sondheim and the Reinvention of the American Musical / Robert
L. McLaughlin.
Description: Jackson : University Press of Mississippi, 2016. | Includes
bibliographical references and index.
Identifiers: LCCN 2016004207 (print) | LCCN 2016005505 (ebook) | ISBN
9781496808554 (cloth : alk. paper) | ISBN 9781496808561 (epub single) |
ISBN 9781496808578 (epub institutional) | ISBN 9781496808585 (pdf single)
| ISBN 9781496808592 (pdf institutional)
Subjects: LCSH: Sondheim, Stephen—Criticism and interpretation. |
Musicals—United States—History and criticism.
Classification: LCC ML410.S6872 M36 2016 (print) | LCC ML410.S6872 (ebook) |
DDC 782.1/4092—dc23
LC record available at http://lccn.loc.gov/2016004207

British Library Cataloging-in-Publication Data available

CONTENTS

PREFACE

"Generally they see things that aren't there. But I don't want to make
fun of them. It's nice to be taken seriously."
—Stephen Sondheim, on scholarly studies of his work.[1]

This book takes Stephen Sondheim seriously. More specifically, it attempts to put Sondheim's work in conversation with its cultural moment.
The two preceding sentences are more complicated than they may appear.

The first complication is the notion of seriousness as applied to the
musical theater. I begin from the premise that the musical theater can be
studied with the same academic methods and intellectual rigor that are
routinely applied to other art forms—literature, drama, film, opera—and
other popular-culture forms—TV, music videos, computer games. Sadly,
there is still resistance in the academic world to the thought that the musical theater is a worthy subject for scholarly study. I hope this book will
collaborate with other recent work[2] to demonstrate that the musical theater can not only sustain the weight of scholarly scrutiny but also reward
that scrutiny.

This is not to say that this book is dry—at least I hope it isn't. This
project has been a labor of love in the sense that in it I bring together two
different kinds of (almost) lifelong loves. The main focus of my academic
career has been postmodern literature and culture, especially postmodern fiction, especially the work of Thomas Pynchon. This literature has
fed my enthusiasm for the experimental and new, for the kind of literature
that breaks the rules so as to suggest other ways of seeing and being in the
world beyond the ones that have been officially defined for us. My other
love, for the musical theater, began long before I imagined myself as an
academic, when the national tour of *1776* came to Rochester, New York.
I had seen stage musicals before—the one that stands out is *Oliver!*—and
enjoyed them, but what I had enjoyed was the story, the book; when the

characters started singing, I waited impatiently for the dialogue to start again. But *1776* was different, or I was different: I not only enjoyed the songs but also understood how they were helping tell the story, define the characters, and develop the themes; I was surprised and delighted by the way this musical took figures I knew only from statues and textbooks and turned them into real people. I had to have the cast recording, and I soon began collecting the cast recordings of other shows—classics like the Rodgers and Hammerstein canon, *My Fair Lady, Fiddler on the Roof, West Side Story*—and reading scripts and histories of the musical theater. (I had David Ewen's *New Complete Book of the American Musical Theater* perpetually checked out of the Avon Free Library.) One day I saw the cast recording of *Company* in the library: I hadn't heard of the show, but I recognized the name Stephen Sondheim from the album of *West Side Story,* so I took it home. The opening number, with its overlapping voices calling out to Bobby, was like nothing I'd heard before. Soon after, I saw the double album *Sondheim: A Musical Tribute* (the Scrabble album) in the record bin at Woolworth's, bought it, and was completely and forever hooked. I chose a college in New York City not least so that I could finally see Broadway shows, and I joined my university's theater club so that I could act and sing myself. Seventeen years after my last college performance, after earning my graduate degrees, after moving to central Illinois, after pretty much ensuring my tenure, I auditioned for a local community theater's production of *A Little Night Music* simply because I'd never had the chance to be in a Sondheim musical. I've been in several more of his musicals since. My point here is that while my academic interests have focused on postmodern literature, my interest in and love for the musical theater and for Stephen Sondheim's words and music have never been far in the background. In fact, over the years I've thought more and more about the connections between the two—postmodern literature and Sondheim's work. I've written a couple of articles and conference presentations on Sondheim, but this book is my most serious attempt to bring the two together, to use postmodernism as a frame through which to look at the musical theater and the plays of Sondheim and his collaborators and to see what new ways of understanding them this approach can offer.

The second complication from my opening sentences has already reared its head in the previous two paragraphs: the problem of "Sondheim's work." The musical theater is necessarily a collaborative enterprise. When librettists, lyricists, composers, directors, choreographers, designers, and actors collaborate on a musical, their individual contributions can be impossible to parse out from the final product, the show on the stage. There are no strict boundaries between a musical's areas of responsibilities. Stephen Sondheim has been generously insistent in crediting his collaborators, bristling, for example, in letters to the *New York Times* when an article refers to a "Sondheim musical" without mentioning the librettist. When he received a Lifetime Achievement Award from the Tony Awards in 2008, his acceptance speech began,

> Thank you all, but this award has to be shared with Julius Epstein, Arthur Laurents, Burt Shevelove, Larry Gelbart, George Furth, Jim Goldman, John Weidman, Hugh Wheeler and James Lapine. These are the men who created the characters that sang the songs, the situations that gave rise to the songs and the criticism that improved the songs. They were my collaborators. They are called playwrights. They invent. They make whole cloth out of nothing. They make a hat where there never was a hat. And they don't just write musicals. I would also share this Award with Hal Prince, but he has one already.[3]

This book, for reasons explained in the following, focuses on the musicals of Stephen Sondheim, but it recognizes that these musicals are not solely the product of Sondheim's imagination, thought, and talent. In concentrating on Sondheim's oeuvre, I am not belittling the contributions of his collaborators, theater giants in their own right. Nor am I going to try to separate Sondheim's music and lyrics from the rest of the play (no brilliant-score-troubled-book readings). I will consider each play as a whole, and there will be times when my attention will be focused on elements of a play that might not seem to be, strictly speaking, Sondheim's contribution. Finally, although I strive to give proper credit to each play's creators, there are times when, for efficiency's sake, I refer to "Sondheim's plays" or "Sondheim's musicals." Please accept that I do this with the understanding that these plays are not Sondheim's alone. After all, no one is alone.

The third complication concerns what it means to put Sondheim's work (see? I've done it again) in conversation with its cultural moment.

By this, I mean that I want to understand the musicals of Sondheim and his collaborators in light of the larger aesthetic and cultural movements in which they were created. To do this, I place this work in two contexts. The first is the exhaustion of the Rodgers and Hammerstein musical in the late 1960s. Because of the success of *Oklahoma!, Carousel, South Pacific,* and *The King and I,* the Rodgers and Hammerstein musical became, in its aesthetic and form, the model for musical plays, and that model dominated Broadway for more than twenty years. As the form became used up, however, composers, writers, and directors looked for new directions for the musical, leading to a period of experimentation in the late 1960s and 1970s. The second context is the postmodernism that pervaded all the arts in the 1960s and 1970s. My first chapter argues that the American musical theater in many ways has always made use of what we now call postmodern characteristics, at least until the Rodgers and Hammerstein–style show introduced an aesthetic of realism to the musical. By the late 1960s, the musical theater returned to these postmodern characteristics with a purpose, using experimentation in form and performance to develop ideas about identity construction, epistemology, history, and representation. These two overlapping contexts created a cultural moment in which Sondheim, his collaborators, and others were able to reinvent the musical theater.

Sondheim's work, across the decades and with a variety of collaborators, stands out in this double context and thus is the focus for this study. His career forms a bridge between the musical theater of his mentor Oscar Hammerstein II and the postmodern musical theater of the 1970s. Moreover, his work of the 1990s and 2000s begins to reflect the possible exhaustion of postmodernism and the desire to return to a real beyond language. Sondheim's work also stands out for its quality: its fearless formal experimentation, its depth of thought, its attention to craft. While Sondheim and his collaborators are not the only musical-theater artists who engaged postmodern thought and experimented in form and style, their work, especially in retrospect, clearly set the intellectual and aesthetic standard for the time and for subsequent generations of writers and composers.

In focusing on Sondheim's work, this book is following a number of other important studies. Craig Zadan's *Sondheim & Co.*, Meryle Secrest's *Stephen Sondheim: A Life,* and Stephen Citron's *Sondheim and Lloyd Webber* put Sondheim's musicals in a mostly biographical or career-arc context, as do Sondheim's own lyric collections, *Finishing the Hat* and *Look, I Made a Hat.* Stephen Banfield's *Sondheim's Broadway Musicals,* Steve Swayne's *How Sondheim Found His Sound,* and the interviews contained in Mark Eden Horowitz's *Sondheim on Music* offer musicological analyses. (In fact, this book is a response to Banfield's call for a variety of scholarly approaches to Sondheim's musicals, including those based in postmodern and poststructural theory.) Joanne Gordon's *Art Isn't Easy,* her essay collection *Stephen Sondheim: A Casebook,* Sandor Goodhart's collection *Reading Stephen Sondheim,* Gina Masucci MacKenzie's *The Theatre of the Real,* and Robert Gordon's collection *The Oxford Handbook of Sondheim Studies* bring a range of theoretical lenses to bear in performing close readings of the musicals. Although I make some use of the biography and music theory, my methodological approach in this book is primarily literary criticism, and so my work is closest to this last group.

Two style notes. First, Mr. Sondheim has requested that all quotations of his lyrics be taken from his two volumes of collected lyrics, *Finishing the Hat* and *Look, I Made a Hat.* After each lyric quotation, I will indicate volume and page number parenthetically, indicating the former volume with *F* and the latter volume with *L.* Quotations from the musicals' dialogue and stage direction will be from the published editions (with a couple of exceptions) as indicated in the notes. Second, because Mr. Sondheim makes frequent use of ellipses in his lyrics, I will indicate my own use of ellipses by putting them inside brackets.

A few paragraphs ago, in talking about the musical theater as a collaboration, I noted that no one is alone. That's also true for writing a book about the musical theater. I've received help and support of all kinds from a range of people, some longtime friends, some strangers, but each contributed something to the completion of this book.

First, I have to thank Stephen Sondheim, pragmatically for permission to quote his lyrics, but, more important, for creating a body of work that has so entertained, challenged, puzzled, instructed, and delighted me, and has gotten so far under my skin and so deep into my mind that I developed the need to write this book.

I want also to thank the many people who have provided support during the writing, revising, and production processes. As my teacher, Larry Stempel provided a model for bringing scholarly brilliance to the subject of the musical theater; as my friend and still my teacher, he was generous enough to read some early chapters and provide sage advice as the manuscript headed toward publication. Connie Tumminelli and Chad Kirvan also read chapters, offered valuable advice, and patiently answered my questions. Others who answered questions, gave feedback, and made things happen that I couldn't do on my own include: Elias Blumm, Robert Gordon, Jim Kalmbach, Joseph Mendola, Shirley Mendola, Roberta Parry, Rick Pender, Paul Salsini, Phillip Sprayberry, Susan Stroman, and the staff at the New York Public Library for the Performing Arts. Leila Salisbury, my editor at the University Press of Mississippi, has been an ideal guide and a good friend.

Earlier in this preface, I talk about scholarly study of the musical theater not being respected in academia. While this is generally true, I am fortunate that it is *not* true of my colleagues at Illinois State University, who have been nothing but supportive of this project. I need especially to thank Christopher Breu, Christopher De Santis, Ron Fortune, Charles Harris, Victoria Harris, Tim Hunt, Joan Mullin, Gary Olson, Gregory Simpson, Jim Skibo, and Roberta Seelinger Trites and her family. I also thank the students in my musical-theater courses, especially Sarah Dzak, Colleen Rice, and Travis Stern.

Many of my ideas about Sondheim and his musicals gestated in conversations and arguments with my friends in Fordham University's theater organization, the Mimes and Mummers. These friendships have continued over the years, as have the conversations. I especially thank Dominic Adinolfi, Jeff Brone, Joe Cronin, Tod Engle, Sarah Engle, Frank Gadler, Barbara Halas, Michael Healey, Tim Kelley, Steve Love, Jose Martinez, Peter Paulino, Joe Pirolli, Gabrielle Sorapure, and Valerie Smaldone, who first suggested that I write a book on the musical theater.

Having the chance to perform in Sondheim's musicals not only gave me greater appreciation for them but also led me to friendships with directors, singers, and actors who enhanced my understanding of the plays, the songs, and the characters. I owe special thanks to Brian Artman, Cris Embree, Sally Hoffmann, Angela Jackson, Sherise Kirvan, Dave Lemmon, John Lieder, Bob Manasco, Barb Mason, Dave Montague, Bruce Parrish, Kathy Parrish, Ed Peck, Mike Reams, Madeline Reed, Dave Schick, Jeremy Stiller, Tricia Stiller, Michael Wallace, and Marcia Weiss.

My family has been patiently and supportively hearing about this project for some time. Thank you Sue King, Cathy McIntyre, Betsy McLaughlin, Tom McLaughlin, Marcia Parry, and Tom Parry. My cat Peaches was a good companion while I wrote this book; I wish he were here to see the finished product. Luckily, his successor, Claudia, is well able to celebrate for two.

Finally, the first conversation I ever had with Sally Parry was about Stephen Sondheim. She had seen the original production of *Follies* (which she has never let me forget), and I asked her some questions about it. We have had many other conversations about Sondheim since then, and I hope we will have many more. Sally is the best part of everything I do. I dedicate this book, with love, to her.

STEPHEN SONDHEIM AND THE REINVENTION
OF THE AMERICAN MUSICAL

One

Instructions
to the Audience

Near the end of Stephen Sondheim and James Goldman's 1971 musical *Follies,* what has been a strange and startling show becomes even stranger and more startling. The four middle-aged principals, while attending a reunion of the casts of a Ziegfeld-style series of Broadway extravaganzas, have been forced to confront their pasts and their present—their discarded dreams, their bad but irreversible decisions, their lost innocence—and have reached a point of crisis. Dramatic structure and even time break down as they confront, at first, each other, and then, surreally, their younger selves, seeking someone to blame for their failed lives. As literal and ontological violence threatens to tear the characters in two, as shouted, overlapping dialogue supplants communication, as the play seems to be about to fall apart before our eyes, the orchestra reprises the crashing chords from the opening sequence, drop after drop hurtles down, transforming a dilapidated theater into a fairyland, and statuesque showgirls and chorus girls and boys enter in costumes that might come from a Victorian Valentine's Day card. Completely disregarding the principals' quarreling, they incongruously launch into a song reminiscent of a 1920s production number, all about the joys of love. We, and the characters, are in Loveland. In the sequence that follows, the past and present embodiments of the principals sing and dance pastiched, high-powered musical-comedy numbers. Individually, each number explores the crisis that threatens the character's identity. Taken together, the songs show the folly of the characters' lives, of their attempts to find meaning in them, and of the songs themselves as vehicles for self-expression. The Broadway theater has rarely seen such exhilarating numbers employed for such a devastating effect.

This transition into Loveland marks a new kind of musical, one that can adopt the musical theater's past, but turn it inside out, exposing its naive innocence, mocking its messages of happily ever after, and using its forms to demonstrate the problems of its contents. In this moment the Rodgers and Hammerstein–style musical and the musical comedy that preceded it collide with the postmodern musical. *Follies* and Sondheim's other musicals of the 1970s changed the rules for the musical theater, redefining what a musical could be and ushering it into the postmodern age.

This book studies the plays of Stephen Sondheim and his collaborators in two contexts. The first is the aesthetic of the Broadway musical as it developed from the musical comedy of the 1920s and 1930s through the Rodgers and Hammerstein era of the 1940s, 1950s, and 1960s to the postmodern musical of the 1970s, 1980s, and 1990s, of which Sondheim's work offers the most compelling examples. The second is the context of postmodernism as a cultural movement that pervaded all the arts in the 1960s, 1970s, and 1980s. Before engaging Sondheim's work specifically, I need to discuss these two contexts, and I begin with what I mean by *postmodern,* a slippery term about which there is no consensus.

In the broadest sense, postmodernism is marked by an awareness—perhaps a hyperawareness—of the ways in which language mediates between us and our experience of the world. To put it more bluntly, we have no experience of the world that is not mediated by language, discourse, or narrative.[1] If we accept this idea, several corollaries relevant to our discussion of the musical theater follow. One concerns self-referentiality, perhaps the most seminal characteristic of postmodern art. Self-referentiality is a direct challenge to the premise of realism, the suspension of disbelief that allows us, while watching a play, to forget that we are in a theater, that the people onstage are actors, and to imagine that we are actually watching scenes from the characters' lives. Put differently, realism as a style and a practice seeks to render invisible the process of representation by which the world is turned into art. By invoking the metaphor of a mirror held up to nature, realism inserts an equal sign between the world and art. Postmodernism, owing to its emphasis on the language-mediated nature of experience, complicates this equation in many ways. It seeks to make the process of representation, not invisible, but translucent so that the viewer is conscious of the art as art and of the difficulty of capturing through representation any experience of the world. This self-reference, this reminder that what the viewer is looking at is not the world but a representation of the world, explodes the suspension of disbelief, demolishes the fourth wall, and asks the viewer to engage the art on levels other than that of empathizing with the characters.[2] This is not to say that postmodern art is nonrepresentational (though it can be). Rather, postmodernism is about art pointing to itself pointing to the world, *world* understood here, not as an objectively knowable essence, but as a construction of language, discourse, and narrative.[3] Examples from the past half-century are legion: Andy Warhol's portrait of a Campbell's tomato soup can, which calls into question the difference between art and advertising; a host of fiction by Jorge Luis Borges, Alain Robbe-Grillet, Thomas Pynchon, Robert Coover, and many others, which makes problematic the narrative conventions by which readers assume novels ought to operate; the proto-postmodern Pirandellian and Brechtian plays in which the characters are aware of themselves as characters in a play, and the plays by Beckett, Pinter, Albee, Stoppard, and others that subvert the conventions of plot and characterization; even the series of *Scream* films, in which the characters are aware of and mock the conventions of slasher films at the same time they are caught within them.

A second, connected corollary is intertextuality. Romanticism has bequeathed us an image of the artist as lonely genius, transforming unique experiences of the world into personally rendered yet universally meaningful art. This is the image of artist as god, creating the world of art ex nihilo. However, postmodernism challenges the idea of anyone's unique experience of the world: since we can know them only through the shared language of our culture, our experiences are more communal than unique. Similarly, the language, discourses, narratives, and conventions artists use to create their art are inherited, not conjured out of nothing. Any expression of the artist's experience of the world in art is—far from the romantic model—automatically articulated through several layers of discourse and so is expressed in and seen, read, or heard through the noise of competing ongoing cultural conversations. As Roland Barthes suggests in his landmark essay "The Death of the Author," authors do not speak texts so much as texts speak through authors.[4] Intertextuality, then, is the concept that when we speak, write, express ourselves in the broadest sense, we do so over, through, and amid the already spoken, the already written, the already expressed.

A third corollary concerns identity and performance. Postmodernism challenges the concept of the autonomous individual. Instead, identity is constructed through the layers of discourses available in our culture to think and talk about ourselves. That is, our culture offers discourses—complete with vocabulary, implied narratives, and assumptions about behavior, appearance, and being—on the various factors that combine to give us a sense of identity, such factors as gender, sexuality, class, race, ethnicity, religion, profession, and on and on. In other words, by articulating membership in any of these factors, we are immersed in the ideologically charged discourses connected with them, ideologically charged because, as we will see in chapter 2, different claims to identity (I am white/I am black, I am a man/I am a woman) position one differently amid the power relations of one's society.[5] Part of this immersion in discourse takes the form of learning how to perform one's identity. As we learn our culture's discourses concerning, for example, gender, we simultaneously learn the expectations for gendered behavior, appearance, and attitudes, and so we learn to perform our gendered role, to perform being a man or being a woman. These performances are generally unconscious; our culture's various discourses so inculcate these constructions of identity into us that we come to think of them as natural, as the way things are, rather than as a social construction, something we might have a choice about.[6] These performances, however, can become self-conscious, performative. When one performs with such awareness, the performer takes an aspect of identity construction that is usually unconscious and invisible and brings it into the foreground for examination. Performativity seeks to make its spectators aware of what they are seeing as performance and of the performances in their own sense of self.[7]

So what does all this have to do with the musical theater? I contend that the aesthetic of the musical theater, the set of artistic principles by which it operates, has had much in common with postmodernism and that looking at the musical theater through the lens of postmodern theory can help us understand the musical, especially the musical of the past forty years, in a new way. Traditionally, the musical theater combines in various proportions the elements of song, dance, comedy, and spectacle. What it does not always have is narrative. The Broadway musical counts among its influences such nonnarrative forms as the revue, the minstrel show, burlesque, and vaudeville. Many of the most successful Broadway musicals in the early years of the twentieth century were revues or blown-up versions of revues, such as the *Ziegfeld Follies* or *George White's Scandals*. (Revue-style shows can still be popular on Broadway: note such narrative-less musicals as *Ain't Misbehavin'* [1978], *Smokey Joe's Café* [1995], *Fosse* [1999], and even *Sondheim on Sondheim* [2010], a revue surveying Sondheim's career and combining live performances with video commentary by Sondheim himself.) Revues large or small made use of the above elements, but they did not have a narrative, a dramatic arc to hold the piece together.

What we think of as the Broadway musical comedy began to form when aspects of the revue, especially popular-based Tin Pan Alley–style music and ragtime- and jazz-inspired dance, combined with the narrative elements of European-style operetta.[8] Something of a plot and something approaching continuing characters would be offered, if not as a dramatic arc, then as a sort of narrative clothesline, on which the songs, dances, and comic routines could be hung. Musical-theater historian Larry Stempel defines the musical comedy as "a revue in which the 'right running order' is governed by a plot." Raymond Knapp describes it as "a show in which the various ingredients matter—songs, dances, comedy, star turns—but somehow not the totality." Musicologist Joseph Swain writes, "The musical comedy that flourished on Broadway in the early decades of the century was a casual and happenstance affair. Constructed as it was from traditions of vaudeville and burlesque combined with some of the procedures of European operetta, a musical comedy was little more than a succession of songs, comedy routines, and dance numbers that as often as not had nothing to do with the progression of a story. [. . .] And even when there was a reasonable plot, the collaborators often took no notice of it."[9] Thus we need to note an important paradox. At the same time that the narrative provides a structure for the show, an excuse for the songs, dances, and comedy, it is also completely malleable, twisting, turning, pausing, or being altogether suspended so that songs, dances, or comedy can take center stage. As longtime reviewer Walter Kerr noted, "The essential purpose of the musical-comedy book was to be interrupted. It's very quality lay in its interruptability. It wasn't supposed to *do* things, it was supposed to get out of the way of other things."[10] Aesthetically, narrative is both central and irrelevant.

The paradox of this aesthetic supports a nondramatic kind of song. Since the songs are not usually expected to further the plot (the plot, rather, readjusts itself to accommodate the songs) or explore character (character is put aside to make way for the performer performing), they engage and entertain the audience in other ways. One way is through the beauty of the music or the emotion of the lyric's sentiment. Another is through a series of punch lines organized around a theme. Yet another is what Sondheim calls "the sheer pleasure of verbal playfulness."[11] Because the musical numbers strove to entertain with only a tenuous relationship to the narrative, songwriters hoped to create songs that would have a life beyond the show they were written for; that is, they wanted hits.

If we think of the aesthetic I have described and how it is manifested in the musical comedies of the twenties and thirties in terms of the postmodern concepts we discussed earlier, we can see that these concepts are present in a seminal if simple way. Musical comedy is self-referential. There is no attempt to build a fourth wall between audience and play. Theater historian Scott Miller notes that the fourth wall was dismantled as early as the George M. Cohan musicals of the early twentieth century: "In a Cohan show, everybody involved admitted plainly and openly that they were making the very artificial art form of musical comedy. The once cherished 'suspension of disbelief' was irrelevant."[12] Further, the lack of seriousness, the very disregard with which the play addresses its own plot, encourages the audience likewise to dismiss any potential connections between the narrative and anything outside of the theater.

Musical comedy is intertextual. Music never functions in a vacuum; rather, listeners recognize elements of the music they hear and connect it to other music they have heard. The style of music, the type of music, and the function of the song within the show all recall in the audience previous experiences of that music and in a way enter into conversation with it.[13] Musical-comedy conventions are themselves intertextual in that an audience familiar enough with musicals will recognize and develop expectations based on the way the conventions are usually employed—for example, the girls' chorus that almost always opened the show and the ballad in front of the curtain that signaled a change of scenery. In a 1970 interview, Richard Rodgers suggested the intertextual nature of the musical comedy and connected it to the conventions audiences had come to expect:

> You had an opening chorus, then sometimes called an icebreaker. This was obligatory. You had to have a fast 2/4 opening number [. . .] then you had a number between the soubrette, in those days she was called the second girl, and the young comedian called the funny boy, not the top banana, then you had your first sentimental song, a romantic ballad between the ingénue and the leading man. It was a 1-2-3-4 order and you didn't break that sequence because if it had been successful once before it was assumed it would be again. [. . .] Shows were put on along an iron-bound formula.[14]

Or as musical-theater historian Ethan Mordden puts it, "Musical plays generally differ from one another; it's musical comedy that has to learn new ways of doing the same things again and again."[15]

Musical comedy is performative. One might argue that theater in general always involves creators, actors, and audiences self-consciously aware of performance. Theater historian Paul Woodruff states, "Theater is the art by which human beings make or find human action worth watching."[16] The mutually dependent elements of performance and spectating are fundamental to anything we call theater. In the musical comedy the self-consciousness of performance and spectating goes much further. Because there is no pretense of a fourth wall between actors and audience, because character functions primarily as a name that tenuously links actor to narrative, and because the success of the show's entertainment depends on the ability of the performers to put the songs, dances, and comedy over, musical-comedy actors did not lose themselves in their characters nor did audiences lose sight of the performers who were putting over the performances. As musical-theater historian Bruce Kirle puts it, "In the 1920s,

1930s, and 1940s, musical theatre actors did not inhabit their roles; they performed them."[17] Whatever the plot, whatever the characters, the audience's attention was most likely focused on the star's performance.[18]

The aesthetic of the musical comedy I have described might seem to presume that musical comedies were all exclusively interested in entertaining and showcasing the great performers doing terrific songs, dances, and comedy, all hung on a disposable plot. We might leap to the conclusion that musical comedies did not have a serious idea in their heads, and in the majority of the cases we would be right. This legacy of mindlessness still haunts the musical theater. When reviewers or audiences cannot imagine that a *musical* might be about something serious, about murderous barbers or presidential assassins, they are drawing on this musical-comedy tradition and aesthetic.

There were, however, even in the 1920s, 1930s, and early 1940s, exceptions, musicals that aspired to serious thought in a nonserious form. Often, when playwrights, lyricists, and composers sought to address serious ideas in the musical form, they turned to satire. One thinks of *Of Thee I Sing* (1931) and its sequel *Let 'Em Eat Cake* (1933), *Hurray for What!* (1937), and *The Cradle Will Rock* (1937), all of which were able to pair the exaggeration of satire to the nonrealistic aspects of the musical form in order to offer social criticism. More interestingly, John O'Hara, Richard Rodgers, and Lorenz Hart's *Pal Joey* (1940) set its character study of a self-absorbed gigolo in the sordid world of cheap nightclub entertainment. This not only allowed the songwriters to insert non-plot-related, musical-comedy-style nightclub numbers, but also provided a dramatic justification for why the characters sing and dance outside of the nightclub scenes.[19] Moss Hart, Kurt Weill, and Ira Gershwin's *Lady in the Dark* (1941) separated its study of a magazine editor struggling with issues of identity, independence, and femininity into two distinct styles: her life awake, which was presented in the form of a realistic play; and her dream life, which was presented as musical comedy. The musical-theater masterpiece of the 1930s, George Gershwin and DuBose Heyward's *Porgy and Bess* (1935), purposely eschewed the musical-comedy aesthetic to embrace the opera form (though there are some musical-comedy elements in it). The musical-theater masterpiece of the 1920s, Jerome Kern and Oscar Hammerstein's *Show Boat* (1927), is, of any play in the era of the musical comedy, the most dissatisfied with the reigning aesthetic. Yes, like the later *Pal Joey*, it is set in entertainment venues, where musical-comedy-style numbers can be inserted, two of them, "Bill" and "After the Ball," that were written years before the rest of the score, and where dances and comedy routines can occur with little concern for plot. Yes, Kern's score is consciously intertextual, striving through echo, allusion, and quotation to offer something of a history of American music. Yes, producer Florenz Ziegfeld mounted the kind of extravaganza audiences associated with his name. Yet there is nevertheless something different going on here, a desire to explore serious ideas in a serious manner, to present psychologically real characters in real situations, to use music and lyrics, not to sever the connection between character and performer, but to open up the characters and make them richer and deeper. In some of his subsequent shows, Hammerstein continued to experiment with what would become a new aesthetic for the musical theater, an aesthetic based in realism, but he would not perfect it until sixteen years later when he collaborated with Richard Rodgers on *Oklahoma!*, the play that changed everything.

What most startled theatergoers when *Oklahoma!* opened at the St. James Theatre on 31 March 1943 was the way it defied musical-comedy conventions, the "iron-bound formula" Rodgers spoke of.[20] *Oklahoma!* and the remarkable series of musicals with which Rodgers and Hammerstein followed it up, *Carousel* (1945), *South Pacific* (1949), and *The King and I* (1951) (*Allegro* [1947], something of a special case, is discussed in chapter 3), perfected what came to be known as the *integrated musical*, in which there must be a dramatic, narrative- or character-driven reason to motivate every element of the play. In the integrated musical, characters sing when song becomes the most effective way to tell the story. Similarly, dance contributes to the telling of the story or the development of character. Humor comes from the characters and the situation, not from gags. Performers enter into the characters they are playing and stay there until the curtain call. In the musical-comedy era, a star was essentially irreplaceable.[21] When Rodgers and Hammerstein and the producers of *Oklahoma!* auditioned John Raitt as a replacement for Alfred Drake's Curly, the concern was whether he could perform the role as written and, Raitt used to joke, whether he could fit into Drake's costumes.

The practice of the integrated musical, as established by the success of the Rodgers and Hammerstein plays and the influence they had on other writers, implies three theoretical premises, which, taken together, make up the Rodgers and Hammerstein aesthetic. First, this aesthetic demands a new attitude toward narrative. Where in the musical comedy narrative was central but malleable and, in the end, irrelevant, in the Rodgers and Hammerstein musical play narrative is the organizing principle that structures the whole. When writers and composers ask if a scene, a song, or a dance works, the answer is to look at whether it helps to tell the story—advance the plot, reveal character, explore a theme. Moreover, every element of the show—scenic design, costumes, lighting—should contribute to the project of getting the story across to the audience.[22] This organizing principle became the standard by which reviewers and audiences judged the success or failure of a musical play.

A second theoretical premise centers on the songs in a musical play. Where before songs were built around beautiful melodies and sentiments, a series of punch lines, or wordplay, in the Rodgers and Hammerstein aesthetic songs function dramatically. We can understand this function in three ways. First, songs are introduced at particular dramatic moments for particular dramatic purposes, and they are written for specific characters to sing at these moments. Hammerstein put it this way: "There are few things in life of which I am certain, but I am sure of this one thing, that the song is the servant of the play, that it is wrong to write first what you think is an attractive song and then try to wedge it into a story."[23]

Second, songs help propel the story. Something must happen during the song; the dramatic situation at the end must be different from what it was at the beginning. Hammerstein was a master of the dramatic lyric. In an interview Stephen Sondheim explains,

> I was essentially trained by Oscar Hammerstein to think of songs as one-act plays, to move a song from point A to point B dramatically. I think of songs in sonata form—statement, development and recapitulation—but in Oscar's terms it was first act, second act and third act. The character singing goes through a development process and comes out with a conclusion emotionally different from where he began, so the song has a sense of moving the story forward even though

it may not move the plot forward. Oscar's attempt was never to have
a song that merely stated one idea over and over again, which had
been the practice of people like Cole Porter and Rodgers and Hart.[24]

This technique of making songs dramatic connects to the larger structural
purposes of songs in a musical play. Legendary music director Lehman
Engel argues that, structurally, songs function both as exclamation points
and index fingers, exclamation points in that they serve as a climax to a
scene's dramatic situation, index fingers in that they point the way to the
next dramatic situation.[25]

A third way songs function dramatically is in the music itself. Burton
Lane, whose career as a composer spanned the musical-comedy and Rodgers and Hammerstein eras, noted, "When books started to have more
meaning and take on more weight, the scores became better because the
books demanded better music."[26] At their best, songs in musical plays
make use of the elements of music—tension and resolution, repetition
and variation—to help define and develop the drama. This goes beyond
the music setting the mood to the music working with or against the lyrics
to accomplish the song's dramatic purpose.

The final theoretical premise implied in the Rodgers and Hammerstein
aesthetic is a broad one, containing everything else we have discussed, and
the one that marks the most significant break from the musical-comedy
aesthetic that preceded it. Because the Rodgers and Hammerstein aesthetic insists that every element of the play be justified in terms of the narrative, that songs be appropriate for the characters and dramatic moment
in which they are introduced, that there be, in fact, a certain naturalness
and inevitability to the introduction of song and dance into the dialogue,
the integrated musical brings something that had never been an element
of musical comedy: realism. Rodgers and Hammerstein, in effect, built a
fourth wall between the actors and the audience.[27] At its most perfect, a
Rodgers and Hammerstein–style musical play makes music and dance
arise from the dialogue so appropriately that the audience is not subject
to the self-referential nudge they are while watching musical comedies
as performer separates from character. At its most perfect, the Rodgers
and Hammerstein–style musical play absorbs the audience into the reality of its characters and their dramatic situation, effecting a suspension

of disbelief that even the introduction of song and dance cannot dispel. This does not mean that the aspects of the musical-comedy aesthetic we discussed earlier, such as intertextuality and performativity, disappear, but that, because of the suspension of disbelief, the audience recognizes them but holds them apart in their minds while they lose themselves in the artificial reality of the play.[28] Larry Stempel writes that "the songs in *Oklahoma!* were performed representationally: They intensified thought or speech without really being songs at all. Only audiences eavesdropping on the characters through the proverbial fourth wall experienced the songs as the musical numbers they actually were."[29] The results, then, of the Rodgers and Hammerstein revolution were a musical theater that took itself more seriously as art, that was more capable of addressing serious themes in a serious manner, and that repressed the proto-postmodern characteristics that had been central to its art for most of the century.

Although other kinds of musicals did not disappear (the 1948–49 season alone saw *My Romance,* a new operetta by Sigmund Romberg, *As the Girls Go By,* an old-fashioned musical comedy with a Jimmy McHugh score, and Alan Jay Lerner and Kurt Weill's proto-postmodern *Love Life*[30]), the Rodgers and Hammerstein aesthetic dominated the American musical theater for more than twenty years, and its influences continue to this day. The Rodgers and Hammerstein musicals of the 1940s were so successful that other songwriters, librettists, directors, and choreographers followed their example, some of them simply imitating the form and others embracing and advancing the aesthetic. Some of the great songwriters of the musical-comedy era ended up doing their best work in the new form, what Irving Berlin dismissively called the "situation show"[31]: Berlin, with librettists Herbert and Dorothy Fields, in *Annie Get Your Gun* (1947, produced by Rodgers and Hammerstein); Cole Porter, with Samuel and Bella Spewack, in *Kiss Me, Kate* (1948); Burton Lane and E. Y. Harburg, with Fred Saidy, in *Finian's Rainbow* (1947). More important, a new generation of musical-theater artists hazarded the high bar set by Rodgers and Hammerstein's accomplishments, embraced the potential of the new aesthetic, and created great work. The aesthetic Rodgers and Hammerstein created became so dominant, in fact, that when the masters wrote *Me and Juliet* (1953), their love letter to the theater and old-fashioned musical comedy, reviewers and audiences were disappointed. Having set the standard for the new, they were not able to go back to the old.

Of course, the new does not stay new forever. While many great musical plays were created in the Rodgers and Hammerstein aesthetic, some elements of the integrated musical's form—not its aesthetic—became overused, formulaic, and tired. (The frequency with which dream ballets appeared in new musicals in the 1950s and early 1960s—in everything from *The Pajama Game* [1954] to *Take Me Along* [1959] to *Bye Bye Birdie* [1960]—suggests that producers must have thought they were contractually required.[32]) In short, as usually happens, a form that at its outset defied conventions and opened up possibilities for the new becomes, with time, conventional itself, thus limiting the possibilities for what can be done.

As early as the mid-1950s but more obviously in the 1960s and early 1970s, there were signs that the Rodgers and Hammerstein–style musical was nearing exhaustion. One sign was nostalgia for the old days of musical comedy. This nostalgia began with popular parodies of musicals of the 1920s and 1930s: *The Boy Friend* (1954, revived 1970) and *Little Mary Sunshine* (1959). Nostalgia for the pre-*Oklahoma!* musical comedy took a more direct approach in *George M!* (1968), part biography of George M. Cohan's life, but mostly a celebration of his greatest songs. Even more directly nostalgic were several successful—and usually heavily revised—revivals of pre-*Oklahoma!* shows: *No, No, Nanette* (1971), *Irene* (1973), *Very Good Eddie* (1975), and *Whoopee!* (1979).

More important, however, than this looking backward were the forward-looking musicals that began experimenting with ways to move in directions different from the Rodgers and Hammerstein musical and that, in doing so, began to rediscover and reinvent postmodern aspects of the musical-comedy aesthetic. *Man of La Mancha* (1965) split its story in two: the frame story of Cervantes being thrown in prison by the Inquisition is presented realistically; but the inner story, in which Cervantes puts on a play about Don Quixote for and with his fellow prisoners, is self-consciously performative. Similarly, *Cabaret* (1966) is split in two, one part the story of Cliff and his relationship with Sally, written and staged like a Rodgers and Hammerstein–style musical, and the other part a metaphysical cabaret, which is both inside the Cliff-and-Sally musical as a setting for action and outside it, commenting on the action, presided over by a demonic emcee, again, self-consciously performative. *Hair* was initially regarded as revolutionary for its score's use of the rock idiom, but in retrospect its more interesting flouting of convention was its de-emphasis of the plot. As in musical comedies, there is a slight through-story that provides a structure to hang a variety of songs on, many of them forthrightly performative.[33] These plays and others hint that the musical theater of the late 1960s was ready to depart in many ways from the conventions of the integrated musical and the theory of the Rodgers and Hammerstein aesthetic.[34] This need to move on would not be satisfied by simply returning to the era of the musical comedy, as the brief *No, No, Nanette–Irene* fad demonstrated. Rather, the groundbreaking musicals of the 1960s suggest that the new musicals of the 1970s and beyond would retain the Rodgers and Hammerstein tradition's commitment to craft and its affinity for the treatment of serious subjects, but reject its style of realism, its fourth wall. In this rejection it would reconnect with the postmodern elements of its musical-comedy past and reimagine them with a seriousness of purpose.

In the climactic scene of Stephen Sondheim and John Weidman's 1991 musical *Assassins,* the various assassins and would-be assassins gather on the sixth floor of the Texas School Book Depository to convince Lee Harvey Oswald to kill President John F. Kennedy. One of the pre-1963 assassins says to Oswald, "You're going to bring us back," and one of the post-1963 group adds, "And make us possible." A few moments later, John Wilkes Booth tells Oswald, "You're the one that's going to sum it all up and blow it all wide open."[35] They see Oswald as a bridge connecting past to future and, more than that, as a person who can provide a summation for the past and bring the future explosively into being. In a similar historical if significantly less violent sense, Sondheim can be seen as a bridge connecting the Rodgers and Hammerstein era to the postmodern era and even beyond. By studying the plays he and his collaborators created in the 1950s and 1960s, we can begin to develop a clearer understanding of how the Rodgers and Hammerstein aesthetic for the musical theater gave way to a postmodern aesthetic, which in many ways recalls aspects of the musical-comedy aesthetic but which, in the cultural context of convention-busting and authority-questioning and in the intellectual context of challenges to the nature of language, representation, knowledge, identity, and reality, offers new opportunities for how musicals entertain, how they work as theater, and, more important for this study, how they make meaning.

The facts of Sondheim's life and career have been presented frequently and thoroughly, especially his tutoring and mentoring by Oscar Hammerstein.[36] At Hammerstein's instigation, Sondheim worked on several apprentice musicals through his years at Williams College and beyond (the first one, *All That Glitters*, a musical version of *Beggar on Horseback*, by George S. Kaufman and Marc Connelly, was produced at Williams).[37] Eventually, he had the chance to submit some songs on spec for a musical adaptation of *Front Porch in Flatbush*, a play by twin brothers Julius J. Epstein and Philip G. Epstein, screenwriters of, among other films, *Casablanca*. The musical was titled *Saturday Night* and was scheduled to open in late 1955. Set in spring 1929, the musical focuses on Gene Gorman, a young man from Brooklyn who wants desperately to live in the circles of wealth, influence, and class. He schemes to make a killing in the stock market for himself and his friends, but uses their money instead to make a down payment on a Sutton Place apartment, then raises the money to invest by selling his cousin's Pierce Arrow. When the stock falls, his house of cards falls with it. He is pursued by his cousin, the police, and a loan shark, he faces jail, and he contemplates suicide. By the end, however, he decides to face up to the consequences of his actions, and, thanks to the intervention of his neighborhood friends and his fiancée, Helen, who has helped him to abandon his unrealistic dreams, his problems are solved. Resigned to a middle-class life, he and Helen look forward to their marriage. Sondheim and book writer Julius Epstein created a play with fun, appealing characters and a clear structure. The songs are well crafted and charming. In short, *Saturday Night* was a well-made musical, light, but in the Rodgers and Hammerstein tradition, similar to other entertaining but easy-on-the-mind mid-fifties musicals about slightly stymied love finally working out.

As it turned out, the world would have to wait quite a while to see *Saturday Night*. Before all the money was in place, producer Lemuel Ayers died and the production was canceled. In 1959 a new mounting was announced, but that too was aborted. *Saturday Night* finally had its world premiere in 1997 at the Bridewell Theatre in London. After Sondheim made some revisions, including the addition of two new songs ("Delighted, I'm Sure" and "Montana Chem"), the play had its first US production at Chicago's Pegasus Theatre, directed by Gary Griffin, in 1999, followed by an Off-Broadway production, directed by Kathleen Marshall, in 2000. By that time, the show was regarded as an interesting footnote to Sondheim's career, what the composer himself likened to his baby pictures.[38]

The most significant result of the failed 1955 production was that it led to the opportunity that would really begin that career: Sondheim was invited to assist Leonard Bernstein with the lyrics for *West Side Story*. By the time the show finished its out-of-town tryout, Bernstein, in what librettist Arthur Laurents calls "the most magnanimous act I ever heard of in the theatre before or since," had given Sondheim sole credit as lyricist.[39] Sondheim was subsequently invited to work with Laurents and director and choreographer Jerome Robbins again and to provide lyrics to Jule Styne's music for *Gypsy*. *West Side Story* and *Gypsy*, with *My Fair Lady* and *Fiddler on the Roof*, are the greatest late expressions of the Rodgers and Hammerstein aesthetic, the most intelligent, most sophisticated, and richest examples of the integrated musical. At the same time, however, as we will see in the next chapter, these plays began straining at the form.

The 1960s, as I have argued, was a time of confusion in the musical theater as the Rodgers and Hammerstein–style musical neared exhaustion and as new forms struggled to emerge from it. The works created by Sondheim and his collaborators, as accomplished as they are, participated in the confusion. *A Funny Thing Happened on the Way to the Forum*, the first produced show for which Sondheim wrote music and lyrics, was a classical farce rethought through the frame of vaudeville, with a fast-paced book and a score that, instead of keeping the plot moving, deliberately stopped the action so that the audience could catch its breath. *Anyone Can Whistle* was a satire that insistently trumpeted its groundbreaking form and style. *Do I Hear a Waltz?* was firmly in the Rodgers and Hammerstein tradition, not surprising since Richard Rodgers wrote the music, while Sondheim returned to lyrics only. *Evening Primrose*, a musical written for television, tempered realism with fantasy as a way of exploring decidedly postmodern themes. Comparing these last two works, premiering as they did only nineteen months apart, can help us understand both the exhaustion of the Rodgers and Hammerstein aesthetic and the birth pangs of the postmodern musical.

Do I Hear a Waltz? was adapted from Arthur Laurents's 1952 play *The Time of the Cuckoo,* with book by Laurents, music by Richard Rodgers, and lyrics by Sondheim.[40] Opening at the 46th Street Theatre (now the Richard Rodgers Theatre) on 18 March 1965, the musical tells the story of a spinsterish American woman, Leona Samish, on vacation in Venice, where she meets a slightly older, handsome, sophisticated, and charming Italian antique-shop owner, Renato Di Rossi. Leona is attracted to him but is afraid that he means to take advantage of her, suspicions that seem confirmed when an eighteenth-century goblet he sells her turns out possibly to be brand new, when she has to pay the balance due for a garnet necklace he gives her, when he apparently earns a commission on what she pays for the necklace, and when she discovers he is married. Leona is lonely but does not connect easily with others. The other Americans at her pensione tend to brush off her nakedly desperate attempts to join them on their outings and become their friend. Yet when Di Rossi makes clear his attraction to her, she resists; internally convinced that she is unlovable, she cannot believe that he or anyone else would love her for herself. Thus she sours their relationship with suspicions about money—whether or not he is playing some kind of confidence game—even though she knows the money in question amounts to only a few US dollars. Leona's story is balanced by a love-triangle subplot concerning an American couple also staying at the pensione, Eddie and Jennifer Yeager. Jennifer is devoted to Eddie and suffers continual little heartbreaks from his more cynical attitude toward their relationship and one large heartbreak when she finds out about his casual affair with Fioria, the owner of the pensione. Eddie has come to Italy to hone his talent as an artist and is frustrated that he cannot work. Yet that he fails as an artist is no surprise as he seems to lack a moral center and cannot or will not connect with others. The musical uses these characters and the conflicts among them to explore the themes of ideal, romanticized love versus practical, real-world love and human connection versus loneliness.

Richard Rodgers and Stephen Sondheim. Credit Line: Photo by Friedman-Abeles/©The
New York Public Library for the Performing Arts

In some ways *Do I Hear a Waltz?* is a comfortable fit for the Rodgers and Hammerstein form and aesthetic, but in other ways the demands of the form seem inappropriate to the story. Where Laurents's play was set entirely in the garden of the pensione, the musical opened the story up to show more of Venice. Yet, given the constricted nature of the American characters, a single, contained set seems to support the narrative better. Similarly, conforming to the demands of convention, the musical employed a fifteen-person singing ensemble and a ten-person dancing ensemble, even though the story and score offer them little to do. (In its original conception, the show was to have no choreography, but after a rocky out-of-town tryout, Herbert Ross was brought in to create some dances.) Theodore Chapin, the executive director of the Rodgers and Hammerstein Organization, sums up the problem: the "original production [. . .] had forced a big musical from a story that lent itself to a chamber-sized work."[41]

More important than these problems, however, is the disjunction between the story and the Rodgers and Hammerstein aesthetic. Looking back at the Broadway production, Sondheim once concluded, "I never thought the play should be a musical. [. . .] The reason, and I still think I'm right, is that it's about a lady who, metaphorically, can't sing. How can you do it as a musical? One way is to do it as a chamber opera or another way is to have a musical in which everyone sings the whole time with the exception of the main character, which I think would have been very interesting—if she wouldn't be able to sing until the climax of the piece, then breaks open in anger and is able to sing."[42] Such a solution would have been interesting, but it would have departed significantly from the Rodgers and Hammerstein formula. As Sondheim notes elsewhere, "Dick [Rodgers] thought in terms of song. And to him it was impossible to have a leading lady who didn't sing. He didn't have that kind of imagination."[43] Nevertheless, a different form for the show would have served the story better.

Connected to this problem of Leona's character not being able to sing is a thematic conflict basic to the show, a conflict about the nature of reality. Leona sees the world as concrete and tangible, a place where emotions and price tags should be equally unambiguous. Leona's worldview is called into question by her relationship with Di Rossi. Di Rossi sees the world much differently from Leona; he refuses to be held to one reality. He can simultaneously be married and court Leona, make her a gift of a necklace and rely on her to pay for it, and sell her an eighteenth-century goblet that is brand new. Despite Leona's suspicions, we never really get the impression that he is a scoundrel or a con man. Rather, never tethered for very long to any one of the multiple realities he lives in, he lives, as he sings to Leona, in the moment. By embracing the ambiguity of reality, Di Rossi lives more deeply and more beautifully than Leona. When Leona asks Fioria if the goblet she has bought from Di Rossi is eighteenth century, the pensione owner responds as Di Rossi would: "Yes, it is. But it is so lovely, what is the difference?"[44] Leona, stuck in her rigid binary world of either/or, cannot see the beauty and cannot make human connections. The play, then, calls into question the validity of Leona's realistic worldview, yet it is written from the Rodgers and Hammerstein aesthetic, which is, as we have seen, essentially an aesthetic of realism. In a way, it undercuts its own artistic premises. In order to develop its themes fully, the story needs another theory of the musical theater to be told in. Arthur Laurents relates that when Herbert Ross joined the out-of-town tryouts as choreographer, he recalled working with Laurents and Sondheim on *Anyone Can Whistle*: "Herb reminded us that with *Whistle* we had been breaking the musical out of the mold in which we were now stuck with *Waltz*."[45]

Some of the same formal, aesthetic, and narrative challenges that faced the creators of *Do I Hear a Waltz?* were handled differently by the creators of *Evening Primrose*. Of course, these different solutions were to a certain extent dictated by a major difference between the two musicals: *Evening Primrose* was a Broadway-style musical written for television, not the stage. It was a one-hour episode of *ABC Stage 67*, a weekly series of arts and educational programs that ran one season. Broadcast on 16 November 1966, with a teleplay by James Goldman (with whom Sondheim had already started writing *The Girls Upstairs,* the musical that would become *Follies*) and music and lyrics by Sondheim, *Evening Primrose* is about a frustrated poet, Charles Snell (played by Anthony Perkins), who decides to escape from the demands and failures of his life by living in a large Manhattan department store. By day, when the store is open, he plans to hide; at night, after everyone leaves, he will make himself at home among the store's products and write. He imagines that this solitude, being the ruler of a kingdom of one, will give him control over his life and result in great poetry. On his first night, however, after avoiding a security guard, he discovers that he is not alone. There is a whole community of people living by night in the store for much the same reason, though most of them seem to have dropped out of society during financial crises like the Great Depression. The community of store-dwellers is ruled over by the autocratic Mrs. Monday (Dorothy Stickney), who jealously guards the secret of the store with threats of the dark men, another strange community that lives in a mortuary and can be called on to rid the department store of unwanted visitors and community miscreants. She welcomes Charles only after he proves he is a poet by reciting some of his (not very good) verse. Settling in, Charles is given a room display to live in and a copy of the security guard's schedule to memorize. He is distracted from his poetry, however, by thoughts of the one unhappy member of the community, Ella (Charmian Carr). It turns out that, shopping one day with her mother when she was a little girl, she fell asleep and was discovered after store hours by the store-dwellers. Mrs. Monday chose to keep her as a servant. She longs for the outside world and so is ostracized by the others and supervised carefully. Defying warnings to stay apart, Charles and Ella make a world for themselves in the backyard-products section of the store while he teaches her reading, math, and history. Ella finally convinces Charles to take her away from the store and start a life in the outside world, but they inadvertently broadcast their plans over the store intercom system, the dark men are summoned, and they end up as bride and groom mannequins in the store window.

In some ways *Evening Primrose* works in the Rodgers and Hammerstein tradition. Most significantly, the songs arise out of the characters' emotions, they reveal character, and they propel the action. In other ways—ways probably dictated by the limitations of the medium—it departs from the formal conventions of the Rodgers and Hammerstein musical, especially in taking the form of the chamber musical *Do I Hear a Waltz?* might have been. There is no singing and dancing ensemble, the number of characters is quite small, and only Charles and Ella—the emotional center of the story—get to sing.

More important, at least for my interests, is its presentation of and attitude toward realism. On the one hand, in accordance with the Rodgers and Hammerstein aesthetic, the songs arise naturally out of character and situation, sustaining the illusion of the fourth wall. On the other hand, the entire story is offered in what might be called *Twilight Zone* realism. The mirror that the story holds up to nature is distorted, maybe a fun-house mirror. The world of the play is reasonably recognizable as being like our own world, but there is something of a twist, an intrusion of the fantastic, that defamiliarizes our world and asks us to look at it in a new light.[46] *Evening Primrose* is not utterly fantastic, something that can be dismissed as pure fiction; rather, it is close enough to our sense of reality that it unnerves us.

This attitude toward the real serves the development of two of the play's interconnected themes. The first is the role of art and the artist in society. In its thematic interest in art the play is self-referential—Charles's striving to create art reflects on the play itself as art—in a way that points toward postmodernism. Charles apparently sees poetry as transcendent, an ideal that rises above the commonplace concerns of a petty society to be forever and always beautiful and meaningful. In "If You Can Find Me, I'm Here," which he sings upon successfully secreting himself in the store, he refers to the things he is escaping from, the things that interfere with his artistic creation—friends, landlords, the hordes who do not appreciate poetry, the equally unappreciative critics, the literal and symbolic noise of living in Manhattan. The only poem of his we hear reveals how the noise of the city has distracted him and polluted his art: the central metaphor for his heart breaking is street crews using jackhammers to break up the asphalt. He imagines that if he can get away from the noise and the demands of the social world, he will have the time, space, and silence in which to create. Aloneness, solitude, separation from society is necessary for the making of transcendent art.

Charles does not, however, retire to a hermitage. Completely unconscious of the irony, he chooses to escape from society by moving into a department store, the symbolic center of an affluent society's consumer culture. Compounding his error, he discovers he is not alone. Far from having escaped society, he falls immediately into the alternate society of the store-dwellers, complete with its traditions, hierarchies, rules, and punishments—all organized around the store and its products. In effect, the store-dwellers' community is a simulation of the society outside the store.

The conflict between the two societies—the one outside the store and the one inside—develops the play's second important theme. Much is made of the distinction between the two worlds. With the exception of

Ella, the store-dwellers, like Charles, have come to the store to escape the chaos of the world outside. We get the impression, since they exhibit a privileged attitude and came to the store in the wake of financial panics, that perhaps they lost their fortunes. At any rate, they vigorously police the border between inside and outside, careful not to let any news of their existence escape to the "outsiders." Burglars, security guards, and anyone else who violates the border and discovers their nocturnal life are sacrificed to the dark men. Ella, who has grown to adulthood in the store, accepts this distinction between inside and outside too. She longs to escape the store world and rejoin the outside world she only vaguely remembers from childhood. In order to have hope for escape from the life in the store, which she finds unbearable, she needs to believe that the outside world is different. In "Take Me to the World" she pleads with Charles to help her escape to this necessarily different and better world: "Take me to the world / That's real [. . . .]" Charles tries to tell her that the world she imagines is a fantasy: "I have seen the world, / And it's mean and ugly" (*L* 392). Nevertheless, he is caught up in her enthusiasm and agrees to escape with her.

After establishing the importance of the distinction between the store world and the outside world, the play goes about breaking down that distinction so as to show that the store world is a very model of the consumer culture outside. The displays in the store are fictional versions of real-life settings—den, library, patio—yet they are designed to inspire desire on the part of consumers, to make them want their real-life houses and yards to look as perfect as the store versions. Which version, then, is more real? The store-dwellers are expert at imitating mannequins to fool the security guards. Shortly after his arrival, Charles is astounded by group after group of apparently inanimate figures in a variety of poses coming to life. Again, the distinction between life inside the store and life outside is blurred: in both worlds identity is inextricably connected to one's role in the consumer economy, and the difference between genuine life and imitation life is by no means clear. When Charles and Ella resolve to escape the store, they are defeated most immediately by the dark men, but symbolically, they cannot escape because there is nowhere to escape to. The play's final image is of the pair turned into mannequins representing a bride and groom at a perfect, window-display wedding. They are observed by a young couple on the sidewalk—at first glance we might have mistaken them for Charles and Ella—who have clearly been inspired by the display to dream of their own wedding, one that might be as perfect as the one in the window. Consumer culture, then, conflates image and reality, and desire is both the generator and the product of the conflation.

This conclusion returns us to the role of the artist. Charles is defeated in his attempt to find a space and a silence in which to write poetry. He is barely in the store before he is dealing with as much noise, literal and metaphorical, as on the outside. Further, his aesthetic of art transcending the social is undercut by the play itself and the way it is presented. That is, the play shows us that identity is ineluctably social, that the artist of the late twentieth century cannot spout romantic dreams of the unique, striving, autonomous individual, the Byronic hero facing down his mendacious society. Rather, art, like *Evening Primrose,* must address the complexly tangled relationship between the person and his social setting. How are we the products of social forces and how do we serve them? To what extent, if any, can we claim ownership of our identity? To what extent can we hope to have an impact on those social forces? How can we rebel against them? In the end, this is perhaps the major difference between *Do I Hear a Waltz?* and *Evening Primrose*: the former explores its characters as psychologically individual; the latter sees its characters as born out of and existing in a web of societal power relations. The former reflects a modern sensibility, the latter a postmodern.

What I have tried to establish in the foregoing is that characteristics of the postmodern have been present in the American musical theater since its inception. These characteristics were generally repressed during the Rodgers and Hammerstein era, when the aesthetic became centered in realism. By the 1960s, however, as the Rodgers and Hammerstein–style musical became played out, a new kind of musical emerged. It inherited from Rodgers and Hammerstein an attention to craft and a commitment to the musical theater as a serious dramatic art form, one that had the potential to explore serious topics in sophisticated ways, but it also began to move away from realism as a style, returning to many of the self-referential, intertextual, and performative stylistics of the musical comedy. However, it returns to these stylistics in the cultural context of postmodernism, imbuing them with intellectual significance. The musical theater thus began to position itself to use its implicitly postmodern form and style to engage and explore these significances. The musicals created by Stephen Sondheim and his collaborators are central to this positioning and the musical theater's movement into postmodernism and beyond.

It is important to remember that aesthetic transformations occur gradually, not overnight. The stylistic revolution marked by *Oklahoma!* began at least sixteen years earlier with *Show Boat*. We must also remember that when a new style becomes dominant, older styles do not disappear. For all its innovations, *Oklahoma!* retains some elements of the musical comedy. In chapter 2 I examine the Sondheim shows from the 1950s and 1960s (with the exception of *Do I Hear a Waltz?* and *Evening Primrose*, discussed previously) in the context of the transition from the Rodgers and Hammerstein aesthetic to a new, postmodern aesthetic. I conclude by discussing *Company* (1970), a truly postmodern musical. In chapter 3 I examine Sondheim's remarkable subsequent collaborations with director Harold Prince: *Follies, A Little Night Music, Pacific Overtures, Sweeney Todd,* and *Merrily We Roll Along*. Coinciding with the high point of cultural postmodernism, these plays formally and thematically break down conventional epistemological systems and open up new possibilities for meaning. In chapter 4 I examine Sondheim's shows from the 1980s, 1990s, and the first decade of the twenty-first century and argue that they mark a transition from the postmodern musical to a new kind of musical, which, while acknowledging postmodernism's critiques of traditional epistemological systems and representational strategies, seeks to reclaim a more solid epistemological footing for claims about people and the social world. Finally, in chapter 5 I return to a broader view of the musical theater to discuss the other ways postmodernism has been manifested and to examine the ways some of the musical-theater artists who have been influenced by Sondheim's work have addressed the challenges of the contemporary world.

And now—We start.

Two

Opening Doors

In the last chapter I argued that the 1960s was a time of confusion for the Broadway musical, as the Rodgers and Hammerstein–style musical became exhausted, rock music began to displace traditional show tunes, and writers, composers, and directors explored new directions, forms, and styles for the musical play. I also argued that Stephen Sondheim's career can be seen as a bridge, not just connecting the Rodgers and Hammerstein musical to the postmodern musical, but summing up the Rodgers and Hammerstein tradition and then exploding it so as to create something new. In this chapter I examine Sondheim's musicals of the late 1950s and 1960s to see the ways postmodern techniques and ideas began intermingling with Rodgers and Hammerstein–type form and style to create new possibilities for meaning and for what a musical can be, until, with *Company* in 1970, a new kind of aesthetic emerged.

West Side Story, which premiered on 26 September 1957, at the Winter Garden Theatre, is in many ways the apotheosis of the Rodgers and Hammerstein–style musical.[1] With book by Arthur Laurents, music by Leonard Bernstein, lyrics by Sondheim, and direction and choreography by Jerome Robbins, it is one of the most successfully integrated musicals ever. Making this point in his memoir, Laurents writes, "What we really did stylistically with *West Side Story* was take every musical theatre technique as far as it could be taken. Scene, song and dance were integrated seamlessly; we did it all better than anyone ever had before."[2] The book establishes its themes economically yet develops them in depth. The songs not only arise naturally from the dramatic moments but also work together as a score, Bernstein's musical themes helping to develop the play's ideas. Although Sondheim is on record as being critical of many of the lyrics for this play, they work with Laurents's dialogue to create a unified discourse for the characters.[3] Most important, Robbins's staging erases the line between stage movement and dance as the characters move seamlessly from one to the other. The choreography often takes on the main burden of telling the story, as in the "Prologue," and of developing the themes, as in "Cool" and the "Somewhere" ballet. Indeed, working within the Rodgers and Hammerstein aesthetic, *West Side Story* reached a level of achievement that would be difficult for subsequent shows to approach, much less match. Reflecting on the show years later, Bernstein concluded, "It changed the nature of Broadway shows in two diametrically opposed ways. It encouraged shows to embrace these various forms of the art and, on the other hand, it discouraged such embracing because there weren't people around to do it. I mean, who could follow Jerry?"[4] While perfecting the Rodgers and Hammerstein–style musical in form, however, *West Side Story* explores ideas about ideology, power, and identity that connect to postmodern theory. It is in these ideas that this musical begins to break with the Rodgers and Hammerstein tradition.

Ideologically, musicals have traditionally functioned much like Shakespearean comedies: they take established social order, shatter it, but then restore it at the end, often with a wedding, a symbol of social unity. With the exceptions we looked at in chapter 1, pre–Rodgers and Hammerstein musicals rarely present any explicit, significant social commentary; implicitly, however, they manage by the end to contain whatever chaotic principle was comically threatening social order. They essentially reconfirm the ideological status quo. More complex ideologically, the Rodgers and Hammerstein canon is infused with Oscar Hammerstein's deeply felt liberal humanism. Here, the social order is threatened more seriously: by Judd Fry's and Billy Bigelow's unbridled ids; by Nellie Forbush's and Lieutenant Cable's inherited racism; by Anna Leonowens's colonial assumptions and the King's chauvinism. However, there is no critique of the underlying liberal humanist ideology that is the basis for American social democracy; rather, the critique is of the people who in their actions and in their lives fail to enact this ideology. Rodgers and Hammerstein's message to audiences of the 1940s and 1950s is that our country's social philosophy is sound, if only we have the strength to really live it.

Postmodern art is rarely interested in reconfirming the ideological status quo, nor is it willing to separate a social philosophy from its practice. The kind of racism that Hammerstein saw as an aberration in a sound social philosophy might be seen from a Marxist-inflected, postmodern point of view as seminal to the operations of a capitalist-dominated social order. In other words, postmodernism examines social practices both as products of ideology and as producers of ideology. Jean-François Lyotard argues that postmodernism is characterized by an incredulity toward master narratives, by which he means the fundamental stories that explain a society to itself.[5] This sums up neatly the attitude of skepticism that postmodern art tends to bring to its own social and ideological contexts (as well as a tendency to question narrative as an epistemological vehicle, as we will see later in this chapter).

To understand how the post–Rodgers and Hammerstein–era musical play both makes ideology part of what it tries to explore and seeks itself to function ideologically, we need to examine postmodern conceptions of power, especially as put forward by Michel Foucault. For Foucault, power does not reside, as we often think of it as residing, in institutions or people: the government, the police, your boss, your teacher. Rather, it exists in the force relations among institutions and people. If we think of the many force relations each of us participates in—between us and federal, state, and local governments; between us and our spouses, lovers, or roommates; between us and our parents, siblings, and other relatives; between us and our bosses and fellow employees; between us and our neighbors; between us and our pets—we can see that it is simplistic to think of any one of those parties as having "the power," while the other is "powerless." Instead, power is in constant negotiation and competition between the parties as each tries to assert force over the other, each acquiesces to or develops techniques to resist the other's attempt to assert force, and each responds to the other's acquiescence or resistance.[6]

The interrelationship between language and power can help us understand how power functions ideologically. Power operates through institutions (government, the justice system, religion, education, the arts, the media, the family) that can disseminate and naturalize a worldview that serves to reify and perpetuate the ideological status quo. Each of us, from birth onward, is the target of ideologically charged discourse—languages that imply a worldview, an understanding of reality, how power operates in it, and our place in it. When the dominant ideology controls most of the institutions (what Louis Althusser calls *Ideological State Appara-*

tuses), it controls most of the discourse (the languages available to us to explain our experiences of the world) and thus is in an excellent position to convince us that the particular worldview that best serves a particular distribution of power is the *only* worldview, that that particular reality is the one and only reality—a process Althusser calls *interpellation.*[7]

Foucault writes that power is best understood in its local operations. This is also the approach taken by *West Side Story*. The action of *West Side Story* never moves beyond a few New York City blocks. Nevertheless, these few city blocks become the site where multiple aspects of power—power manifested institutionally and locally, power as violence, and power as ideology—come together.

Like its source, *Romeo and Juliet, West Side Story* is about two young people trying to fulfill their love in a hostile social environment. But whereas Shakespeare's play identifies and brings onstage several sources of its society's power—the Prince of Verona and the Capulet and Montague patriarchs—in *West Side Story* the effects of power are everywhere, but their source is unidentified, offstage, and amorphous. The Jets and the Sharks speak of their parents, but the family has no evident control over these children, and the parents never appear onstage. The adults who do appear onstage all represent institutions through which power operates—Schrank and Krupke represent the law enforcement and justice systems, Glad Hand represents the social welfare system, and Doc, the pharmacist, represents science. Yet they are all ineffectual, unable to work their power on the teens in any productive way. In "Gee, Officer Krupke" the Jets express their collective contempt for all these systems and their representatives—cop, judge, psychiatrist, social worker—and mock the ways these representatives are less interested in helping a delinquent teenager than in passing the problem off to someone else. The song also demonstrates the skill with which the Jets have learned to deal with these representatives of authority: in a manner reminiscent of Henry Louis Gates Jr.'s articulation of the practice of signifying, they use the discourse that each authority figure expects to hear, but in a knowing, parodic way that allows the teens to affirm the auditor's power and undermine it at the same time.[8] The play's adults, then, far from being sources or instruments of the power against which the Jets, Sharks, Tony, and Maria must struggle, are themselves powerless, or, as the stage directions at the very end of the play tell us, "The adults—DOC, SCHRANK, KRUPKE, GLAD HAND—are left bowed, alone, useless."[9]

The play seems purposely to deny the characters and the audience a source for the power the effects of which we see playing out onstage. This is part of the reason for the characters' anger: the conditions in which they live are intolerable, but there is no identifiable root cause for these conditions against which to respond. Rather, the conditions are the results of the workings of an ideology that seeks to rigidly define social reality so as to control it. The Jets, in "Gee, Officer Krupke," sense this ideology at work as they parody the cop's, judge's, psychiatrist's, and social worker's attempts to define the problems of the delinquent (played by Action) so as to label him and deal with him. As Action puts it, "To them we ain't human. We're cruddy juvenile delinquents" (113). This ideology of control is manifested in the process of creating exclusive categories, drawing boundaries between them, and refusing to let anything cross the boundaries or transcend the categories. Control is maintained by enforcing rigid intellectual, social, ethnic, national, and even neighborhood boundaries. The play, in its original production, expressed this idea through Oliver Smith's set design, emphasizing streets and alleys and the boundaries they create. (This same idea was beautifully put forth at the beginning of the film version of *West Side Story* by the languorous overhead shots of New York City streets, the camera looking straight down and thus depicting the graph-paper-like layout of the city—almost a maze for laboratory animals—until finally moving in on the one small neighborhood that will be the setting for the action.) The connection of city streets and their buildings, each with a number, and boundaries creating and maintaining order and control is most evident in the "Somewhere" ballet, where Tony and Maria, after the rumble and the deaths of Riff and Bernardo, dream of escaping the city and the power of division and control it represents. The stage directions describe the action, starting in Maria's bedroom: "the walls of the apartment begin to move off, and the city walls surrounding them begin to close in on them. Then the apartment itself goes and the two lovers begin to run, battering against the walls of the city, beginning to break through as chaotic figures of the gangs, of violence, flail around them. But they do break through, and suddenly—they are in a world of space and air and sun" (106–7). After a brief idyll, in which Jets and Sharks interact without division, prejudice, and hate, "The harsh shadows, the fire escapes of the real, tenement world cloud the sky, and the figures of RIFF and BERNARDO slowly walk on. The dream becomes a nightmare: as the city returns, there are brief re-enactments of the knife fights, of the deaths" (108). The city itself is a manifestation of the ideology that controls the characters, and they cannot escape the city or the effects of that ideology.

West Side Story's plot is about how the characters—the Jets and the Sharks, Tony and Maria—respond to the ubiquitous effects of this all-encompassing ideology. Ideology, as we saw earlier, seeks to naturalize and replicate itself. Invisible, it becomes its subjects' reality, a reality they then help to reproduce and pass on to others. This effort is only partly successful among the play's characters. The Jets, as we see in "Gee, Officer Krupke," have at least an unsophisticated understanding of the prevailing ideology, how it operates, and how it seeks to label, objectify, and control them. Their skepticism helps to disrupt the smooth transmission of ideology, as in this exchange:

ACTION: Them PRs're the reason my old man's gone bust.
RIFF: Who says?
ACTION: My old man says.
BABY JOHN (To A-RAB): My old man says his old man woulda gone bust anyway. (8)

In one sense, then, the Jets refuse to capitulate to the forces that seek to label them, objectify them, put them in the pigeonhole where they will best serve the dominant ideology. In "Krupke" they reject the advice to get a job, "Like be a soda jerker, / Which means like be a schmuck" (*F* 50), an oblique criticism of Tony, who, at the beginning of the play, has given up the Jets to work at Doc's drugstore. From the skeptical point of view of the Jets (except for Riff, for whom Tony can do no wrong), Tony has been absorbed into the system they try to resist.

What the Jets do not see is that in trying to resist, in seeking to claim power for themselves, they replicate the operations of power they want to escape: they create territory- and identity-based boundaries and enforce them rigorously. In a weird, stunted, urban version of Frederick Jackson

Turner's frontier thesis, the Jets base their sense of power and identity in the effort to claim, hold, and control a chunk of land, a section of a city street. Doc expresses the pathetic absurdity of this: "Fighting over a little piece of the street is so important?" (62). To the Jets, however, it is their raison d'être. At the very beginning of the play, they answer Schrank's challenge, "you hoodlums don't own the streets" (6), with the declaration, "A gang that don't own a street is nuthin'!" (7). Just as territorial boundaries must be protected, strict figurative boundaries must be maintained between those inside the group and those outside. Group membership becomes synonymous with identity; the Jets understand themselves and others by their status as inside or outside of the group. The potentially constructive and destructive aspects of this kind of boundary making are laid out in "Jet Song." In an effort to buck up the gang members in preparation for challenging the Sharks, Riff reminds them of the benefits of belonging to a group:

> When you're a Jet,
> If the spit hits the fan,
> You got brothers around,
> You're a family man.

> You're never alone,
> You're never disconnected.
> You're home with your own—
> When company's expected,
> You're well protected! (*F* 31)

But this idea of mutual identity, support, and protection turns belligerent after Riff leaves. Now, membership in the group is used as a position from which to claim superiority over those not in the group:

> When you're a Jet,
> You're the top cat in town,
> You're the gold-medal kid
> With the heavyweight crown! (*F* 31)

The Jets go on to express their determination to enforce the boundaries defining their group:

We're drawin' the line,
So keep your noses hidden!
We're hangin' a sign
Says "Visitors Forbidden,"
And we ain't kiddin'! (*F* 31)

To empower themselves, they have adopted the methods of control used by the dominant ideology, the same ideology that they feel oppressing them and seek to resist.

The Sharks as a gang maintain similar boundaries in similar ways, but for different reasons. They and their families, come to New York from Puerto Rico, find themselves Othered, labeled as different and not allowed to become a real part of American society, perpetual outsiders. We see the backstory of the formation of the Sharks in the dance that begins the play. When the attempts of Bernardo and then two or three other Puerto Rican teens to join the Jets are rebuffed, they react by forming their own gang, defined, presumably, by the need for mutual identity, support, and protection, by the desire to claim territory of their own, and by antagonism for the Jets. Anita and the Sharks' girls mock Bernardo for his apparently frequently repeated claim that Puerto Ricans came to New York, "ready, eager," with hearts and arms open (48), only to be rejected, but to him, it is true, as is the injustice of Puerto Ricans earning less money and prestige than white Americans for the same jobs. Bernardo recognizes the absurdity of this Othering when he compares Puerto Ricans to other immigrants who are not Othered, who are welcomed on the local level as part of the Jets and on the national level as "real" Americans. Anita recites his speech from memory, apparently having heard it so often: "The mother of Tony was born in Poland; the father still goes to night school. Tony was born in America, so that makes him an American. But us? Foreigners!" (48).

Both gangs work to maintain their boundaries through the arrangement of physical space, through violence, and through language. The original production's staging emphasized physical separation. In the dance at the gym, "The line between the two gangs is sharply defined [. . .]" (28), and under the highway, before the rumble, "they fan out on opposite sides of the cleared space" (89). At the gym, Glad Hand attempts a get-together dance, but when couples end up mismatched, Jets with Sharks' girls and Sharks with Jets' girls, the gang members reclaim their dates and lines are redrawn. The only time the gangs voluntarily intermingle before the final scene is during the war council at Doc's; when Schrank enters, they rearrange themselves in a mock integration that fools no one. That they try to maintain boundaries through violence is obvious from the dance prologue onward. The violence can be fighting, as in the "Prologue" and "The Rumble," or dancing, as in the contest that develops between Bernardo and Anita and Riff and Velma after the get-together dance fails. In maintaining boundaries through language, the gangs adopt a method of control used by the dominant ideology. As we see in "Krupke" and as we see in the Jets' collective annoyance at being labeled "hoodlums" (62), language can be used to objectify and control. Once again replicating the ideology that oppresses them, the gangs use language—derogatory words for national, ethnic, and racial background—to stereotype, to deny the individuality and the humanness of another. This use of language contributes to the Othering of the Puerto Ricans in New York: the Sharks and their girls recount being called "Foreigners!," "Lice!," and "Cockroaches!" (48), all things that those safely inside the boundaries of the social body want to keep outside so as to preserve the health and purity of the body. The gang members, Jets and Sharks alike, are throughout the play victims of this kind of labeling, but they themselves label, seeking to make others their victims. The conflict between the gangs, then, operates on many levels, but it centers on the need to maintain a strict boundary. Riff sums it all up at the war council: "You crossed the line once too often" (65).

All the methods of maintaining boundaries come together in a scene where another character crosses the line. Near the tragic climax of the play, Maria sends Anita to Doc's to tell Tony that she will be delayed because she is being questioned by Schrank. In order to do this, Anita has to transcend her own sense of group membership and her grief over Bernardo's death, but this transcendence is both misunderstood and threatening to the Jets, who immediately work to reestablish the gang boundaries.

The trouble begins when Anita violates the Jets' physical space, coming into Doc's drugstore. The Jets react with a slowly building antagonism. With a pun, Snowboy refuses her entry into their space: "She's too dark to pass" (132). The Jets' initial sarcasm in response to her questions segues into a parodic mocking of Anita's language: "*Por favor,*" "*Non comprende,*" "*Gracias,*" "*Di nada*" (135). When Anita says she wants to help Tony, the language becomes brutal in an effort to force her back to her side of the line: "Bernardo's tramp!," "Bernardo's pig!," "Spic!," "Gold tooth!," "Pierced ear!," "Garlic mouth!" (134–35). The Jets then turn physically violent, brutalizing and sexually assaulting Anita until Doc interrupts them. As a result of all this, Anita is forced back across the line, out of the Jets' physical space and, more important, back inside her own mental boundaries. She says, "Bernardo was right . . . If one of you was bleeding in the street, I'd walk by and spit on you" (135). This scene is the Jets' least sympathetic moment. The gang members unself-consciously and mercilessly employ the methods of control that the dominant ideology has used to create the oppressive social situation in which they find themselves; instead of following through on their earlier attempts to resist this ideology and its operations, they thoughtlessly replicate them. As it turns out, they are not able to think beyond the ideological situation in which they have been placed. At the end of this scene, when Doc shouts at them, "*You make this world lousy!,*" Action's only response is, "That's the way we found it, Doc" (136).

The gangs' contradictory response to their ideological setting—dissatisfaction and resistance on the one hand and, ultimately, acceptance and reproduction on the other—is contained in the philosophy of cool. This philosophy counsels emotional detachment as a way to respond to and protect oneself from the social environment and the operations of power. As Riff explains in his introduction to the song "Cool," "No matter who or what is eatin' at you, you show it, buddy boys, and *you are dead.* You are cuttin' a hole in yourselves for them to stick in a red-hot umbrella and open it. Wide. You wanna live? You play it cool" (63). In addition to "Cool," we see this philosophy in action at the dance in the gym. The stage directions tell us, "Both gangs are jitterbugging wildly with their bodies, but their faces, although they are enjoying themselves, remain cool, almost detached" (28). The problem with the cool philosophy is evident throughout the play: repressing intense emotions is unhealthy, resulting in violent and destructive outbursts. In the dress shop, Maria asks Anita why the gangs are having the rumble:

ANITA: You saw how they dance: like they have to get rid of something, quick. That's how they fight.
MARIA: To get rid of what?
ANITA: Too much feeling. (75)

Ultimately, the cool philosophy, by feigning indifference to the social world and by regulating destructive outbursts, serves to protect, not the gang members, but the dominant ideology of control.

All this, then, constitutes the ideological and social context within which Tony and Maria's love story is set. By falling in love with each other, Tony and Maria manage to violate both the rigid ideological boundaries of their society and the cool philosophy of their immediate social groups. That they violate the cool philosophy is obvious; although they know they should keep their relationship a secret, Doc, Anita, Chino—practically everybody—guess right away. By showing their emotions so openly, they leave themselves vulnerable to the violence of others. On a broader scale, unlike the Jets and Sharks, who want to resist the dominant ideology but end up replicating it, the lovers try consciously to transcend and obliterate ideological boundaries. At the beginning of the play, as we have seen, Tony has slipped away from gang membership as a means of responding to the dominant ideology and has seemingly acquiesced to societal expectations by becoming a soda jerk and taking a place in the economy. However, even in this role he is dissatisfied; he longs to break the boundaries that define him. He tells Riff that every night he wakes up, "reachin' out" for something "right outside the door, around the corner" (19), for something, that is, outside the boundaries of the ideological box he is in. Similarly but more practically, Maria strains against the short leash her family, particularly her brother Bernardo, keeps her on. She has been in New York for a month, she complains to Anita, but she has done nothing but work in the dress shop. Her marriage to Chino is apparently all planned despite her reservations. Bernardo even dictates the style dress she can wear. Like Tony, she's waiting for "something" to happen (24), something, presumably, that will break down the walls of the too-planned-out life that awaits her.

After Tony and Maria meet, their love becomes the means by which the walls, labels, and boundaries their society and the gangs would seek to enforce are broken through. In the original production Jerome Robbins emphasized this through the staging and the scenic design. When Tony and Maria see each other across the gym during the dance, "The lights fade on the others, who disappear into the haze of the background [. . .]" (30). Later, on the fire escape (symbolic of the escape from social control the lovers will attempt), as they begin to sing "Tonight," the buildings and the streets, which, as we have seen, represent the ideology of control, disappear, "leaving them suspended in space" (42). This scenic effect enhances the song's lyrics, as Maria sings, "I saw you and the world went away" (*F* 40). Rejecting the ideological forces that would pigeonhole them, they sing, "Today, the world was just an address, / A place for me to live in [. . .]" (*F* 42). Earlier, in "Maria," Tony implicitly rejects the use of words as labels that constrain, stereotype, and control; instead, he finds the power of language to signify infinitely. The word "Maria" represents "All the beautiful sounds of the world in a single word" (*F* 37). Through each other, Tony and Maria find an identity outside gang membership. At the dance, when Bernardo asks her, "Couldn't you see he's one of them?," Maria responds, "No; I saw only him" (32). As the second act nears its climax, even the boundaries between the lovers as individuals break down. Maria sings, "everything he is / I am, too" (*F* 52).

This comprehensive breaking down of social, gang-related, and individual boundaries, made possible through their love, accounts for Maria's impossible demand to Tony that he stop the rumble. She says, "*Any* fight is not good for us" (77). She understands that any fight reifies the lines between the gangs, the lines that she and Tony seek to transcend. Maria's plea leads into another mock-integration scene, but unlike the earlier scene at the drugstore, where the gangs intermingled insincerely as a way of thumbing their nose at Schrank, here the lovers indulge in a gentle fantasy, arranging the mannequins in the dress shop to represent their families and friends. In so doing, they also reimagine the boundaries that keep their families and friends apart in real life. Anticipating the "Somewhere" dream ballet, they create the relationships among their intimates that will allow for them to be together. Indeed, it is only after the mannequins have been harmoniously arranged that the lovers can hold their symbolic wedding.

Where this and the other scenes of integration—the get-together dance, the war council, the "Somewhere" ballet—have been failures, parodies, or fantasies, the end of the play offers a sincere moment of integration of the gangs. After Chino has killed Tony, and Maria has threatened the gang members with Chino's gun, she breaks down and then, after a moment, brings together two Jets and two Sharks to bear away Tony's body. Then, "The others, boys and girls, fall in behind to make a procession, the same procession they made in the dream ballet [. . .]" (143). They enact, at least momentarily, the ideal of social unity in the face of ideologically inspired divisions that the ballet represented. That this ending is less certain, more ambiguous, than the coming together of the Capulets and Montagues at the end of *Romeo and Juliet* suggests the complexity of the ideological forces and the operations of power in contemporary society. *West Side Story*'s final message is multiple and contradictory. On one level it does offer the possibility of hope, the possibility that the Jets and the Sharks, like Maria and Tony, can rise above the divisions that have been encouraged by the dominant ideology, divisions that they themselves have self-destructively replicated, to respond together in productive ways to the forces that have been oppressing them. On another level, however, we might ask if this one final moment, balanced against so much labeling, objectifying, hating, and killing in the rest of the play, can really support such a hopeful interpretation. Does the play really give us strong reason to hope that when the sun rises tomorrow the ideals of the dream ballet will still be played out on this city block? On a third level, we might wonder to what extent the ending functions ideologically to ameliorate the social critique that has preceded it. Is this a restoring of the social order, reassuring audiences that the basic liberal humanism on which our society is based will come through if only we can all learn to enact it? More likely, the play gestures sentimentally toward this possibility but knows—and expects its audiences to know—that this final coming together cannot offer a cure to the disastrous social effects of the operations of the dominant ideology we have seen throughout the play. Lacking a catharsis that might send us out of the theater confident in the goodness and rightness of the ideology in which we live, *West Side Story* leaves us disturbed, aware of the heartlessness of the dominant ideology and of the deleterious effects of the operations of power that support it.

Sondheim's second Broadway musical, like *West Side Story*, is in form and style very much a part of the Rodgers and Hammerstein tradition, but, also like *West Side Story*, its ideas connect to postmodern concerns about the construction of reality and the construction of identity. The opening chords of the overture to *Gypsy* establish the major musical and intellectual theme of the play: I had a dream. This musical, which opened at the Broadway Theatre on 21 May 1959, had much of the same creative team as *West Side Story*; book, lyrics, and direction were again by Arthur Laurents, Sondheim, and Jerome Robbins, and the music was by Broadway and Hollywood veteran Jule Styne.[10] Styne's four-note I-had-a-dream theme recurs at key moments throughout the show and reminds us of the importance of dreams—in this case, dream as a vision for the future—as a motivating force for the character of Rose and as a fundamental part of the American experience. Four years after *Gypsy* opened on Broadway, Martin Luther King Jr. would make famous the image of dream as a vision of a social future in his "I Have a Dream" speech. The two visions—personal and social—are brought together in the concept of the American Dream, which we usually think of as some sort of personal goal, the achievement of which is made possible by the particular social context provided by an idealized version of America, the land of opportunity, where one can go from rags to riches and where any kid can grow up to be president.

Rose's dreams are primarily visions of a personal future, but they are linked to a social vision and to a larger mythos of America by an offhand remark Herbie makes. He tells Rose that when he first saw her, she "looked like a pioneer woman without a frontier."[11] The frontier thesis, as articulated by Frederick Jackson Turner, is a particular manifestation of the American Dream in which the continual movement west in the nineteenth century was a means both of personal advancement (owning land, expanding business, starting over, striking it rich) and of societal evolution (claiming territory, controlling it, exploiting it—all justified and mandated by the guiding master narrative of Manifest Destiny). But by the 1920s, when pioneer woman Rose and her brood set out in pursuit of her dream, there is no more frontier—the West Coast, where the action of the play's first scenes takes place, is settled. It seems significant that Rose's father worked for the railroad, that key player in the expansion westward, but is now retired.[12] No longer able to head west toward a frontier, Rose loops back into already settled America, Manifest Destiny's straight, east-to-west line now giving way to a circle, the vaudeville circuit. *Gypsy* makes use of dreams in multiple senses to articulate a vision of an American society folding back on itself entropically and becoming an image—a dream—of its own myths.

Much of the dramatic tension in the play comes from two competing versions of the American Dream. The first, associated with Rose and, to a lesser extent, June, is the dream of stardom. Here the goal is to become a star, to become famous and wealthy as the result of the recognition of one's talents. All of Rose's dreams articulate one goal: as she puts it, "Just let me get June's name up in lights so big, they'll last my whole life" (36). In "Some People" the dream she narrates is about June making it on the Orpheum Circuit. Similarly, in the theatrical hotel in Akron she tells June, Louise, and the newsboys that she dreamed about a cow: "That dear fat cow looked me right in the eye and said: 'Rose, if you want to get on the Orpheum Circuit, put *me* in your act'" (26). The result is the new farm-boy act. At the end of act 1, after June has run off with Tulsa to find their own path to success, Rose's dreams of stardom turn to Louise in "Everything's Coming Up Roses." The second version of the American Dream, associated with Herbie and Louise, is the more traditional and more humble dream of home and family. Here the goal is secure family relations and a secure place to live. This vision is most simply and charmingly put by Louise in "If Momma Was Married":

> If Momma was married, we'd live in a house,
> As private as private can be:
> Just Momma, three ducks, five canaries, a mouse,
> Two monkeys, one father, six turtles and me . . . (*F* 65)

Perhaps minus the menagerie, this vision is the same as Herbie's. When they first meet, Herbie tells Rose, "I don't have a home" (16), and his desire through the rest of the play is to get one. He demonstrates in his speech to Rose after June leaves that he has a vision for the future as vivid as hers: "I can go back in the candy business. It's steady: fifty-two weeks all year every year. I'll work my fingers to the bone; I'll do twice what I did before and that was pretty fair. Rose, I could be a district manager and we could stay in one place. We could have our own house. Louise could go to school. [. . .] O.K., the act's finished. But you and me and our daughter, we're going to have a home [. . .]" (57–58).

Rose and Herbie's relationship is defined by a tug-of-war between the dream of stardom and the dream of home and family from their first scene together, where candy-salesman Herbie, seeking marriage, is pulled back into show business by Rose, through the Chinese restaurant scene, where Herbie presses Rose to marry him and give the girls a normal life and is once again placated, to the act 1 finale, where Rose torpedoes Herbie's vision of a traditional life together by shifting her dream of stardom to Louise. The tug-of-war finally seems to go Herbie's way when the act is booked into a burlesque house in Wichita: Rose, admitting defeat, finally agrees to give up the act and marry Herbie. On the day of the wedding, Herbie, gushing like a bride, imagines hanging the marriage license over the mantle of their home and exults, "I'm finally getting everything I wanted!" (88), but Rose is morose at the death of her show-business dream. Thus when the opportunity arises for Louise to go on for a missing stripper, Rose grabs it. She has previously looked down on burlesque as immoral and as inferior entertainment, yet it offers the last chance to fulfill her dream. As she tries to explain to Louise, "it's the star spot! I promised my daughter we'd be a star! Baby, it's all right to walk out when they *want* you. But you can't walk out when after all these rotten years, we're still a flop. That's quitting. We can't quit because we're a flop! [. . .] Just do this, and then we can walk away proud because we made it! Maybe only in burlesque, maybe only in second-rate burlesque at that—but let's walk away a star!" (89–90). This time, Herbie will not be pulled back into Rose's dream; he leaves, and the dream of home and family is lost for Rose and Louise. In its place, the dream of stardom rises unexpectedly and weirdly triumphant.

Before exploring the weirdness of the resultant dream of stardom, I want to go a bit further with Rose's ability to pull others into her dreams and connect it with a different kind of dream: not a vision for the future, a goal to be achieved, but a fantasy, an alternative reality. In her obsessive desire to make her daughters stars, Rose creates fantasies and then treats them as reality. This is most easily seen when June gripes to Louise, "Momma can do one thing: She can make herself believe anything she makes up. Like with that rhinestone finale dress *you* sewed for me. Momma wants publicity so she makes up a story that three nuns went blind sewing it! Now she believes it" (47). June adds, "She even believes the act is good" (47). That the lousiness of the act comes as a surprise to Louise is testament to Rose's ability, through her force of personality, to drag others into her fantasies—the act is good; the boys are no older than twelve; June is nine; Louise can replace June; they are all one break away from stardom. Removed from Rose's influence, the other characters can see the reality of their situation: the act isn't very good; vaudeville is dying; Louise isn't talented enough to replace June. But in Rose's presence, they see everything through her eyes, and when Rose despairs, as when she faces the grim reality of being booked into a burlesque house, the others take up her vision, reassuring her with her own fantasies.

The result for the characters and the play is a Baudrillardian hyperreality in which image has become disconnected from reality. In "The Precession of the Simulacra," Jean Baudrillard argues that in contemporary culture the function of the image has changed with deleterious effects for society. Where once the image pointed toward the object it sought to represent or stood in for it or even marked its absence, in postmodern culture the image has its own autonomous status, no longer in relation to the object, and, in fact, frequently preferred to the object. It doesn't *matter* if it's live or if it's Memorex.[13] This confabulation of image and reality is most obvious in *Gypsy* in the song "Little Lamb." Here, after the excitement of the surprise party, the presentation of gifts, the confrontation with Mr. Kringelein, and the celebration of Mr. Goldstone booking the act on the Orpheum Circuit, Louise sits quietly alone and contemplates her birthday. She sings to the real baby lamb Rose and Herbie gave her as a gift, to a stuffed bear, to a wooden hen, to a stuffed cat (another present), and to a drawing of a fish (given to her in lieu of a real fish). What is striking here is that she treats them all—real animal, stuffed and wooden animals, a *drawing* of an animal—equivalently. To Louise, raised in the theater, thoroughly under the influence of her mother's fantasies, and tremendously lonely, there is no significant difference among them. They are the things to which she attaches emotionally in reaction to being denied attention and love from her mother. We see her lost amid the images and confused about her own sense of self, what is real about her.

Gypsy uses its theater setting to establish this concept of hyperreality, the idea that image takes precedence over object, and then uses this concept to develop the theme of the dream and to connect it to a vision of contemporary America. To see this, we need to return to the dream of stardom and the dream of home and family. In "Some People" Rose establishes her commitment to the dream of stardom. In the middle section, introduced by the I-had-a-dream theme, she tells her father of her dream, "All about June and the Orpheum Circuit— / Give me a chance and I know I can work it" (*F* 58). In the dream Mr. Orpheum himself catalogs the trimmings needed to make June more professional and concludes, "in jig time / You'll be being booked in the big time!" (*F* 58). This middle section is sandwiched by the main sections of the song in which Rose contrasts herself to and contemptuously dismisses "some people," the sweater-knitting, bingo-playing, rent-paying people who make up the bulk of the population. What, for Rose, separates the "some people" from the people praised (imaginatively) by Mr. Orpheum? Talent. For Rose, the people who pursue and achieve the dream of stardom are special people, people made special by talent. In Gypsy Rose Lee's memoir, which was the source for the musical, one of the veteran performers appearing with Baby June and company on the Pantages Circuit longs for a return to the big time, and tells June's mother, "There's something about the Big Time I can't explain. [. . .] When you walk in the stage door it sort of hits you. You *feel* important. You know you wouldn't *be* there if you weren't good."[14] This, then, is the foundation of Rose's dream of stardom: the assumption that those who achieve this dream and become stars are special; their talent makes them different from the mass of "some people." For Rose to give up the dream of stardom—to accept Herbie's marriage proposal and his vision of a normal, stationary, job-house-backyard-school life after June leaves or after the act is booked into the Wichita burlesque house—is not only to admit failure but also to admit that she and her daughters are not special; they're just "some people" like everybody else.[15]

The "some people," of course, the ones Rose says "sit on their butts" (*F* 58), are the people devoted to the dream of home and family. For them, having a secure place to live and secure family relationships is the goal at which their work and dreams are aimed. In the early-twentieth-century context of the completion of Manifest Destiny and onset of the Great Depression, during which most of the action of *Gypsy* takes place, the dream of home and family seems to be a watered-down version of the frontier myth—the process of moving west and claiming and settling land replaced by stasis and the desire for safety. This replacement suggests an entropic degeneration whereby the myth that for good or bad created the United States became empty, a myth without meaning. We see this in *Gypsy* in the numbers the vaudevillians perform. In these numbers characters achieve something approaching the dream of stardom only to reject it in favor of values associated with the dream of home and family. The best example is the "Farm Boys" number, created by Rose to show-case June and seen by us when the act auditions for Grantziger's Palace. June is established as a farm girl with a special friendship with her cow, Caroline. But when the chance comes up to accompany several dancing chorus gents to New York to be a Broadway star, June, "dazzling, glamor-ous" (41), is ready to give up the farm and Caroline. At the last minute, however, June stops the train, giving up her Broadway dream to stay with Caroline. In an overrehearsed speech, she explains that "everything in life that really matters is right here! What care I for tinsel and glamour when I have friendship and true love?" (42). June's character gives up the dream of stardom and embraces the dream of home and family, and Rose has made this embracing the punch line of an act the purpose of which is to propel June to stardom. The image of the dream of home and family is invoked but divorced from any meaning beyond an anticipated visceral, sentimental reaction from the audience.

In the world of the play, then, the dream of home and family has be-come an image of itself, a corny, crowd-pleasing show-business device and a rhetorical posture, a myth about America that can be occasionally alluded to but one only the sappiest characters (Louise and Herbie) be-lieve in. Yet the play reveals the dream of stardom to be equally hyperreal, an image of itself that has lost its meaning. Earlier I asserted that Rose's dream of stardom comes true in an unexpected and weird way. It comes

"Dainty June and Her Farm Boys": Lane Bradbury (June), Ethel Merman (Rose), and the original cast of *Gypsy*. Credit Line: Photo by Friedman-Abeles/©The New York Public Library for the Performing Arts

true unexpectedly when Louise, after Rose urges her to go on for the AWOL stripper, actually becomes a star. In the montage sequence, we see her move from the burlesque house in Wichita to ones in Detroit, Philadelphia, Boston, and finally to Minsky's in New York, her act becoming more confident and polished at each stop. The dream comes true weirdly because Louise lacks the one thing that for Rose separates stars from the "some people": talent. In her memoir Gypsy Rose Lee recalled her reaction to her first appearance as a stripper: "I didn't have to sing or dance or do anything. I could be a star without any talent at all, and I had just proved it."[16] In the play Louise knows that she does not have any talent. "I don't really mind," she says, "except Momma would like it better if I did" (47). Later, however, in the burlesque house, Tessie Tura answers Louise's admission of having no talent with "to be a stripper all you need to have is no talent" (82). This claim presages Louise's rise to stardom and undercuts Rose's ideas of both stardom and show business. It also points toward stardom at the turn of the twenty-first century, when celebrities are famous, successful, and wealthy not because they are talented but because they are famous, successful, and wealthy.

The play ends with Louise and Rose ensconced in a culture of hyperreality. Louise, who, as we saw earlier, was so thoroughly interpellated into her mother's show-business fantasies that she marked no difference between real and representation and so felt herself disconnected from the real emotional attachments that might give her a solid sense of identity, now embraces the image of stardom, the success without talent, and the ambiguity of an image-created identity. In an argument with Rose in her Minsky's dressing room, she says, "*Nobody laughs at me*—because I laugh first! *At* me! ME—from Seattle; me—with no education; me, with no talent—as you've kept reminding me my whole life. Look at me now: a star! [. . .] I'm having the time of my life because for the first time it *is* my life! I love it! I love every second of it and I'm damned if you're going to take it away from me! I *am* Gypsy Rose Lee! I love her [. . .]" (101). Note the confusion in Louise's referring to Gypsy Rose Lee in both the first person and third person; she is impossibly both an image—a role played by Louise—and Louise's identity. Again, image and reality are conflated, and the difference between them is made irrelevant.[17]

For her part, Rose wants to hold on to the conviction that achieving stardom requires talent. Her frustration with Louise's no-talent stardom is the cause of her bickering with Louise in the dressing-room scene and is the impetus for her great eleven o'clock number, "Rose's Turn." This song begins as a desperate cry for attention, a recognition that Rose herself has the talent, the specialness, that makes a real star. She says, "With what I have in me, I could've been better than ANY OF YOU! What I got in me—what I been holding down inside of me—if I ever let it out, there wouldn't be signs big enough! There wouldn't be lights bright enough!" (104). As she sings, she again makes the distinction between herself and the great mass of untalented "some people":

Some people got it and make it pay,
Some people can't even give it away!
This people's got it [. . . .] (*F* 75)

As the song goes on, Rose comes to realize what her daughters and the audience have recognized for some time: that her ambition for her daughters to be stars is her own displaced desire to be seen as special. As she embarrassedly admits to Louise, who has observed the song from the wings, "Just wanted to be noticed" (107).

On the most immediate level the play ends ambiguously. Rose and Louise reach a cautious reconciliation, though viewers might wonder if Rose's epiphany has changed her so much that they will not be fighting again the day after the play ends.[18] This reconciliation is effected through a new dream of Rose's: "It was a big poster of a mother and daughter— you know, like the cover of that ladies' magazine. [. . .] Only it was you and me, wearing exactly the same gown. It was an ad for Minsky—and the headline said: MADAM ROSE—AND HER DAUGHTER, GYPSY!" (108). The stage directions tell us that Rose indicates that Gypsy gets top billing. This image seems to do two things. First, it is a restatement of the dream of stardom; the image Rose describes suggests that the two women have wealth, fame, and talent. Second, it is a restatement of the dream of family, if not home; the image stresses the family relationship between the two women. On one level we might assume that this final dream marks a reconciliation of the two women and the two dreams. Yet we have to notice that Rose does not describe the reconciliation—she describes a photograph, a poster, an advertisement of the reconciliation. That the play insists that this is an image of mother and daughter united in stardom rather than the actual thing returns us to the theme of the hyperreal. The America of the play is one in which the dreams that have historically motivated its people and have given them a vocabulary to articulate the meaning of their country and their lives have become images, useful nostalgically to raise an emotion in a vaudeville audience, but no longer connected to any real meaning or real experience.

To further emphasize America's nineteenth-century certainties folding in on themselves to become a series of images, a twentieth-century fun house of distorting mirrors, the play itself is presented not as the direct, realistically depicted adventures of Rose and her daughters but as a theatrical representation of those adventures. In Jerome Robbins's original staging, vaudeville-style placards were built into the proscenium to announce each scene as if it were an act on the Orpheum Circuit. In

Sam Mendes's 2003 Broadway revival, the physical design of each scene allowed the audience to see backstage at the Shubert Theatre, including stagehands observing the action from the wings. In Arthur Laurents's 2008 Broadway revival, the actual proscenium, with changing placards, was mirrored by a second, false proscenium, which was tattered and broken in a way that was reminiscent of the Weismann Theater in *Follies*. One amateur production I saw in Rochester, New York, had the background for each setting painted on canvas that was hung between stanchions; with each new scene, the stagehands brought out the new painted canvas and stanchions. Each of these design strategies emphasizes the theatricality of the play, that the audience is watching a theatrical representation—an image—of the action.

Gypsy, then, uses a show-business metaphor to depict the nature of post-pioneer, post-frontier, post–Manifest Destiny America. The dreams and master narratives that gave meaning to the nineteenth century collapse as the continent is settled and fall back onto themselves, looping entropically, drained of meaning, existing only as images that take on a life of their own, no longer providing cultural or societal meaning but proliferating nonreferentially to create a culture of images to mask the run-down, used-up, dead-like-vaudeville thing America has become.

Sondheim's next show, *A Funny Thing Happened on the Way to the Forum*, also recalls vaudeville, but not for a meditation on the exhaustion of the American Dream. Instead, *Forum* takes old comic shtick from vaudeville and uses it to treat even older shtick—plots from the classical Roman comedies of Plautus. The result is a wickedly funny, lowbrow farce. The first produced show for which Sondheim provided both music and lyrics, *Forum* opened at the Alvin (now Neil Simon) Theatre on 8 May 1962, with book by Burt Shevelove and Larry Gelbart and direction by the venerable George Abbott, with substantial out-of-town assistance from Jerome Robbins.[19] Based in and celebrating older comedic forms and having as its main purpose making the audience laugh itself silly, *Forum* lacks the seriousness of theme of *West Side Story* and *Gypsy*, but in two ways, like them, it fits uncomfortably in the Rodgers and Hammerstein tradition and stretches itself beyond its conventions. The first way is in its score. If the goal of a Rodgers and Hammerstein–style show is to integrate the songs completely into the plot, *Forum* is remarkably unintegrated. Sond-heim has said, "*Forum* is not generally recognized as being experimental [. . .] but I find it very experimental. *Forum* is a direct antithesis of the Rodgers and Hammerstein school. The songs could be removed from the show and it wouldn't make any difference." Shevelove maintains that the songs, rather than advance the plot or develop character, provide a respite from the breakneck pace of the plot: "Without the songs, the show would become relentless. It would exhaust you and you wouldn't get any breath-ers, any savoring of certain moments."[20] This disconnection between the songs and the book is in some ways a return to the pre–Rodgers and Hammerstein musical comedy, a disconnection that will be mined more deeply for its thematic potential in some of Sondheim's later shows.

The second way in which *Forum* moves away from the Rodgers and Hammerstein tradition is in the area of narrative. In one sense the play's narrative seems to function traditionally. Like the Shakespearean com-edies I referenced earlier, it shatters the social order of its setting, a street in ancient Rome, spinning it into chaos, only to restore order at the end. In another sense, however, it is through the unleashing of narrative, disso-ciating it from its representational function, or, perhaps more accurately, reversing its representational function so that, instead of mirroring real-ity, narrative creates reality, that the play smashes order and generates chaos. To understand this, we need to examine the play's main character, Pseudolus. Pseudolus is a slave who seeks his freedom; this motivation fuels the main dramatic arc of the play. As befits a man who desires to overturn the social order (a slave becoming free!), Pseudolus continually challenges authority by mocking, parodying, and thus undermining those who attempt to exercise power on him. He is something of a deconstruc-tive agent, using wordplay—puns, jokes, non sequiturs, signifying—to defuse the operations of power of those above him in the social order, who, him being a slave, is just about everyone.

Connected to this wordplay is his use of narrative, by which I mean the story he tells the audience (the plot of the play, how he will get his free-dom) and the stories he tells the other characters (as he attempts to get his freedom). What is striking about the first use of narrative is that Pseu-dolus is not bound by a definite plot. As circumstances change ever more chaotically around him, he continually revises his story: he will buy Philia so that Hero will free him; he will arrange for Hero and Philia to sail away together; he will drug Philia so that she will go with Hero; he will convince the captain who has bought Philia that she has died so he will go away and Philia can go with Hero; and so on. The events of the play are such that they cannot be contained by a single narrative arc. Narrative as a controlling, ordering device is exploded. Pseudolus's second use of narrative fuels much of the play's humor. At the same time that he is revising the play's main story (how he will become free), Pseudolus is creating narratives for the other characters, some of them true, some of them partly true, some of them completely false. He tells Lycus that Philia has the Cretan plague. He tells Senex that Philia is a new maid. He tells Erronius that his house is haunted. He tells Miles Gloriosus first that he is Lycus, then that his bride has escaped, then that his bride has died. And so on. The humor comes from the way that these narratives generate their own reality; each of the characters to whom Pseudolus tells a story accepts that story as the truth, as representing reality, and then acts according to that reality. To Lycus, Philia is dying and may contaminate his other girls. To Senex, Philia is a maid who lusts for him. To Erronius, the house is haunted, and he must run around the seven hills of Rome seven times to exorcise it. To Miles, Senex's house is the house of Lycus, and his bride has died. There is barely an exchange in the play in which Pseudolus does not generate a new reality for one of the characters, and by the chase scene near the end of the second act, these various realities are crashing into each other and provoking confusion over the very nature of reality.

Erronius's announcement about his kidnapped children being identified by a ring with a gaggle of geese and the realization that Philia and the captain are sister and brother work to revise the play's narratives, shift character relationships, allow Philia and Hero to be together, and give Pseudolus his freedom. So even though it all indeed turns out all right, the play has raised interesting questions about the limitations and possibilities of narrative as well as about the process of narrative representation. These ideas will be treated with more seriousness and in more depth in later plays.

Earlier, in our discussion of *West Side Story*, we looked at how identity is constructed by means of ideologically charged discourse, how a sub-ject position offers the possibilities to resist or replicate the dominant ideology, and how a sense of identity is achieved by the maintenance of strict boundaries. All of these ideas are corollaries to the postmodern skepticism about the concept of identity based in a stable, autonomous individual. Exploring the limitations and possibilities of identity in a post-modern world is the main thematic focus of *Anyone Can Whistle*, which opened at the Majestic Theatre on 4 April 1964 with music and lyrics by Stephen Sondheim and book by Arthur Laurents. *Anyone Can Whistle*, a determinedly groundbreaking musical, was a celebrated failure, its nine-performance run inspiring pans and praise, fault-finders and fans. One fan was Columbia Records president Goddard Lieberson, who decided to make the cast recording despite the brief run, thus preserving the original performances and earning such gratitude that Sondheim dedicated the score to him.[21]

Anyone Can Whistle is set in a town whose economy is based in the manufacture of a product that never wears out. When the market is sati-ated, of course, the town falls into ruin and its citizens into poverty and despair. An offstage narrator establishes the play's concern with identity when he introduces a group of ragged, depressed citizens and says, "It'll take a miracle to make them human again. [. . .]"[22] A miracle of a kind is arranged by Mayoress Cora Hoover Hooper and her corrupt admin-istrators, Treasurer Cooley, Chief of Police Magruder, and Comptroller Schub: they set up a pump to spurt water from a rock, which is taken for a miracle. Although the style of "Miracle Song" suggests a religious revival, there is more Edward L. Bernays than Aimee Semple McPherson in its message. The miracle is aimed at the townspeople and, eventually, pil-grims who are desperately dissatisfied with their lives and seek some sort of opportunity for transformation. The townspeople, who immediately buy into the transformative potential of the miracle, sing, "It's a miracle that's going to change your life!" (*F* 117). For them, it offers "hope," "an answer," "New life," "True happiness" (*F* 117). For Cora and her henchmen, however, the miracle is designed to line their own pockets, and it is sold as any other product is sold: by appealing to consumers' dissatisfaction and promising to alleviate it. In this case, the miracle is sold much as mouthwash, the latest fashions, or the newest tech toy is sold: by promising the townspeople that their existential crises can be resolved by buying it. Cora sings,

> Come and take the waters
> For a modest fee.
> Come and take the waters
> And feel new.
> Come and take the waters
> And with luck you'll be
> Anything whatever, except you. (*F* 117–18)

She follows this claim for total transformation with Madison Avenue–style promises:

> Come and take the waters,
> And with luck you'll be
> Happy and successful! [. . .]
> Liked and loved and beautiful and perfect! [. . .]
> Healthy, rich, handsome, independent,
> Wise, adjusted and secure and athletic! (*F* 118)

That the townspeople and tourists flock to the rock shows how well Cora and company have estimated the market for their product and how desperately people want to abandon the identity they find themselves in and to become something different. Unfortunately for them, this fake miracle ends up making them, not more human, but only excellent consumers.

This general existential situation is localized in the Cookies, the inmates from Dr. Detmold's Asylum for the Socially Pressured, the polite name for the town's insane asylum; the impolite name is the Cookie Jar. The Cookies are succinctly described by Fay Apple, the head nurse at the Cookie Jar and a devotee of science, reason, and order: "Quarantined out of fear their disease may be contagious, they are people who made other people nervous by leading individual lives" (34). The implication is that the Cookies, presumably unlike the so-called sane townspeople, refuse to conform to the socially constructed expectations for their identities.

Where the townspeople dislike their lives but act to change them only in approved ways (like the miracle), the Cookies apparently have acted in unofficial and thus disapproved ways. The Cookie about whom we know the most is a perfect example. J. Bowden Hapgood arrives in the town and is mistaken for a new doctor for the asylum. He later reveals to Fay, however, that he is in fact another, just-committed Cookie. Once a logician and an adviser to the president, Hapgood realizes one day that logic can be used "to prove any side of any question" (126), so he travels the world performing stunts that reveal the contradictions and absurdities at the heart of the official operations of power. He boasts to Fay of his arrests: "Once I held an aquacade off a testing island. That was my hundredth arrest. Then day before yesterday, I went to the UN—and played 'Auld Lang Syne' on my horn" (127). His refusal to conform to others' ways of thinking and his insistence on challenging the ideological status quo have resulted in his being committed to the Cookie Jar. The diagnosis of insanity, then, is not indicative of something wrong with the Cookie but fear of what the Cookie represents: the possibility of creating an identity outside the workings of the dominant ideology and the possibility of challenging that ideology. It is thus not surprising that when Fay and Schub are arguing over whether the Cookies can take the miraculous waters (Schub is afraid that if they do and are not visibly cured, the miracle will be exposed as a hoax), the Cookies mingle with the townspeople and pilgrims and nobody can tell the difference.

The methods by which the Cookies are eventually returned to the Cookie Jar in act 3 reveal much about identity construction. The first is naming. As we saw in our discussion of *West Side Story,* naming and labeling provide a means of knowing, understanding, containing, and controlling. In *Anyone Can Whistle,* the town's corrupt administrators use labels to discredit and disempower those who try to challenge them. For example, when Fay tries to announce that they faked the miracle, they respond by calling her "Anarchist!," "Atheist!," and, anachronistically, "Suffragette!" The townspeople quickly join in with "Communist! Fascist! Red! Pink! Cheat! Liar! Fraud! Foreigner! Stoolpigeon! Embezzler! Capitalist! Egghead!" (170–71). That many of these labels are contradictory matters less than that they serve as ways of demonizing Fay as an outsider, a nonconformist, and a threat.

A second way the Cookies are controlled is through their dossiers. The dossiers represent all the discourse about the Cookies, gathered into one place. We can imagine the type of information the dossiers hold: name, age, sex, employment, criminal record, voting record, financial record, and on and on. This information—and the ideologically charged discourse in which it is represented—creates the officially defined identity for each Cookie. It is an objective representation of the Althusserian process of interpellation, or construction of subjectivity, that we discussed earlier. Recognizing the power these dossiers have to define and control the identities of the Cookies, Hapgood urges Fay to destroy them. He says, "Most people'd like to be torn up and set free. [. . .] They could stop pretending to be like everybody else and go back to living the way they want; they could enjoy!" (120). In the original production, when Fay began tearing up dossiers, a ballet ensued wherein, as each dossier was destroyed, its corresponding person began to dance, as the stage directions explain, finally able "to be what they want" (130).

The third method of controlling the Cookies is the most straightforwardly repressive way: their being committed to the Cookie Jar, an asylum where all their actions, movements, and speech can be supervised. Hapgood, exhausted from his idealistic attempts to save the world, faces the prospect of confinement with relief. He says, "I'm free now! [. . .] I'm not responsible to or for anything or anyone" (128). However, this is a freedom—the freedom to hand over the responsibility for one's identity to an institution—that is not free at all. Institutionalized, the Cookies not only eschew responsibility and agency but also, ironically, end up conforming, marching and singing together and all exhibiting the same eerie smile on their faces. Their identities are lost in the overarching, overwhelming, and officially dictated identity of Cookie.

All these official means of controlling the Cookies' identities are subverted by one of Hapgood's stunts. Mistaken for the new psychiatrist, Hapgood arrives in the town square just in time to be called on to separate the Cookies from the townspeople and pilgrims, all now indistinguishable. Thus begins "Simple," a long musical interrogation scene in which Hapgood, rather than reestablishing the Cookies', townspeople's, and pilgrims' identities, attacks the foundations of identity construction in the service of ideology. The first way he does this is through asking each

"Simple": Janet Hayes (June), Harvey Evans (John), Harry Guardino (Hapgood), and the original cast of *Anyone Can Whistle*. Credit Line: Photo by Friedman-Abeles/©The New York Public Library for the Performing Arts

person he examines for his or her watchcry. As he explains to George, the first man he interrogates, "when you were a child [. . .] I'm sure there was a saying you learned that you have used ever since to govern your life. A motto, a watchcry" (54–55). George responds, "I am the master of my fate / And the captain of my soul!" (*F* 120), and Hapgood uses that as the basis of his questioning:

HAPGOOD: Married?
GEORGE: Yes, sir.
HAPGOOD: Two children?
GEORGE: Yes, sir.
HAPGOOD: Two TV sets?
GEORGE: Yes, sir.
HAPGOOD: Two martinis?

GEORGE: Yes, sir.
HAPGOOD: Bank on Friday?
GEORGE: Yes, sir.
HAPGOOD: Golf on Saturday?
GEORGE: Yes, sir.
HAPGOOD: Church on Sunday?
GEORGE: Yes, sir.
HAPGOOD: Do you vote?
GEORGE: Yes, sir.
Only for the man who wins. (*F* 120–21)

Hapgood's inquiries reveal George's perfect interpellation into the expectations of his society. Hapgood reveals that George's watchcry is a mockery (he is obviously far from being the master of his life) and demonstrates the process by which, from childhood, we are all the targets of discourse that tells us what to think, what to believe, how to act, and how to be.

The second way Hapgood subverts the processes of identity construction is by questioning naming and tearing down the boundaries that limit identity. When asked to identify who on the line waiting to take the miraculous waters is a Cookie and who a genuine pilgrim, he begins by asserting the principle he secretly plans to explode:

Grass is green,
Sky is blue,
False is false
And true is true.
Who is who?
You are you, I'm me! (*F* 120)

To this way of thinking, distinctions between true and false are definite, and boundaries between individuals—you and me—are secure. However, when he calls on the first person to interrogate, George, he calls him by his own name, Hapgood. The dialogue that follows creates further confusion and seems more Abbott and Costello than Freud and Jung:

HAPGOOD: Now then, Mr. Hapgood—

GEORGE: Call me Happy, Sir. Or George.
HAPGOOD: All right, Georgie.
GEORGE: Thank you, George. (54)

Where a few minutes before, the distinction between me and you was secure, now Hapgood sings, "You be you / And me to some degree" (*F* 121). Connections between name and person are breaking, and boundaries between individuals are falling.

The third way Hapgood subverts the social construction of identity is the division of all the intermixed Cookies, townspeople, and pilgrims into two categories: Group A and Group One. Cora and the administrators assume at first that one of these groups is for the townspeople and pilgrims and the other is for the Cookies; they imagine a straight binary opposition—sane/insane. It soon becomes clear, however, that there is no logical scheme behind the categorization. As the song goes on, Hapgood sorts the crowd into the two groups quite casually and arbitrarily. At what is perhaps his most forthright moment, he explains the appeal and the use of groups:

The opposite of safe is out.
The opposite of out is in.
So anyone who's safe is "in." [. . .]
That's how groups begin! (*F* 121)

This is all familiar from our discussion of *West Side Story*: the Jets and Sharks take their identity from group membership; the group creates and maintains boundaries; the group provides protection; the group creates a sense of superiority over those outside the group. For the Jets and Sharks, however, there is a fairly clear basis for determining membership, who's in and who's out. Group A and Group One have no such basis, and that's the point. Hapgood is revealing the arbitrariness, not necessarily of the basis for determining group membership, but of using group membership as a means of creating a sense of identity.

So on the one hand, Hapgood, by dividing everyone into these two groups, is exposing one means by which ideology constructs compliant subjects and is liberating the townspeople and pilgrims from their officially approved subject positions, but on the other hand, he is demonstrating that group membership, regardless of how arbitrary or even silly the basis for the group is, is dangerous and threatens a complete loss of individuality in group identity.[23] Near the climax of the interrogation scene, after all the people on the line have joined a group, Hapgood shows their mindless conformity by having them alternately and then together rub their stomachs and pat their heads while saying, parrot-like, "Good" and "Hello" (*F* 123). At the very beginning of act 2, both groups celebrate themselves in a march:

> GROUP A: Hooray for A,
> The Group that's well-adjusted,
> Everyone can be trusted
> In Group A.
> GROUP ONE: Have fun with One,
> The Group that's not neurotic,
> Everyone's patriotic
> In Group One.
> BOTH: Dignity, integrity, and so on,
> We haven't much to go on,
> Still we go on.
> We've a platform strong enough to grow on.
> GROUP A: Whenever they cheer, we're incensed!
> GROUP ONE: Whatever they're for, we're against! (*F* 125)

This is almost a parody of "Jet Song." Group membership provides an opportunity for self-aggrandizement, a chauvinistic superiority over outsiders, and self-definition based in an opposition to non-group-members. Group membership is also dangerous in the abrogation of agency it offers. Both groups sing, "As long as we're told where to go, / There isn't a thing we need to know!" (*F* 125). Having been freed from the controlling power of Cora and her henchmen, the townspeople submit themselves to Hapgood, following his directions, carrying him about the town, and singing his praises. However, part of Hapgood's point in all this seems to be that whether a dictator is oppressive or benevolent, he or she is still a dictator. The interrogation and the division into groups have exposed much of the ideological workings of subject construction, but it has not created a way for the townspeople to be responsible for their own identities.

Connected to the process of the social construction of identity is, as we saw in chapter 1, the idea of performance. Through a variety of means—parental example, education, religion, politics, art, advertising, the media, popular culture—we are taught both our identities and how to perform them in socially approved ways. We even learn, as Beats, Hippies, or Punks, to perform our nonconformity. In short, in learning our identities, we are much like actors preparing to play a role, although in our cases the preparation and role-playing are usually unconscious. This idea is introduced in *Anyone Can Whistle* at the very end of act 1, after Hapgood's interrogation has created chaos among the townspeople, pilgrims, Cookies, and administrators. Hapgood, in an almost complete blackout, looks straight at the audience and says, "You are all mad" (80). The lights then come up, and, according to the stage directions, "we see the company sitting in theatre seats and laughing and applauding louder and louder [. . .]" (80). Not only has another boundary been punctured, the boundary between actors onstage and the audience, but also, in suddenly switching roles, in pointing at, laughing at, and applauding for the audience, the people onstage force the audience members into the role of the actors, the spectacle rather than the spectators. This potentially uncomfortable moment asks the audience, in the wake of the interrogation scene, to think of the ways their identities are wrapped up in performance.

This concept of identity as performance can be seen at work in the play's three main characters, Cora, Fay, and Hapgood. Cora's character is the most obviously performative, but Cora is also the least self-conscious about her performance. Her main numbers—"Me and My Town," "A Parade in Town," and "I've Got You to Lean On"—stand out from the rest of the score in their brassy, larger-than-life, Broadwayness. Sondheim says of these songs, "All the numbers Angie [Angela Lansbury, who created the role] sang in the show were pastiche—her opening number, for instance, was a Hugh Martin–Kay Thompson pastiche. The character always sang in musical comedy terms because she was a lady who dealt in attitudes instead of emotions."[24] For example, in the second act, when Group One and Group A march Hapgood around the town and Cora feels abandoned and unloved, she sings "A Parade in Town," a song similar in style and content to songs from two musicals that had opened earlier in the 1963–64 season: "Before the Parade Passes By," from *Hello, Dolly!,* and "Nobody's Gonna Rain on My Parade," from *Funny Girl.* Both of these songs are sung by dynamic leading ladies at moments when they need to make life-changing decisions, but, of course, both are presented realistically, in the Rodgers and Hammerstein sense. In *Anyone Can Whistle* the moment is presented, not realistically, but self-referentially. Faced with a crisis, Cora responds with a song because that is what the conventions of the Broadway musical demand for a musical-theater diva. It does not transform her or give her character a new resolve or direction—it just gives her a number. The only problem it solves is Cora not being the center of attention: thanks to the number, she gets to take center stage. Thus the audience sees that Cora is a character who lacks character. Her performance is her character.

Nurse Fay Apple's performance and identity situation is more complex. Her character, as Fay tells us repeatedly, is based in science, control, and order. An empiricist, she believes only that which can be proven logically and scientifically—thus her skepticism about the miracle and her determination to prove it false. As she says in her long, character-defining speech in act 1, "I *am* in love with reason and against any balderdash superstition that holds up progress, and those dripping waters of yours not only hold it up, they flood and drown it" (35). On the one hand, her devotion to science, control, and order provides a basis for her challenging the machinations of the administrators. On the other hand, however, her denial of the miraculous, of the reality of anything that cannot be proven logically, leaves her unable to effect any real change. She is critical of the status quo but unable to imagine a better future. In that sense, she is interpellated into the dominant ideology as effectively as the townspeople.

Of course, this is the identity she unself-consciously performs, the woman of science, the devotee of logic, reason, and order. The very nature of this performed identity implies a self-control, a repression of all aspects of her character that stray from the reasonable and the ordered. That there are other aspects of her character is hinted at in the song she sings as she flees the administrators who want her to identify the Cookies on the line for the miracle, "There Won't Be Trumpets":

There are heroes in the world,
Princes and heroes in the world,
And one of them will save us! (*F* 119)

Here she reveals a romantic desire shaped by childhood fairy tales. Later, under Hapgood's probing, she admits that a part of her hopes the miracle is real for the Cookies' sake and her own. She says, "[. . .] I *need* a miracle!" (106). She longs to escape the planned and the proper, to be spontaneous, intuitive, unbound by rules and convention.

She deals with this aspect of her character through her performance as the Lady from Lourdes. As the Lady from Lourdes, Fay wears a costume—a sexy red dress, an extravagantly feathered coat, and a red wig—and self-consciously acts, speaking in, the stage directions tell us, "one of the thickest French accents in captivity" (84). The costume, especially the wig, allows the ego-dominated Nurse Apple to open up to her id. She explains, "Eight years ago, at the hospital where I was training, we put on a graduation play. I was what I still am—control and order—so everyone thought it would be funny to make me be a French *soubrette*. This was the dress; zis was ze accent; and (*She holds up the wig*) I put it on; I wore it to the party afterwards. A week later I woke up in a hotel room in Cleveland with an interne" (104). Fay is so insistent on control that she blames something external to herself—the wig—for aspects of her own character she does not want to admit to. Only in performance as the Lady from Lourdes can her whole identity, in all its complexity and contradiction, come out. Then, she is a person capable of claiming agency and engaging the ideologies of control. In the act 3 "Cookie Chase," when the administrators decide to lock up as Cookies the first forty-nine people they can capture, Fay in her role as the Lady from Lourdes is an agent of chaos, disrupting the plan by repeatedly releasing the just-captured people, leading their escapes, and singing a warning to the town. However, after she is recognized by Dr. Detmold and her wig is removed, Fay succumbs to Schub's faux-logical appeal ("We are going to lock up forty-nine people, Nurse Apple. Whether that includes the innocent—depends on a lady who claims she fights for justice" [171]) and, defeated, recites the names of the Cookies. As Nurse Apple, all ego, logic, order, and control, she despises the administrators, but she is helpless to fight them.

Hapgood is in many ways Fay's opposite. As Sondheim, looking back at the show, put it, "Our two principal characters were an idealist who turns out to be a cynic and a cynic who turns out to be a romanticist."[25] Where Fay is controlled, Hapgood is spontaneous. Where Fay insists on logic as a definitive means of knowing the world, Hapgood sees it as a game that serves whoever masters it. Where Fay relies on a wig to create a performance that she can claim is out of her control, Hapgood accepts whatever performance opportunities are presented him as a way of subverting officially defined reality. We have seen the kinds of stunts he engages in as a way of protesting the operations of power; not coincidentally, they all—aquacade, trumpet playing, "Doctor" Hapgood—involve some kind of performance, or rather performances, as the roles he plays change in relation to specific operations of power. This constant re-self-creation becomes in essence his identity, an identity the coherence of which lies in its opposition to officially promulgated ideologies. This continual reinvention is apparently effective in some ways, but it is also wearing. That is why, on one level, he welcomes his commitment to the Cookie Jar: he has an identity-providing label that relieves him from his responsibility as perpetual protestor. He says, "I'm a retired Don Quixote!" (128).

As we saw earlier, however, Hapgood's relief at entering the Cookie Jar, at retiring from trying to save the world, is only partly true. Given the chance, as when he is mistaken for a doctor and asked to identify the Cookies in the crowd, he takes on a new role and uses it to kick the shins of those in power. His desire to be saved from a life of world-saving comes at least partly from his weariness and the repeated failure of his efforts. We see this in his blasé reaction when Groups One and A turn against him after the administrators shut down the miracle: "That's par for people" (152). Fay is defeated because she reverts to her position of angry helplessness against the operations of power; Hapgood is defeated because, despite a life of performative activism, he never expects to win. Neither accepts the possibility that he or she may have agency to affect significantly the official construction of reality.

Where, then, are Fay and Hapgood left? It is a cliché that opposites attract, yet each of them desires in the other what he or she lacks. In Fay, Hapgood sees stability and the ability to get things done; in Hapgood, Fay sees faith in the possibility of making the world over. These desires, however, are what they fear make it impossible for them to remain together. Their society offers them no unambiguous place or way to be. In this sense, they are like Tony and Maria in *West Side Story,* looking for a "Somewhere," a place where they can be together outside the ideologies of power. Fay and Hapgood, however, are more sophisticated than Tony and Maria. They understand that a place and a way to be may be claimed only contingently. In their final duet, "With So Little to Be Sure Of," Hapgood sings,

> If there's anything at all,
> I'm sure of here and now and us together.

> All I'll ever be I owe you,
> If there's anything to be. (*F* 138)

Here, knowledge and identity are unmoored from certainties, absolutes, and ideologies, but such an unmooring can exist only temporarily, for "a moment" (*F* 138). However, even a moment can be a miracle.

While the plays we have looked at so far—*West Side Story, Gypsy, Anyone Can Whistle,* and, in its way, *A Funny Thing Happened on the Way to the Forum*—explore ideas that are associated with postmodernism, their form and structure, and by extension their aesthetic, are for the most part grounded in the Rodgers and Hammerstein tradition. Their themes are developed in the context of characters moving through a narrative plot, a context that provides the aesthetic justification for the musical numbers. If on the one hand we can see *West Side Story* and *Gypsy* pointing toward the future of the musical theater, we can on the other hand see them, along with *My Fair Lady* and *Fiddler on the Roof,* as the fullest realization of the Rodgers and Hammerstein aesthetic. *Company,* which opened at the Alvin (now Neil Simon) Theatre on 26 April 1970, with music and lyrics by Sondheim, book by George Furth, direction by Harold Prince, and choreography by Michael Bennett, does something different.[26] *Company* is arguably the first musical of the postmodern era because it bases its self-reflexivity, its self-conscious attention to its own form, in an eschewal of narrative structure. In so doing, the play dramatizes the postmodern dilemma: how to find meaning in a culture where inherited certainties have been discredited and traditional narratives have failed.

Before going on, we should understand the nature and significance of narrative structure. Put simply, traditional narrative structure implies a set of events turned into a story through the organizing principles of beginning, middle, and end. This basic structure, however, is significant beyond providing a way of thinking about drama or fiction. Narrative is a means by which human beings take phenomena that would otherwise be disconnected and organize them into an epistemological structure. Such theorists as Lyotard, Bauman, and White have argued that narrative is basic to our culture's ways of knowing.[27] In *The Order of Things*, Michel Foucault describes what he calls the *modern episteme*—the fundamental structure by which knowledge is constructed in a particular era—as consisting of origin, end, and the cause-and-effect sequence that connects origin to end, a structure that narrative shares. Some important implications arise from this. First, knowledge exists in time; to be known, phenomena must be understood as being in process. Second, nothing can be known completely and finally until it is part of a completed structure, until its end has been reached. This offers something of a contradiction: on the one hand, phenomena must be known in time, in process, in history; on the other hand, for phenomena to be known finally, time must be stopped—phenomena must reach the end of their process. This contradiction is finessed by our projecting forward an anticipated end that will complete the structure and imagining a conceptual structure (what Foucault calls *History*) that we see simultaneously with the actual, in-process structure (what Foucault calls *history*). For example, Christian faith conceptualizes a History marked by original sin, Christ's sacrifice and redemption, and the anticipated return of Christ at the end of time. This conceptual structure, completed by an anticipated ending, helps make sense of the in-process history Christians experience day to day. If the anticipated end, Christ's return, should never happen, the conceptual structure, incomplete, fails.[28]

One of the tenets of postmodernism is that narrative structure, while central to Western culture's epistemology, is not only not universal and necessary but also potentially imprisoning in the way it constructs and limits how we can know the world. Hayden White argues that narrative is not a neutral, transparent means of organizing knowledge. Narrative's structure—the chronological ordering, the insistence on cause and effect, the meaning-providing closure—shapes the phenomena it is organizing, forcing them into a certain form and thus into a contained set of meanings. The organizing structure affects how the phenomena it orders are known.[29] Zygmunt Bauman, taking a different tack, argues that the narrative structure of knowledge, especially as inflected in modernism, seeks to dominate. A narrative gains its power as knowledge by being the *correct* narrative, by being the most persuasive in its attempts to contain and account for all phenomena or by being supported by the most raw power. Alternative narratives, which seek to explain the same phenomena differently, threaten the power of narrative-based knowledge and its insistence on one totalized truth.[30]

To escape totalizing narrative structure, to escape it even incompletely, or at least to escape its claims to absolute truth, is a kind of liberation. It gives us the critical distance we need to examine the basis for our culture's assumptions and beliefs. It offers us the possibility of discovering different kinds of knowledge, meaning, and ways of being. It offers us, through the acceptance of multiple narratives with their multifarious and contradictory truths, relief from the will to dominate and the ideology of control. At the same time, however, it recognizes that this critical distance is not the same as separation. We can never liberate ourselves completely from narrative epistemology or the cultural systems it expresses. It leaves us simultaneously inside and outside, critical of, yet implicated in, our culture's master narratives.[31]

Narrative structure as both an aesthetic property and an epistemological paradigm is central to *Company*. The play focuses on Robert, a Manhattan bachelor, and five married couples who gather to celebrate his thirty-fifth birthday. There is no plot as such. Rather, a series of scenes follows in which Robert interacts with the couples and with three girlfriends and through which the play explores marriage and personal relationships. The play renders chronology irrelevant. Many of the scenes and songs could be put into a different order without affecting our understanding of the play or the characters. In this sense *Company* reminds us more of a revue than of a Rodgers and Hammerstein–style book musical, what Sondheim calls a "twilight-zone revue."[32] And here, the songs, which in a

"Company": Dean Jones (Robert) and the original cast of *Company*. Credit Line: Photo by
Friedman-Abeles/©The New York Public Library for the Performing Arts

Rodgers and Hammerstein–style musical seek to arise seamlessly from
characters and plot, seem detached from both. In some songs, "The Little
Things You Do Together" and "You Could Drive a Person Crazy," for example, the characters singing are commenting on a scene in which they
are not physically present. In others, such as "Getting Married Today"
and "The Ladies Who Lunch," characters step out of their physical and
dramatic setting to sing. Sondheim recalls, "Every time I tried to develop
a song out of the dialogue it didn't work. Which is why all the songs in
Company are either self-encapsulated entities or Brechtian comments on
what is happening. In the score of *Company*, nothing comes out of the
play, nothing. It's absolutely the reverse of what Oscar taught me."[33]

What, then, provides a structure for the play? Rejecting the forward-
moving, time-bound schemes of traditional narrative, the authors instead
employ a pair of cyclically repeated devices. The first is Robert's thirty-
fifth-birthday surprise party, which occurs at the opening of the play, the
end of act 1, the opening of act 2, and the end of the play. This repetition

offers some significant implications. One is that while this particular moment is repeated four times, each time it is presented differently—different dialogue and different songs. These variations liberate the birthday party and, by extension, the play as a whole from the tyranny of time. The birthday-party scenes suggest that each moment is a launching pad for multiple possibilities, all of which can exist simultaneously, with no one of them clearly the "true" one. This cyclical structure undercuts audience expectations for a forward-moving narrative with its implications about the characters' progress or growth.[34]

The second repeated device that provides structure for the play is the "Bobby Baby" musical theme. This song, in which the couples call out to Robert to talk to them and join them in various activities, recurs vocally and instrumentally throughout the play. It often returns us to the birthday-party scene and also serves as something of a musical question mark, recalling us time and again to one of the play's central concerns: Robert's identity—who is Robert? The "Bobby Baby" theme arises from the cast or orchestra at those moments large and small when Robert's sense of self is disturbed.

Company's structural experiments create a tension that contributes to the play's main thematic conflict: the world of the busy signal versus the world of relationships. The world of the busy signal is introduced with the "Bobby Baby" theme; the rhythm and dissonance of the opening vamp suggest a telephone busy signal. (In a nice touch, producer Thomas Z. Shepard inserted an actual busy signal into the opening track of Columbia's 1970 original cast recording.) Later, to reinforce this image, when Marta asks Robert what the pulse of New York City is, he replies, "A busy signal."[35] But what does the busy signal suggest about New York and Robert's life? As the "Bobby Baby" theme indicates, the world of the busy signal is full of constant activity. The couples, eventually joined by the three girlfriends, in their overlapping voices implore Robert to join them in a host of activities, activities that fill every day of the week. The "Bobby Baby" theme segues into "Company," in which Robert describes his life and his relationship with the others:

Phone rings,
Door chimes,

In comes company!
No strings,
Good times,
Room hums, company!
Late nights,
Quick bites,
Party games,
Deep talks,
Long walks,
Telephone calls. (*F* 170)

Robert neatly sums this all up when discussing his apartment with April: "[. . .] I've always liked my apartment but I'm never really in it. I just seem to pass through the living room on my way to the bedroom to go to the bathroom to get ready to go out again" (85). Robert's time is filled with unending activity, activity that is, like the play's structure and like the "Bobby Baby" theme, cyclical—repeated with variations but without moving forward in a narrative sense. Robert's life is stuck in a cycle of pleasurable but pointless activity.

The play goes on to expand the world of the busy signal from the specifics of Robert's life to the broader canvas of New York City. It does this first in the song Marta sings to punctuate the brief conversations Robert has with each of the girlfriends in act 1, scene 5: "Another Hundred People." The song describes the people who come to New York looking for something, the activities they get swept up in, and the difficulty of their being able to connect with others. Linking Robert's situation to what Marta sings, the "Bobby Baby" theme is embedded in the accompaniment, and like the "Bobby Baby" theme, "Another Hundred People" is cyclical: it is sung through two and a half times, complementing the cyclical life of the city the lyrics describe:

Another hundred people just got off of the train
And came up through the ground
While another hundred people just got off of the bus
And are looking around
At another hundred people who got off of the plane

And are looking at us
Who got off of the train
And the plane and the bus
Maybe yesterday. (*F* 179)

Set within this cycle of people coming to the city are the activities the city offers, seemingly endless, yet also impersonal:

Or they find each other in the crowded streets
And the guarded parks,
By the rusty fountains and the dusty trees
With the battered barks.
And they walk together past the postered walls
With the crude remarks,

And they meet at parties through the friends of friends
Who they never know.
Will you pick me up, or do I meet you there,
Or shall we let it go?
Did you get my message, 'cause I looked in vain?
Can we see each other Tuesday if it doesn't rain?
Look, I'll call you in the morning
Or my service will explain . . . (*F* 180)

The world of the busy signal offers crowds, parties, dates, but in it personal connection does not seem possible. As the busy signal suggests, chances for communication, on which a relationship depends, constantly fail. The world of the busy signal is a world of unread posters, dirty graffiti, and lost messages. It is a world where answering services substitute for conversation and where parks, which should be oases from the noise and grime of the city, are unsafe and unused. (In the conversation they have in this scene, Kathy tries to make Robert appreciate a park and tells him that she, like the park, is out of place in New York [53].) Marta sums this all up: New York is "a city of strangers" (*F* 179).

The world of the busy signal extends beyond the play's physical setting, New York City, to its historical setting, 1970. Although productions of *Company,* including the show's two major New York revivals, set the play in the present, the script implies a late sixties or early seventies time period.[36] Some references, like Marta's to answering services in "Another Hundred People," point to the past, as does some of the slang: in "Have I Got a Girl for You," the husbands sing of girls who "swing," of "chicks," and they sum up, "Marriage may be where it's been, / But it's not where it's at" (*F* 178–79). If the husbands sound here like a middle-aged Frank Sinatra, trying to seem with it, well, that's the point. The significance of the 1970 setting is that it suggests, never center stage but always in the background, the sixties youth culture of sex, drugs, and rock and roll, of rebellion for the sake of rebellion, all the fun that Robert's friends, having come of age in the 1950s, just missed.[37] Their frustration at having missed it comes out repeatedly. After the pot-smoking experiment, Jenny says, "Bobby, we're just too old! We were all—trying to keep up with the kids tonight" (45). In the nightclub scene, Joanne complains, "Do you know that we are suddenly at an age where we find ourselves too young for the old people and too old for the young ones. [. . .]" (105). This just-missed-it theme is most explicit in some dialogue between Robert and Peter:

PETER: Are you excited about the younger generation?
ROBERT: At moments.
PETER: Jesus, Robert, this is when *I* should be being born. This is *my* age. Wild-ass kids with probing minds rebelling against all the crap. I identify with those kids.
ROBERT: Shouldn't. You're the enemy the same as their parents.
PETER: No, sir, not I.
ROBERT: Peter, we're square to those kids. (102)

Peter feels most acutely what all Robert's friends feel to some extent: a longing for the freedom and the pleasure-seeking of the younger generation.

This longing also helps to explain the fascination that Robert holds for the couples. Despite his protestations to Peter, Robert, in embracing the world of the busy signal, has very much embraced the activities of the sixties youth culture, although in a depoliticized way. The result is perpetual pleasure-seeking. The pot-smoking scene with Jenny and David suggests that he is experienced in using marijuana and adept at obtaining it. His many sexual relationships demonstrate his enlistment in the sexual revolution. Moreover, he admits to Peter that he has had homosexual experiences. Some have latched onto this to argue that Robert's resistance to marriage is based in his homosexuality, but that's not the point. The point is that Robert, near-hedonistically immersed in the world of the busy signal, is open to anything—any action, any experience, any pleasure. As he says at the beginning of the play in response to the many messages on his answering machine, "whatever you're calling about my answer is yes" (4).

Set up in conflict with the world of the busy signal is the world of relationships and marriage. This world is in many ways a response to the busy signal: it seeks a point in the pointlessness, a goal to aim for—marriage—that promises completion and an identity, an identity made possible through a relation to another person. Jenny, David, and Robert bring out this idea in the pot-smoking scene. Jenny says, "To me a person's not complete until he's married" (39). David, in a drug-induced stupor, reasons, "Actually a man should be married. Your life has a—what? What am I trying to say? A point to it—a bottom" (39). Both Jenny and David connect marriage to ideas about narrative completeness. To their way of thinking, the world of the busy signal is the problem, because it is cyclical and pointless, and commitment to another person through marriage is the solution, because it provides a direction, a point, narrative completion, and meaning. Marriage is the happily ever after, the endpoint that resolves complications. Robert seems to sense this idea of structural completion as he tries to explain his objections to marriage. One problem with it, he says, is that "you can never not have been married again" (40). Narrative, linked as it is to the one-way flow of time, is not reversible and repeatable, as the cycle of the busy signal is. Identity implies a life story, which in turn implies a life lived in time.

Of course, *Company* offers a more complex view of marriage and relationships than the fairy-tale-ish. At times, the couples may rhetorically buy in to the happily-ever-after idea of marriage, envisioning it as offering completion and rescue from the whirl of the world of the busy signal. At other times, however, they recognize that marriage, as commitment to another, does not necessarily provide a stable, completed, purpose- and identity-providing narrative structure. In "The Little Things You Do Together," which the couples sing while observing Harry and Sarah demonstrate karate for a horrified Robert, "perfect relationships" are defined by the activities that husbands and wives perform together, but much of the humor of the activities comes from the fact that they suggest people in conflict, not collaboration:

DAVID: It's things like using force together,
LARRY: Shouting till you're hoarse together,
JOANNE: Getting a divorce together [. . . .] (*F* 175)

It is within this structural and thematic tension that Robert exists, thoroughly at home in the world of the busy signal, yet pressured by his friends and social convention to enter the world of relationships and marriage. We saw earlier the extent to which Robert is immersed in the world of the busy signal; we also saw that one of Robert's objections to marriage is its irreversibility, that in its goal-oriented, narrative-based structure it links one's life to time's arrow. One implication of the repetition with variations of Robert's thirty-fifth birthday party is that it shows us a character who is not moving forward, changing, or aging.[38] Robert might, like a thirty-five-year-old Peter Pan, sing "I Won't Grow Up." The play emphasizes this over and over. At one of the birthday parties Larry says, "It's amazing. We've gotten older every year and he seems to stay exactly the same" (80). Later, Susan says to Marta, "Is our Robert not a thing of beauty and a boy forever?" (100). Finally, near the end of the play, after Joanne shocks Robert by propositioning him and he begins thinking his way through relationships in "Being Alive," she says, "You're not a kid anymore, Robert. I don't think you'll ever be a kid again, kiddo" (115), hinting that Robert, as he moves toward his revelation, has been thrust into time.

The play suggests that Robert, by choosing to immerse himself in the world of the busy signal and by resisting the narrative constraints of marriage, has a lifestyle more than a life. What may seem to be freedom and independence lacks substance. In a telling moment, during "Side by Side by Side," David says of Robert, "You know what comes to my mind when I see him? The Seagram's Building. Isn't that funny?" (80). The Seagram's Building, designed by Ludwig Mies van der Rohe and Philip Johnson, is, famously, a glass box that reflects its surroundings; when you look at it, you see it *and* you see the neighboring buildings reflected in it. This image helps us understand Robert's character: as he exists throughout most of the play, there's no *there* there. Perhaps the reason Robert spends so much of the play observing the couples is that there is too little substance in his own life to bear examination.

If Robert has, as a rival artist's wife sings of George in *Sunday in the Park with George*, "No life in his life!" (*L* 12), it is the result of his resistance to a life story with an anticipated goal for its completion. Robert lives pleasurably, in constant motion, ceaselessly active, yet he lives superficially. His relations with the couples and the girlfriends seem less emotionally meaningful than they do potentially awkward social situations he is perpetually trying to negotiate. He speaks in clichés ("when you've got friends like mine" [6]) and apparently rehearsed speeches ("Thank you for including me in your thoughts, your lives, your families" [5]), which no one really listens to. He substitutes a carefully planned and apparently proven seduction strategy (his speech to April about the girl in Miami he left in a motel and then couldn't find again) for true emotional contact. On the morning after his night with April, in "Barcelona," he plays a scene about his wanting her to stay with him and then is horrified when she takes him seriously. When Peter tries to express his sexual attraction for him, he backs out of a difficult emotional moment by pretending that he thinks Peter is joking. For a man devoted to a life of pleasure, he seems to lack any real feelings: he is all performance—mock-sincere, mock-in-love, mock-friend.[39]

Through most of the play, Robert even pretends to have a goal for his life and to desire completion. In "Someone Is Waiting" he imagines just the right woman waiting for him, a woman who is a combination of everything he finds attractive in the wives. A problem with such an impossible combination as a goal is that this "someone" is a fantasy, no one Robert knows or is likely to find in the real world. To set as one's goal an impossible Miss Right is to avoid having a goal at all. At the end of the first act,

Robert sings another song addressed to "someone," "Marry Me a Little," originally written as the play's finale in an early draft. Here, Robert drops the mock-romanticism of "Someone Is Waiting" for a more sincere statement of his goal. As the title suggests, his goal is not marriage in the way his friends are married, but a kind of marriage, a kind of commitment that won't require him to give up the world of the busy signal. He sings his conditions for this kind of marriage: "Keep a tender distance, / So we'll both be free"; "Want me more than others, / Not exclusively"; "We won't have to give up a thing, / We'll stay who we are" (*F* 185). His idea of marriage here is a both-and that will allow him to be married but remain unchanged and unchanging. Although at the end of the song Robert sings, "I'm ready!" (*F* 186), he clearly isn't. His idea of commitment here is a commitment that puts no limitations on him or his imagined partner, a relationship without constraints. His goal is, in the end, as unrealistic as his fantasy in "Someone Is Waiting." In the play's various birthday-party scenes, Robert fails to blow out all the candles on his cake, and he denies having made a wish. This may be his most sincere statement of his goal, the endpoint that will provide a structure and meaning for his life story—he doesn't have one and doesn't want one.

In his final song, "Being Alive," Robert comes to a subtler, less definite, but more mature conclusion about commitment and relationships.[40] As we noted earlier, the motivation for Robert singing this song is Joanne's propositioning him. As Joanne stares him down, Robert tries all his usual tricks for avoiding intimacy. In a rambling, semi-drunken speech he tries mock-sincere and rehearsed conversation, he skims over possible conversational topics, and, when Joanne propositions him, he tries to dismiss her with a joke. When none of these strategies dissuades her, when he can find no escape from the spotlight she has put him in, he asks two revealing questions: "who will I take care of?" and, speaking of relationships, "What do you get?" (111). The latter question indicates a desire for a goal, a point, a forward-moving narrative that, up until now, he has resisted. The former question indicates a desire for a life story that can contain another's story. Together, the questions motivate the exploration he conducts in "Being Alive." He begins by listing his criticisms of marriage:

Someone to hold you too close,
Someone to hurt you too deep,
Someone to sit in your chair,
To ruin your sleep ... (*F* 193)

But with coaching from the couples, Robert discovers that these criticisms culminate in a sense of "being alive" (*F* 195).

The emphasis on action implied by the participle *being* is significant. As Robert enters into the main iteration of the song, Amy pleads, "Blow out the candles, Robert, and make a wish. *Want* something, Robert! Want *some*thing!" (*F* 195). She urges Robert to see and accept the idea promulgated by the couples throughout the play—that meaning for one's life comes from completion, the reaching of an endpoint that is a fulfillment via a relationship with another person—but in his song Robert proposes a different possibility for meaning. As in "Someone Is Waiting" and "Marry Me a Little," Robert addresses an unspecified and presumably unknown person, a "somebody," but here, that somebody isn't a vague and unrealistic straw woman that supports his own indecision and avoidance. Here she is a necessary element to his ability to live, to have a life story, to have a meaning for his life. Here Robert's complaints about marriage are turned into virtues. Here Robert realizes that the meaning a relationship with another person can offer isn't in the reaching of a goal, the completion of a structure, the finishing of a story with its "happily ever after." Rather, the meaning comes from the ability of a relationship with another person to force him to go beyond skimming life's surface and to make him experience life in its details, its trivia, its richness. Robert's final realization is that the meaning of a life comes not from the endpoint, looking back at a completed structure, but from being immersed in the process of living. He sings,

Somebody crowd me with love,
Somebody force me to care,
Somebody let me come through,
I'll always be there

As frightened as you,
To help us survive
Being alive, being alive,
Being alive! (*F* 195)

Life is frightening because it is unfinished, in-process. Its meaning isn't clear to us because it isn't completed, a structure that can be contemplated retrospectively from an endpoint. Its meaning must be found in the depth of the everyday and the indeterminacy of the now. Robert ends by anticipating that an intimate relationship with another person—the kind of relationship he has so far avoided—can help him discover this kind of meaning. Immersed finally in time, Robert understands that the both-and of marriage is the enfolding of another's in-process narrative into his own.

To suggest a clear, linear evolution of ideas from *West Side Story* to *Company* would go against the spirit of the postmodern analysis I am performing. Still, it's not going too far to suggest that the ideas about power, identity, narrative, and knowledge that plays like *West Side Story, Gypsy, Forum,* and *Anyone Can Whistle* were exploring would eventually demand a form of expression beyond the conventions of Rodgers and Hammerstein–style realism, and that in *Company* this new, postmodern form had its first complete articulation. In the next chapter we examine the subsequent Stephen Sondheim–Harold Prince collaborations, plays produced during the height of cultural postmodernism in the United States.

Three

With So Little to Be Sure Of

A lthough Stephen Sondheim and Harold Prince had been friends since the late 1940s, and Prince had produced *West Side Story* and *A Funny Thing Happened on the Way to the Forum, Company* was the first time they had worked together as composer/lyricist and director.[1] It was the beginning of the most important musical-theater collaboration since Richard Rodgers and Oscar Hammerstein. For eleven Broadway seasons, from 1970 to 1981, Sondheim, Prince, and their collaborators presented an unprecedented six brilliant musicals, all of which experimented in form, style, and content, and which, together, like the Rodgers and Hammerstein musicals before them, changed the rules for how musicals work, raised the expectations for the quality and intelligence of musicals, and transformed the possibilities for how musicals can mean. Produced during the height of postmodern experimentation in all the arts, these musicals challenge the formal conventions of musical theater and basic narrative structure as a means of exploring issues of identity and knowledge. Although the title of this chapter comes from a song written for 1964's *Anyone Can Whistle,* it is appropriate for a series of plays that leaves us questioning how we know ourselves and our world.

About midway through *Follies,* after just having led the show-stopping production number "Who's That Woman?," Stella Deems says to no one in particular, "Wasn't that a blast? I love life, you know that? I've got my troubles and I take my lumps, we've got no kids, we never made much money, and a lot of folks I love are dead, but on the whole and everything considered . . . *(She loses the thread)* Where was I?"[2] This attempt to sum up one's life into a grand statement and derive meaning from it and then to lose the narrative glue that holds it together is paradigmatic of the play as a whole. Like *Company, Follies* purposely lacks a narrative and explores the possibilities for and limitations of narrative as a meaning-providing vehicle. In an interview, Sondheim discusses the plotlessness of both shows:

> [*Follies*] started out as a sort of "who'll do it," not a "whodunit," in which we brought four characters together to a party who'd had a complicated relationship in the past, and their old angers and insecurities and passions are reignited at this reunion, and at the end of the first act, they each had a reason to wish one of the others was dead. So the so-called suspense was: who's going to attempt to kill whom? And then we gradually realized that every time, in each rewrite, we would read each version and it was too plotted, and so we would take out a little of the plot and just have the party, and then it still was too plotted. We finally woke up to the fact that we should have no plot at all. It should just be these emotional relationships at a party. They all get drunk, they resolve or don't resolve their problems, and they go home. [. . .]
>
> That's what it shares with *Company*. Neither of those shows have a plot. They're entirely different as structures, and in every way, except neither of them has a plot. [. . .]
>
> [Harold Prince] agreed to do *Follies*, but he only agreed to do it if we did *Company* first. *Follies* had started years before *Company* came up. And so in a way, the plotlessness of *Follies* helped us have the courage to have a plotless *Company*.[3]

To Goldman and Sondheim's concept of a plotless play where the setting of a Ziegfeld Follies–type reunion provides the opportunity for the hopes and regrets of the past to bubble back to the surface of the present, codirectors Prince and Michael Bennett provided a visual style of cinematic surrealism, where the rules of time and space are suspended and past and present embrace and clash. When *Follies* opened at the Winter Garden Theatre on 4 April 1971, it was, in one sense, a sweet farewell to a bygone era of entertainment, and, in another, a spotlight pointed at the future of the musical theater.[4]

In the last chapter we saw how *Company* engages and challenges the idea of narrative, with its origin, end (or anticipated end), and the connecting cause-and-effect sequence providing a structure for organizing, making sense of, and potentially controlling phenomena. In *Follies* these same concepts that connect narrative to knowledge and meaning are applied to the life story. One of the ways, probably the most important way, in which we try to understand our lives, their meaning and purpose, is to cast the things that happen to us in the form of a narrative. The narratization of a life implies some specific applications of the narrative theory we looked at in the last chapter. We saw that a narrative is dependent on its endpoint to give it a complete, interpretable structure. In a life narrative, this endpoint is translated into the narrative standpoint, the point from which the narrator looks back at life; this standpoint, what the narrator has become, what is "now" at the moment of conjuring the life story, is the end toward which all the narrated events of life move.

There are several important implications that derive from this premise. One is that the standpoint is changeable: one could write an autobiography at forty and another at sixty, and, because the standpoint has changed, the story leading to the standpoint will have changed too.[5] Another implication is that, in looking back at life events, the narrating subject selects which events to include in the story (after all, everything can't be included) and that this selection of what is important enough to include is governed by the narrating standpoint. The narrator chooses those events that seem to have worked together to lead to the place that is "now," at the time of writing. The upshot of this is that the significance of life events is perceivable only retrospectively, after a standpoint has been reached, and that the meaning of life events is knowable only after they become part of a narrative structure.[6] A third implication of the importance of narrative standpoint is the distinction between the narrating subject and the character being narrated, even though they purport to be the same person. That is, as a text, a life story has two rhetorical aspects: the narrator, the voice looking back at life and narrating the events; and the character, the narrator's past self, who is acting out the events, the person who is on the way to becoming the narrator. We might argue that there is more than one of these past selves: the narrator as a child, in college, in midcareer, in retirement. Why do we think of these multiple selves as coherent, one person, instead of dispersed fragments? One reason is the life story itself, the way that narrative form imposes a cause-and-effect-based structure on events so as to show a contained and meaningful progression from past selves to present self. Another reason is the personal pronoun *I*, which rhetorically holds together these fragmented selves and creates an illusion of unity, a single, coherent, consistent identity.[7] In a rhetorically successful life story, the bringing together of past and narrating selves must be seamless; the reader should never doubt the coherence of the story or the life being narrated. A fourth implication is the inherent tension between the implied concept of a life being lived progressively yet having meaning only retrospectively. In the words of Søren Kierkegaard, "It is quite true what philosophy says: that life must be understood backwards. But then one forgets the other principle—that it must be lived forwards. Which principle, the more one thinks it through, ends exactly with the thought that temporal life can never properly be understood precisely because I can at no instant find complete rest in which to adopt the position: backwards."[8]

The life story, then, is a specific application of narrative as epistemological structure and is vital to our understanding of our identity in that it provides a sense of coherence to our lives, linking together all of our past selves, and it provides a means by which we can interpret our lives and find their meaning and purpose. *Follies* presents characters struggling to find the coherence, meaning, and purpose of their lives, but the play in its form, style, and content, instead of providing the narrative structures via life stories that might help them, undermines and strips away the devices of the life story, calling into question this particular narrative device and, by extension, narrative in general as a meaning-providing vehicle. It leaves its characters stripped bare and faced with the challenge of finding other ways of making meaning.

One necessary faculty for conjuring a life story is memory. In order to sort through our life events and select and order them, we must first remember them. *Follies,* however, complicates the notion of memory. Most obviously, there is the problem of failing memory. The characters here, who have returned for the reunion, were in their youth or prime during the heyday of the Weismann Follies, a production every year between 1918 and 1941, and so in 1971, when the play is set, the youngest among them are around fifty and many are much older. In introducing himself,

Weismann teases "those of you whose memories may be going" (7), but later, embarrassingly, he can't quite place who Sally is. Other failures of memory, however, imply further complexity. At one point, erstwhile operetta star Heidi Schiller hears the band play her signature song, and she says, "It's my waltz they're playing. Franz Lehar wrote it for me in Vienna. I was having coffee in my drawing room—in ran Franz and straight to the piano. 'Liebchen, it's for you.' Or was it Oscar Straus? Facts never interest me. What matters is the song" (17–18). A little later, the Whitmans, a couple who did a comedy act, have this exchange:

> EMILY WHITMAN: We met at an audition. Teddy was a doughboy, weren't you, dear? You'd just come back from France and when we danced, my blouse kept getting stuck on all your medals.
> THEODORE WHITMAN: Emmy, that's an act we did.
> EMILY WHITMAN: Why, so it was. But acts are real, they happen, and I met you, didn't I? (31–32)

Heidi and the Whitmans suggest that recovering specific facts isn't the only point of memory. The key points—that the waltz was written for Heidi, that Ted and Emily met—are important, but the "facts" that led to these points are not; they may be irrelevant or they may just be a good story. The Whitmans' dialogue also suggests that memory combines "facts," what really happened, with art, imagination, hopes, things that might have happened. Memory becomes not simply a record of what occurred, but a dynamic mixture of one's experiences, one's consciousness, one's imagination, one's cultural context. This idea helps us better understand Ben's comment when first entering the decrepit Weismann Theater: "I sometimes wonder why our memories don't go the way these walls have gone. Our bodies do: our plaster flakes away and yet the fool things we remember stay as fresh as paint" (5–6). Ben, Phyllis, Sally, and Buddy are about to spend an evening encountering their memories in this sense: everything that was around them, everything they were, everything they wanted to be, everything they have become.

This concept of memory works with the play's form and style to subvert the illusion of a coherent identity produced by a life story. An atmosphere of dynamic memory dominates the Wesimann Theater, creating a setting where time and space are disjointed. This effect is created in a number of ways. In the Prince-Bennett staging, characters occupying the stage at the same time were understood to be in different locations. Similarly, time is disrupted. In the original Broadway staging, during the party scenes, an onstage band played background music, songs from the score, including some cut from the show. But as the focus moves from one conversation to another, the stage directions tell us, "There is a little jump in time as the band, like a push-button radio, cuts from one dance tune to another [. . .]" (11). These jumps, together with the cinematic and seemingly random sequence of party scenes, undercut the audience's expectations for a chronological, cause-and-effect-based narrative structure.

The disjointedness of time and space as established by the play's style makes possible the fragmentation of the illusion of the coherent self. The disjunction of the present self and a younger self is emphasized repeatedly throughout the play. In "Beautiful Girls," while the tenor Roscoe recounts the almost indescribable beauty of the girls coming down the staircase, we in the audience see the old women they have become. Similarly, much of the humor of "Broadway Baby" comes from the fact that this song about a young actress trying to make it in New York is sung by a far-from-young woman; in the original production it was Ethel Shutta, the oldest person in the cast. More poignant are numbers like "One More Kiss," where old Heidi Schiller sings her waltz with the ghost of her younger self, and "Bolero d'Amour," where the aging dance team of Vincent and Vanessa perform simultaneously with the ghosts of their younger selves. In both these numbers we see the effects of age—the notes that can no longer be hit; the difficult dance moves that have been made easier—and a picture of what a life story tries to do: create a narrative that links the younger self and the older self so as to make it appear they are the same.

The play's use of ghosts as the dramatization of the characters' past selves is best seen in the case of the four principals, Ben Stone, Phyllis Rogers Stone, Buddy Plummer, and Sally Durant Plummer, who exist on stage in both their older, 1971 versions and their younger, 1941 versions. The younger selves are both memories, appearing occasionally as visualizations of an incident that one of the older selves recalls, and ghosts, literal presences in the Weismann Theater, perpetually performing their Follies numbers, curious about their older selves and able to observe them. The play posits the interesting notion that our past selves, instead of folding ineluctably into our present selves, have an independent existence in some other dimension, in this case, twenty-one forever. The blasting of the rhetorical illusion of the coherent self contained by the personal pronoun *I* starts in small ways but quickly escalates. Sally, so eager to return to her past that she is the first to arrive at the party, drops her married name and declares herself to be Sally Durant, as if becoming her 1941 self again. Later, when Sally and Ben try to rekindle their thirty-year-old affair, the two eras collapse into each other as Ben sings "Too Many Mornings" to Young Sally, embracing her while older Sally "moves precisely as YOUNG SALLY does, as if the two of them were one" (62). Older Sally merges with her younger self here, speaking as if it is 1941: "I don't mind giving up the stage [. . . .] I can wait until the war is over" (62). Still later, when the characters reach their moment of crisis, chaos reigns as the older selves confront and threaten their younger selves, blaming them for having ruined their lives. It is in this atmosphere of fragmentation and subverted narrative coherence that the principals attempt to understand how they became what they have become, to find the meaning of their lives, to know, finally, who they are.

To understand the failure of Sally's life narrative, we need to return to the Foucauldian concept of the narrative construction of knowledge, which we discussed in relation to *Company*. Foucault makes the distinction between History, a completed narrative structure with an origin and a cause-and-effect-based sequence of events leading to an anticipated end that results in a completed structure, and history, the in-time, in-progress events as they are actually experienced. For Sally, the projected end that provides a structure and meaning for her life story is marrying Ben. This was her goal in 1941, and it is still her goal in 1971. In the "Too Many Mornings" scene, where past and present collapse into each other and older Sally and Young Sally recite their dialogue together, they say to Ben, "I can wait forever just so long as at the end of it there's you" (62). Her commitment to this endpoint helps explain her situation at the beginning of the play. Sally did not marry Ben back in 1941; he threw her over for Phyllis. Nevertheless, throughout the years of her marriage to Buddy and raising two children, she has stayed committed to the endpoint of Ben. The seemingly irreconcilable gap between her History, a fairy story with marriage to Ben providing closure, and her history, life with Buddy, accounts for her mental instability. It is no accident that her Loveland song, which contrasts the mundane details of a quotidian existence with the ever-present thoughts of a dream lover, is called "Losing My Mind."[9]

Sally comes to the reunion, then, determined to erase thirty years of her life story and rewrite it so that it will have the ending she has always longed for: marriage to Ben. This is why she is so eager to get to the theater and so quick to revert to Sally Durant, Weismann Girl of 1941. And although Sally seems girlish, with her naïveté and spontaneity, her campaign to win Ben is very calculated, a well-plotted revision of her life story. She reveals this most baldly in "Too Many Mornings," after she thinks Ben loves her:

> How I planned:
> What I'd wear tonight and
> When should I get here,
> How should I find you,
> Where I'd stand,
> What I'd say in case you
> Didn't remember,
> How I'd remind you— (*F* 224)

We see here that all that has come before has been a performance designed to attract Ben: her small-town-girl-in-the-big-city persona suggests a return to the innocence of youth; her song "Don't Look at Me" is a plea for exactly the opposite; even "In Buddy's Eyes," which on the surface is a statement of her satisfaction with her life with Buddy, is a calculated lie. Sondheim has explained that the key to understanding the song is in Jonathan Tunick's orchestration: "Every phrase in the song which refers to her husband is dry, all woodwinds. Whenever she refers to herself it's all strings again."[10] When the older characters turn on their younger selves, her main charge against Young Sally is, "You could of had him [*sic*] but you played it wrong" (80). For Sally, the reunion is the occasion for returning to her 1941 self and revising her life story, but she wants to retain her older self's ability to plan, plot, and manipulate so as to have more control over her story than she did the first time around.

Where Sally is fixated on the endpoint her life story never reached, her old roommate Phyllis Rogers Stone finds herself and her life story confused about the connections between the past and present. She says to Ben as they arrive at the reunion, "I wanted to come back, Ben. One last look at where it all began. I've been devoting my attention to beginnings lately. I wanted something when I came here thirty years ago but I forgot to write it down and God knows what it was" (6). Having lost her sense of the origin and goal of her life story, Phyllis has also lost her sense of the life events in between. She tells Buddy that she and Ben live a life without events: "We don't do things any more; we say them. Our life is like a sound track; words and words with all the action missing" (21). She elaborates on this idea in a later conversation: "One makes bargains with one's life. That's what maturity amounts to. When we're young and every road looks clear, we take them all, ignoring Newton's laws of motion, going every way at once. Star, mother, hostess, hausfrau. So I learned to be an artist with my life. I constantly select, as if each day were a painting and I had to get the colors right. We're careful of our colors, Ben and I, and what we've made is beautiful" (42). Interestingly, Phyllis replaces the familiar metaphor of life as a journey with one of life as a painting. The journey metaphor implies motion, a movement from there to here resulting in a complete journey. The painting metaphor implies a freezing of motion, the taking of something vital and confining it as representation within the boundaries of a frame. That Phyllis sees her life events as a series of separate paintings, no matter how beautiful, suggests a loss of a sense of narrative connection.

As a result of having become disoriented in her own life story, Phyllis has no sense of coherence to her identity. She sees no connection between herself now and the person she was in 1941. She tells Buddy, "When I see pictures of myself back then, I think, 'Somebody's put a stranger in my scrapbook'" (23). The real problem, however, is that the Phyllis she has become—the 1971 Phyllis—is a stranger to her. In a key, recurring 1941 moment we see Young Phyllis, in accepting Ben's marriage proposal, demonstrate an insecurity about her worth. She says, "I'll try. Oh, Ben, I'll try so hard. I'll study and I'll read—I'm not much now, I know that—and I'll walk my feet off in the Metropolitan Museum . . ." (42). She determines to reinvent herself into a woman who is an appropriate wife for mover and shaper Ben Stone. Ben, she says, "taught me everything I know" (56), and even now he occasionally corrects her grammar, as if to accuse her of still not being good enough. At the moment of crisis, when the four principals confront their younger selves, Phyllis rejects the person she's become, finding value in her younger self: "I tried so hard. I studied and I read—I thought I wasn't much: I was terrific—and I walked my goddamn feet off. (*Turning to* YOUNG PHYLLIS) What happened to you, Phyl?" (78). This dilemma becomes the basis for her Loveland number, "The Story of Lucy and Jessie," in which, instead of narrating a story that will provide her with a coherent identity, she turns her past and present selves into separate characters: Lucy is her juicy and racy but dull and drab younger self; Jessie is her dressy and lacy but cold and hard present self. Ironically, each wants the other's virtues without recognizing her own. Phyllis sings,

> Poor, sad souls,
> Itching to be switching roles.
> Lucy wants to do what Jessie does,
> Jessie wants to be what Lucy was. (*F* 236)

Phyllis as Phyllis enters the song only near the end, when she expresses her wish in the first person:

> If Lucy and Jessie could only combine,
> I could tell you someone
> Who would finally feel just fine. (*F* 236)

This trick, however, is one that Phyllis is still unable to pull off.

To understand the complications of Buddy's life story, we need to return to a concept we discussed in relation to *Gypsy*: the dream of home and family. This dream offers as a goal a stable home and a loving family, maybe a house in the suburbs and enough money to afford a few luxuries—a common dream among post–World War II Americans. In one sense, Buddy appears to have everything he wants; he has achieved the anticipated endpoint to his life story. Leaving law school behind him, he married his dream girl, Sally, served in the army during the war, got a job as a salesman (Sally says that "when the war was over, Buddy couldn't wait to start in making money" [43]), and, although he's had to move around to a number of different cities, he's had a home, a wife, and children. As he says to Ben early in the evening, "you grow up hearing it's the little things that count, and you know what? It's true. I come home and I'm welcome. I see Sally and I'm glad to see her" (16–17). While he is sincere in his belief that the little things add up to happiness, he hides from Ben the problems in his relationship with Sally. Still, his solution to his problems, like the problem of Sally running away to come to the reunion, is always home: "Come on, kid," he says, "let's go home" (54).

The glitch in Buddy's dream is that his dream girl has always been in love with Ben and sees life with Buddy at best as a consolation prize and at worst as the failure of her dream literalized every day. This results in an unhappiness that disrupts Buddy's dream and, as suggested earlier, a mental instability that infects their day-to-day life. We get quick images of what their life together is like. Buddy complains, "I've spent my whole life making things the way you want them, and no matter what we do or where we go or what we've got, it isn't what you want" (70). They both know it's because she can't have what she wants: Ben. Buddy describes Sally's behavior: "The mess, the moods, the spells you get, in bed for days without a word. Or else you're crying. God, the tears around our place— or flying out to Tom and Tim [their sons] and camping on their doorstep just to fight—" (70). Significantly, when Buddy takes a lover, she is not some glamorous alternative to a dull housewife. Rather, she is a woman who can give him a reasonable facsimile of home. He describes his time with Margie: "she's got a little house. It's quiet there. She gives me books to read each time, and when I'm there we talk for hours. And she cooks for me and sews my buttons on, and when we go to bed, it's like she thought I was some kind of miracle" (55). Later, in his song and dance, "The Right Girl," Buddy imagines being with Margie:

Hey, Margie,
You wanna go dancing? You wanna go driving?
Or something?
Okay, babe,

Whatever you say, babe—
You wanna stay home.
You wanna stay home! (*F* 225)

This is the life he desires with Sally but has never attained.

Buddy's life story breaks down, then, because of a split in the narrative resulting from a split in the endpoint: home without love with Margie; and love for Sally without being loved in return and thus without home. This bifurcation and the tension between the two narratives increasingly come to define his sense of self. We see this in Buddy's Loveland number, "The God-Why-Don't-You-Love-Me Blues." According to the program, this song takes place on "A Thoroughfare in Loveland," and in the original staging Buddy appears as a baggy-pants vaudeville comic, and, "Suspended from his waist, traveling salesman that he is, is a plywood model car big enough to sit and scoot around in" (95). The setting reminds us of the life-story-as-a-journey metaphor. Here, however, instead of a straightforward journey, Buddy's little car goes every which way, chasing and being chased by the actresses representing Sally and Margie. The comic confusion of the staging reflects the song Buddy sings, in which he rejects what he can have and pursues what he cannot. What he desires, what he can obtain, where he is headed on his life journey and in his life story are all confused for him now, with the result that he is uncertain of his identity. The intensity of this uncertainty, as well as the bifurcation in his life story, is seen in "The Right Girl." The song itself is divided, with two angry sections, in which Buddy sings of the importance of having the right girl, connected by a mellow, lyrical center section, in which he describes his time with Margie. The song is further divided when, at the end of the angry sections, words are no longer sufficient and he has to express himself through dance. Interestingly, given Buddy's problems defining an endpoint for his life story, the song does not really end. The stage directions read, "The dance is more than angry now; it's desperate as BUDDY hurls himself about the stage at non-existent barriers" (70). The original Buddy, 1950s film dancer Gene Nelson, performed with an athletic style only hinted at in the stage directions; he leaped from platform to platform and swung himself around poles, suggesting a man trying to tear himself in two. The incompleteness and violence of this song dramatize the failure of Buddy's life story. His once-secure endpoint is now problematic, and narrative uncertainty has undercut his sense of self, purpose, and meaning.

Where Buddy's life story is governed by the dream of home and family, Ben's is governed by something akin to the dream of stardom found in *Gypsy*. Ben, of course, does not dream of show-business stardom; rather, he dreams of the success that is associated with wealth and influence. This is the endpoint toward which he aims his life story, and, more than the other principals, he reaches it successfully. He has a sense of narrative direction for his life story that both Phyllis and Buddy lack, and, unlike Sally's, his calculations work out. The Ben Stone we meet at the Weismann reunion has achieved influence—he apparently has been involved in national politics, served in some high-profile post at the United Nations, and is currently the head of a foundation; he is also the author of several notable books and gives speeches regularly—and he has achieved fame—Sally tells Phyllis that she saw their living room in *Vogue,* and former Follies star Hattie Walker asks for *his* autograph. That this status has been the goal of his life story is clear from some dialogue we see in flashback to 1941. After he has to borrow money and a car from Buddy to go on a date, Young Ben has this exchange with Young Phyllis:

> YOUNG BEN: Borrowed money, borrowed car. Some day I'm going to have the biggest goddamn limousine.
> YOUNG PHYLLIS: We've got each other, Ben. What difference does it make?
> YOUNG BEN: All the difference. (39)

Ben's problem here is not that he is poor, or at least that's not his primary problem. He desires money and a fancy car not as ends in themselves but for what they represent—control. The problem with borrowed things is that one doesn't control them. One needs to own something in order to exert power over it. Ben wants to be in a position to control his environment, to be the master of it, so as to reach the position of influence, power, and fame that is his dream.

This desire, this narrative impulse, becomes so overwhelming in his character that it warps his ability to love. Connected with his dream is the desire to be loved, not necessarily as a person, but as a charismatic figure. Having people buy his books and read his speeches and ask for his autograph is important to him; they are tangible signs that he is loved. It also explains his bristling when Carlotta says to him, "I haven't seen your picture in the papers lately" (18). Being loved, however, is not the same as being able to love. Ben sees the other people in his life, especially the women, as part of the environment he seeks to control, as territory to conquer. We know that back in 1941 he had simultaneous sexual relationships with Phyllis, Sally, and Carlotta, and, given his character, there may be others we don't know about. (One wonders how he had time to finish law school.) We know too, by his own admission, that since his marriage to Phyllis, he has continued to play around, including one fling on the afternoon of the reunion. Sex, for Ben, brings together his two needs—the need to control and the need to be loved—but he feels no need to love in return. Indeed, his impulse to control others works against his being able to love them because it dehumanizes them. When he proposes to Phyllis, he doesn't mention love. He says, "You'll make a good wife, Phyl" (42). As we saw when we looked at Phyllis's character, he means exactly what he says here: Phyllis is someone he can make over into a woman who will be a proper consort to the man he intends to become. Ben is not even aware of the process by which, as he dehumanizes others, he gradually dehumanizes himself.

The reunion offers a setting and a moment that force Ben to reflect on his life story and confront the identity it has created for him. Despite his remark on his entrance about the vividness of memories, Ben spends much of the evening denying that he remembers much of anything about 1941 and his time with the others, whether it's buying corsages or going to Tony's, the two young couples' restaurant of choice. When Buddy tells him that he thinks about the past a lot, Ben replies, "There's not much to think about" (15). A bit later, when Sally asks if he wishes he were still young, he says, "Once was bad enough. I wouldn't want to face all that again" (24). Still, like the others, he gets swept into the past while singing "Waiting for the Girls Upstairs," and, with the others, is both entranced and shaken by the memory. Trying to lighten the intensity of the memory, the four sing of their past selves, "Everything was possible and nothing made sense [. . .]" (*F* 207), a feeling they have apparently lost, because they have since become committed to their life stories. When young, they find everything to be possible, because, as Phyllis suggested, every road, every possible story, is open to them; nothing makes sense, because, as yet, they haven't chosen a story that will order their experiences and make them understandable. This song presents the younger selves on the verge of, but not yet begun, narrating their life stories.

This moment of returning to the past is an important one for Ben. From here on, he has more and more trouble denying that the past has an effect on him and more and more trouble resisting the contemplation of his own life story. We see the beginnings of his breakdown in his song "The Road You Didn't Take." This song is the play's most elaborate development of the life-story-as-journey metaphor. On the surface, Ben, singing to Sally, tries fatalistically to assert that one can choose only one road/life story and so there is no point in agonizing over the choice one made—better to forget past opportunities and possibilities. He sings,

> You take one road,
> You try one door,
> There isn't time for any more.
> One's life consists of either/or.
> One has regrets
> Which one forgets [. . . .] (F 211)

Ben's confidence in this assertion, however, is undercut by the music. The agitation of the accompaniment and the alternation of the time signature between 3/4 and 2/4 belie the rhetorical position of calm retrospection Ben would like to take. Another interesting effect in the accompaniment further undercuts Ben's claims. At three points in the song, there is a five-note dissonant blare on a solo horn (repeated the last time). This horn suggests both a car horn, as if to criticize Ben for his single-minded pursuit of success down his road, and a mocking laugh for his trying now to deny any second thoughts about his choice. In trying to convince Sally of the rightness of his life choices, the coherence of his life story, Ben has instead undermined his own confidence and opened the door for second-guessing about alternate life stories and "The Ben I'll never be" (F 217).

This unwelcome reflection and reconsideration lead Ben to see the fail-

"The Road You Didn't Take": John McMartin (Ben Stone) and Dorothy Collins
(Sally Durant Plummer) in *Follies*. Credit Line: Photo by Martha Swope/
©The New York Public Library for the Performing Arts

ure of his life story and to try to revise it. In his conversation with Phyllis
after "Who's That Woman?," he says, "I used to wish that life were work
and sleep and nothing else, that I could go from bed to desk to bed again;
and now I look at what I do and find it meaningless" (56). Bed and desk—
the locations for sex and job—are the two places Ben has exerted power to
gain control to reach the projected endpoint of his life story. That he now

finds them meaningless indicates that he has lost faith in his endpoint and the narrative leading to it. Later, with Sally, he says, "I've done it wrong. This isn't what I meant. [. . .] I don't know who I am" (62). Recognizing that he has messed up his life story—done it wrong so that it has the wrong meaning—he concludes that he has lost his sense of identity. At this point he begins to wish that he could start over with a new narrative. Where before he denied wishing he were young again, he now says to Sally, "I would give—what have I got?—my soul's of little value, but I'd give it to be twenty-five again" (61). Here, Ben's desire to start over intersects with Sally's dream of revising the past, and Ben imagines that a new projected ending, life with Sally, would give his life meaning, and he even imagines, in "Too Many Mornings," that this has been the ending he has always desired. He sings to his memory of Young Sally, "Too many mornings / Wishing that the room might be filled with you [. . .]" (*F* 224). The intersection of the two characters' narrative revisions does not last long—Ben realizes the absurdity of what he's doing when Sally says they should get married, and Sally goes off lost in the folds of her own fantasy—but it lasts long enough for Ben to confirm the identity crisis he's facing—"I'm not myself," he says (67)—and to recognize that although he has earned fame and acclaim and a lifetime's worth of sex, he has never been loved in the sense of private, personal love, the kind of love suggested by the lyrics he has just sung.

Acting on this recognition, Ben tries a different revision of his life story—telling Phyllis he wants a divorce, thinking he can find love with someone else. He tells her, "God, I see lovers on the streets—it's real, it's going on out there and I can't reach it. Someone's got to love me and I don't care if it doesn't last a month, I don't care if I'm ludicrous or who she is or what she looks like, I don't care" (75). Phyllis, however, sees immediately that Ben's new narrative must fail. She says, "You haven't got a clue what love is" (75). Love, for Ben, as we have seen, has been a dehumanizing process of conquest and control, a process that has dehumanized him as well. Ben has created, not a life, but an image of a life. At his moment of crisis, he tells Phyllis that he's a fake: "I know it. Doesn't everybody? Jesus, can't they see it? Are they blind? They look at me and I keep waiting for them all to point and say, 'You! Stone! I know what you are'" (75). Shortly thereafter, as the four principals and their younger selves confront one another, Phyllis says to Ben, "I see you now, right through you. Hollow, that's what you are. You're an empty place" (81).

Ben's Loveland number, "Live, Laugh, Love," is significantly different from the other principals.' Sally, Phyllis, and Buddy all directly address their existential crisis. Ben's song, like his life narrative, is a lie. Like Rose in *Gypsy*, Ben creates a conflict in his song between the some people who "sweat / To get / To be millionaires," who read "Proust and Pound," who "get a boot / From shoot- / Ing off cablegrams," who "break their asses / Passing their bar exams" (*F* 238, 241) and himself:

Me, I like to live,
Me, I like to laugh,
Me, I like to love! (*F* 238)

The lie, of course, is that Ben Stone is one of the some people the song describes, not the carefree, unambitious guy who likes to live, laugh, and love. Ben can maintain the lie of the number no better than he can maintain the lie that is his life. He forgets the lyrics, mangling them into "Me, I like— / Me, I love— / Me" (*F* 241), which forces him into the admission, "I don't love me!" (*F* 241). His inability to love anyone, even himself, has resulted in his desperate need to be loved and has turned his success, fame, and achievements into lies. As Ben, his song, and Loveland break down, "The chorus line goes on dancing, as if he didn't exist" (108). Lacking a coherent life story he can believe in, he in some ways doesn't exist.

Taking a broader view of the play, we see that the failure of the principals' life stories is reflected in a larger problematization of narrative. The play is, as we saw earlier, a plotless musical, denying us a beginning, middle, and end and the straightforward working out of a conflict. More than that, the play emphasizes an absence of narrative in its structure and style. Ben's story is a good example. We see Young Ben, with his ambitions and his complicated love life, we see 1971 Ben, stately, polished, at ease with his success, and we hear things about him, but the play never fills in the gaps between these bits of information: it's up to us in the audience to do that imaginatively, to create a life narrative for Ben out of fragments. The same process is at work with the supporting characters: we get glimpses of the lives of the partygoers as they speak to each other, but they are like lives in shorthand, squeezed into the party's conversational exchanges, with many incidents and most of the connective narrative left out. The best example is Carlotta's song "I'm Still Here." In it, Carlotta, a survivor—Weismann Follies performer, movie star, TV actress—reviews her life, but does so in terms of incidents, not narrative:

> I've been through Reno,
> I've been through Beverly Hills,
> And I'm here.
> Reefers and vino,
> Rest cures, religion and pills,
> And I'm here.
>
> Been called a pinko
> Commie tool,
> Got through it stinko
> By my pool.
> I should have gone to an acting school,
> That seems clear.
> Still, someone said, "She's sincere,"
> So I'm here. (*F* 221)

This stanza is typical, with its slew of incidents and apparently scrambled chronology. Occasionally the song will give us narrative cause and effect, as when a "big financier" rescues her from the Depression (*F* 221), but mostly it offers incidents from her life (as in the quoted lyrics) and times ("Windsor and Wally's affair," "Five Dionne babies," and so on [*F* 221]). Unlike the principals, Carlotta seems unconcerned with creating a coherent narrative of her life events—there's no evidence of selecting and sorting or narratively linking here. What's important to her is her standpoint—"I'm here"—and "here" is the sum of everything she's experienced and been through, not forced into a narrative form or connected to any overarching, conceptual History. "I'm Still Here" offers the audience a model of how to understand the play's form: we can work to infer the implied narrative, and/or we can start to think of means of knowing that are not narrative based.

Up to this point I have been treating the Loveland numbers as equivalent to the other songs in the show, but we need to understand as well just how unconventionally this section of the play works. There are three kinds of musical numbers in *Follies*. The first are the book songs, sung for the most part by the principals as they consider their past and present lives. They include "Don't Look at Me," "Waiting for the Girls Upstairs," "The Road You Didn't Take," "In Buddy's Eyes," "I'm Still Here," "Too Many Mornings," "The Right Girl," and "Could I Leave You?" These songs function very much in the Rodgers and Hammerstein tradition. The second kind are numbers from the Weismann Follies, and these belong to two categories. One is the Follies numbers that are being performed presentationally at the reunion, "Beautiful Girls" and "Who's That Woman?" The other is the Follies numbers that are performed in memory, often with older and younger selves of the characters singing or dancing in tandem. These include "Listen to the Rain on the Roof," "Ah, Paris!," "Broadway Baby," "Bolero d'Amour," and "One More Kiss." These songs are pastiches, composed in the style of songwriters of the twenties and thirties.[11] The third kind are the Loveland numbers: "Loveland"; "You're Going to Love Tomorrow," sung by Young Ben and Young Phyllis; "Love Will See Us Through," sung by Young Buddy and Young Sally; "The God-Why-Don't-You-Love-Me Blues"; "Losing My Mind"; "The Story of Lucy and Jessie"; and "Live, Laugh, Love." These songs, like the Follies numbers, are pastiches, but we are not supposed to think that they were originally performed in the Weismann Follies; rather, the play itself takes on the style of the Follies as a way of confronting the breakdown in the principals' life stories.

At the beginning of chapter 1, I described the startling weirdness of the transition from the Weismann Follies reunion to Loveland. At the moment when each of the principals' existential crisis has reached its emotional peak and when the principals old and young turn on each other and themselves, the set becomes a beautiful, stunningly artificial world of bright colors and sunshine, and the ensemble enters singing of romantic love. This is not, however, a musical-comedy deus ex machina come to resolve the characters' problems. Rather, it is a smiling nightmare world, where the futility of the characters' desire to make meaning for their lives will be exposed.

The Loveland sequence is emphatically self-referential: everything about it calls attention to its own theatricality and artificiality. It ups the ante on something the play has been doing all night: fogging up the usually transparent relation between life and art, the process of representation, the means external to ourselves by which we organize, structure, interpret, and understand our world and ourselves. Here, the play and the characters are delivered out of narrative: Loveland's revue form is essentially nonnarrative; but more important, Loveland is removed from history, chronology, time's arrow, on which narrative is dependent. The first words sung as we move into Loveland are, "Time stops [. . .]" (*F* 229). Loveland is a different kind of representation, in a way pure representation, because, in its celebration of its own form and style, no attempt is made to disguise it, to make it seem to be actual life. The characters, struggling with their own failed narrative representations, are folded into pure representation, where they are simultaneously observers, performers, and subjects of their own performances. The distinction—and distance—between narrating subject and narrated character is broken down entirely. Narration, along with the personal pronoun *I* as a means of holding that narration together, collapses. In its place, we have the distinctly nonnarrative form of the Follies—sketches, songs, and dances, presented one after the other in no chronologically or causally determined sequence. Randomness governs the organizational scheme. This form works against what the characters—and probably the audience—want: a coherent, linear, meaning-providing narrative. The form also, in its very name, mocks the characters' follies, both the folly of their life choices that have led to the dilemmas they are in and the folly of trying to find the meaning and purpose of their lives in narratizing them.

After Ben's breakdown precipitates the dissolution of Loveland, the principals find themselves back on the stage of the Weismann Theater, the party apparently long over, a hole in the back wall signaling the beginning of the demolition and allowing the morning light to creep through. Loveland, instead of repairing the failure of their life stories, has stripped the stories away and left them to face tomorrow narrativeless. For Sally and Buddy, the stage directions tell us, "There is no hope at all" (110), because they cannot let go of the endpoints that would have given their lives meaning. Sally says that "there is no Ben for me, not ever, any place"

(109), and she cannot imagine any other narrative structure to replace the failed one. Buddy turns again to the now-discredited dream of home. He says to Sally, as if it were an answer to their problems, "Come on. I'll take you home" (109). But clearly, the idea of home is empty. The situation for Phyllis and Ben is somewhat more hopeful. Left without their governing narratives, they respond, not with despondency, but with anger. Ben says, "There has to be a way . . . I won't face one more morning feeling— (*Impatiently*) Despair: I'm sick to goddamn death of it" (110). Phyllis concurs and offers a way: "Amen. It's easy; life is empty, there is no hope. Hope doesn't grow on trees; we make our own and I am here to tell you it's the hardest thing we'll ever do" (110). Implied here is the idea that meaning must be created—not found—in the process of living in incompletion, not a finished narrative structure. Like Robert at the end of *Company*, Ben and Phyllis reject narrative structure as a way of finding meaning and cast themselves into the process of the moment. We don't know if they will succeed in making meaning and purpose, but we know that there is hope in their breaking away from the conventions and strictures of the narrative knowledge that has failed them to this point.

Where *Company* and *Follies* were purposely plotless and interpretively indeterminate, *A Little Night Music*, the next Sondheim-Prince musical, has, as Harold Prince puts it, "enough plot for two musicals,"[12] and narrative closure. *A Little Night Music*, with music and lyrics by Sondheim, direction by Prince, and book by Hugh Wheeler, opened at the Shubert Theatre on 25 February 1973.[13] Based on an Ingmar Bergman film, *Smiles of a Summer Night* (1955), it is set in turn-of-the-century Sweden and tells the story of several mismatched lovers. In the Egerman household, middle-aged lawyer Fredrik is married to eighteen-year-old Anne, still a virgin after eleven months of marriage. Fredrik's son Henrik, a seminary student, is secretly in love with Anne and is also the target of the casual flirtations of Petra, the maid. Fredrik turns for comfort to his onetime mistress, the well-known actress Desirée Armfeldt, with whom, unbeknownst to him, he has a child, Fredrika, who lives with Desirée's mother on a country estate. Desirée's current lover is a pompous and not-very-bright army officer, Count Carl-Magnus Malcolm, whose wife Charlotte is aware of and despondent over the affair. All these characters descend

on Madame Armfeldt's estate for a weekend and, after many farcical complications, miraculously end up with the right partners. Although *A Little
Night Music* seems far removed from *Follies* in terms of setting, content,
and tone, it shares with that play a certain surreality in style, with Boris Aronson's scenic design suggesting that all the action takes place in a
magical forest, rather like *A Midsummer's Night Dream,* where the rules
by which reality functions in the city break down and other realities become possible.[14] It also shares with *Follies* an interest in the fragmentation
of the coherent identity.

The principal characters in *A Little Night Music* have competing narratives or, perhaps better in this case, fantasies—mininarratives encapsu-
lating a desire or wish—governing their sense of identity. Their ontological troubles as well as their conflicts with others come from their each
turning to two contradictory fantasies and trying to believe the different
things they say about their identities at the same time.

That these fantasies are irreconcilable motivates the characters' troubles and generates the action of the show. Henrik wants to be both a man
of God and a man of the flesh. His ambition to be an exemplary Lutheran
minister is threatened by his sexual desire for Anne, his stepmother. Anne
wants to be both a child and a wife. To stay a child, she resists Fredrik's
attempts to consummate their marriage, but as a wife, she is jealous of
his rekindled affair with Desirée. For his part, Fredrik wants to be young
again but also wants the gravitas gained from maturity. Interestingly, he
is more childlike in his adventures with age-appropriate Desirée than he
is with Anne, with whom he often has to play the role of a parent ("Don't
tease him, dear," he warns Anne when she makes fun of Henrik).[15] Desirée,
to use terminology from the discussions of *Gypsy* and *Follies,* wants both
stardom and home and family. She lives her life as an actress on the road,
but she longs for a life with her daughter. Count Carl-Magnus wants to
be both a faithful husband and an adulterer. He demands all-consuming
relationships with both his wife, Charlotte, and his mistress, Desirée, and,
not being a deep thinker, he doesn't even recognize the contradiction.
Charlotte wants both a passionate love relationship with her husband
and to play the role of the scorned wife. Jonathan Tunick, who orches-
trated the show, writes in his introduction to the published edition of the
play that the movement of the plot is from love triangles (Henrik-Anne-

Fredrik; Anne-Fredrik-Desirée; Fredrik-Desirée-Carl-Magnus; Desirée-Carl-Magnus-Charlotte; Frid [Madame Armfeldt's butler]-Petra-Henrik; Petra-Henrik-Anne) to couples. He writes, "In each of these connected relationships, the unstable number three is drawn to the stable two, as the various mismatched couples disengage and find their proper partners."[16] This is true, of course, but it is accompanied by another movement from the two fantasies competing to govern each character's sense of identity, to one, a single, coherent sense of self with which each character ends. This is what Desirée offers Fredrik and what they and the other characters end the play with: a "coherent existence after so many years of muddle" (168).

The movement from two fantasies to one occurs in a setting, like *Follies*'s, where the rules of space and time are suspended. I have already mentioned how Boris Aronson's scenic design for the original production used gliding trees to suggest a magical forest, a traditional device in drama and literature to penetrate the masks and pretensions that dominate in settled, civilized areas.[17] Further, the playwrights use the Scandinavian setting's high latitudes to free the action from the tyranny of linear time. The topsy-turvy treatment of time is stressed at the beginning of the second act by the Liebeslieders, a five-member Greek—no!—Swedish chorus that comments in song on the action.[18] In "Night Waltz" they sing of the long summer day in Sweden, with its sun never quite dropping below the horizon:

> The hands on the clock turn,
> But don't sing a nocturne
> Just yet. (*F* 272)

In "Night Waltz II" the quintet punctuates the predinner maneuvering of the principals with comments on the discombobulation of the sun, the moon, and time of day.[19] The opportunity for personal revelation that such a surreal treatment of place and time offers is augmented by the mysterious wine Madame Armfeldt serves at dinner. She says of it, "The secret of its unique quality is unknown, but it is said to possess the power to open the eyes of even the blindest among us . . ." (159). In this setting, with this wine, and with the aid of the night's smiles, the characters give over their fantasies and begin a movement to a coherent self.

An alternative to the notion of identity implied by the characters' dual fantasies moving into one is offered by Petra in her song—the last new song in the show—"The Miller's Son." Petra is an interesting character, both participant (she flirts with Henrik and is Anne's sometime confidante) and observer (being from the servant class, she is enough detached from her employers that she sees the folly in what they think is serious and offers the occasional subversive remark). In "The Miller's Son" Petra reveals that she has fantasies too. She imagines her life as it might be if she married the miller's son, a man from the working class, or if she married the businessman, a bourgeoisie, or if she married the Prince of Wales, an aristocrat. Each of these fantasies would bring a different kind of life for her and, presumably, a different kind of identity. Interestingly, however, her emphasis in the song is not on the fantasies—on her wanting to be something—but on the "meanwhile," the interval between now and whatever is to come. She sings that the fantasy fulfilled is likely to become mundane and disappointing, but the journey to the fulfillment can be full of fun:

> It's a wink and a wiggle
> And a giggle on the grass
> And I'll trip the light fandango,
> A pinch and a diddle
> In the middle of what pass-
> Es by. [. . .]
> In the meanwhile,
> There are mouths to be kissed
> Before mouths to be fed,
> And a lot in between
> In the meanwhile.
> And a girl ought to celebrate
> What passes by. (F 279)

Petra recognizes the rapid movement of time's arrow toward death and is intent on enjoying as best she can everything that happens as time passes, until time stops. She sings,

There's a lot I'll have missed,
But I'll not have been dead
When I die! (*F* 280)

In the 2009 Broadway revival performance of "The Miller's Son," Leigh Ann Larkin as Petra played this theme, moving from the celebratory to, after the quoted lyric, a devastated awareness of the inevitability of death.

As noted earlier, *A Little Night Music* offers more definite narrative closure than either *Company* or *Follies*. Madame Armfeldt dies, giving her story completely unambiguous closure. Henrik and Anne run off together, while Carl-Magnus becomes a champion for Charlotte; both couples seem to promise a happily-ever-after ending. Fredrik and Desirée end up together and, with Fredrika, form a ready-made family. Two details, however, prevent the thematic movement of triangles into couples and dual fantasies into single, coherent identities from being complete. First, as they are about to head off into happily ever after, Desirée tells Fredrik that she is committed to a weeklong engagement of *Hedda Gabler*. The resolution of her fantasies still has a loose end. Fredrik replies, "what's wrong with Purgatory before Paradise?" (184), putting emphasis, like Petra in "The Miller's Son," on the meanwhile, the time in between, rather than on the end that marks the completed structure. Second, and more obvious, Petra's story remains unresolved. When, in the final waltz, the couples reappear, now dancing with the correct partner, Petra dances with Frid. There's no reason, however, for the audience to suppose that they are together happily ever after or even happily past this weekend. Petra understands that this is temporary. She says to Frid, "I'm just passing through" (165). This incongruity among the dancing couples serves to underscore the point of "The Miller's Son": the desire for identity-providing fantasies, for completed narrative structures, for happily ever after, is at the root of the characters' follies. In urging us to find ourselves in the process rather than the product, in the movement of time rather than the end of time, *A Little Night Music* lightheartedly joins *Company* and *Follies* in questioning the notion of the autonomous self and the dominance of the narrative construction of knowledge.

* * *

In a decade of surprising musicals, *Pacific Overtures,* the next Sondheim-Prince collaboration, was the most startling, and not just for its content and its large, all-Asian cast. *Company* and *Follies* had decentered plot, but *Pacific Overtures* decentered character. Although there are some continuing characters—Kayama, Manjiro, Abe, and, of course, the Re-citer—the real characters here are nations, Japan and the United States, and the ideological worldviews they represent. The bringing together of these nations and their worldviews sparks the conflict that generates the drama: an exploration of the operations of colonial power. *Pacific Overtures,* which opened on 11 January 1976 at the Winter Garden Theatre, focuses on the 1853 opening of Japan, which for the previous 250 years had isolated itself from foreigners and foreign influence, by the fleet of Commodore Matthew Calbraith Perry, representing the United States.[20] In order to dramatize this story, Prince borrowed and adapted many de-vices from traditional kabuki theater, including an all-male cast playing both men's and women's roles (until the finale, set in contemporary Japan, when a few women appeared); the use of a *hanamichi,* a runway from the stage through the audience; stylized makeup and vocalizations; and stagehands dressed all in black to signal their invisibility. These content-based and formal choices are caught up with the play's thematic interests. Where *Company, Follies,* and *A Little Night Music* were, as we have seen, focused in various ways on issues of ontology and epistemology—cri-tiquing narrative-based knowledge as a means of understanding iden-tity—*Pacific Overtures,* probably owing to the influence of book writer John Weidman with whom the idea for the play originated, is focused more specifically on the sociopolitical and ideological. Even given that both *West Side Story* and *Anyone Can Whistle* explored the operations of power and the reproduction of ideology, *Pacific Overtures* was Sond-heim's most specifically political musical to that point in his career and, if we consider the original production's 1976 opening coming in the wake of the United States' failure in Vietnam, the most ideologically relevant to its initial audiences. By dramatizing the historical incidents wherein the United States forcibly opened Japan, *Pacific Overtures* explores the operations of power between two nations in a colonial relationship; by presenting its story in such a defamiliarizing manner, it asks its American audience to view these incidents through the eyes of the colonized Other and to recognize its own implication in the operations of colonial power.

Before looking at any other aspects of *Pacific Overtures,* we need to discuss its treatment of and attitude toward history. Broadly, the plot is based on the historical record, though some creative license is taken and historical characters intermingle with fictional ones.[21] The first act introduces the closed, rigidly hierarchical, and intricately structured Japanese society and the threat to that society represented by the intrusion of Perry's fleet in July 1853. The Japanese struggle to maintain the inviolability of their islands and the power of their laws while recognizing the reality that they are incapable of resisting American firepower. They compromise by meeting with Perry and his officers in a specially constructed treaty house at the specially prepared cove at Kanagawa: the beach is covered with mats, so that once the Americans depart, house and mats can be destroyed and foreigners will not technically have stepped on Japanese soil. The second act covers more than one hundred years as we see the United States return, soon followed by other Western nations that, in effect, turn Japan into an unofficial colony. The Japanese bitterly debate how to respond—accommodation or resistance—until Emperor Meiji declares that the nation's policy will be to imitate the Westerners, building a modern army and navy, introducing Western technology, and colonizing neighboring countries as Japan was colonized. He says, "The day will come when the Western powers will be forced to acknowledge us as their undisputed equals. [. . .] And all of this will be achieved—sooner than you think."[22] The final number, "Next," propels us into contemporary Japan, where we see the results of the emperor's decision, and ends with the incongruity of two characters from 1853, dressed and acting traditionally, appearing suddenly in the midst of what Japan has become.[23] This final stage moment wrenches the play off the historical continuum and juxtaposes two historical moments: 1853, before Perry's arrival, and 1976, when the consequences of his arrival have played out for 123 years. What has been gained is set against what has been lost.

While making use of the historical record, *Pacific Overtures* is also conscious of history as a mode of knowledge. That is, history is not equivalent to what happened in the past; history is a means of knowing about what happened in the past. It is a form of representation that casts the events of the past into the form of a narrative, and, as such, it is subject to some of the same postmodern-inflected critiques of narrative-based knowledge that we have discussed in relation to *Company, Follies,* and *A Little Night Music.* In thinking about history as a form of narrative knowledge, we need to start with two basic points. First, contrary to some misrepresentations of postmodern thought, to say that history is a narrative construction of the past is not to say that the past never happened, that it's not real. Rather, it's to say that once an incident occurs, the chance to experience and know it directly is lost. Our knowledge of it must come through discourse: eyewitness accounts, letters, diaries, newspaper reports, and so on. *Pacific Overtures* points toward the textuality of history when the Reciter quotes from Perry's personal journal and Kayama's letters to Abe, the shogun. Second, casting events of the past in the form of a narrative does not call out of them some buried or implied narrative pattern; rather, as Hayden White argues, the narrative form imposes an order and implied meaning—an interpretability—onto events that may have had neither. The process of narratizing history is similar to the process of creating a life story that we discussed in relation to *Follies.* Again, there is the matter of defining a starting point and an endpoint, the sorting and selecting of events, the linking of events in a causal sequence, and the establishing of a narrative standpoint, the observing and interpreting mind that will do the defining, sorting, selecting, and linking. A corollary follows that a different observing and interpreting mind, operating from a different narrative standpoint, might make a different narrative out of the same events. Indeed, White argues that all historical narrative is essentially persuasive, trying to convince the reader that one particular ordering and interpreting of events is the most likely to be true. These ideas about historical narrative as a process of representation are telegraphed in the old saying "the winners write the history."[24]

Pacific Overtures presents history through the eyes of the "losers," the Japanese, whose country was essentially turned into a colony by the United States and several European powers in the aftermath of Perry's initial incursion. The play thus asks us to think about how history—the story of what happened in the past—is constructed and the purposes particular constructions can serve. The vehicles for examining historical narrative are primarily the character of the Reciter and the song "Someone in a

Tree." The Reciter functions as the storyteller, the person who transmits much of the historical information to the audience and who, more important, provides a narrative standpoint for that information. The Reciter's relationship to the characters and the action of the play is a complex one. He sometimes enters the action, taking on the role of one of the characters, including the mostly silent role of the shogun during the act 1 "Chrysanthemum Tea" and the Emperor Meiji in act 2. More frequently, however, the Reciter remains outside the time, place, and action of the play. He is a critical observer, able to comment on the action, sometimes sympathetically, sometimes skeptically, sometimes sardonically, sometimes angrily. It is through his attitudes that the audience is encouraged to understand the action. Note, however, that, although the Reciter usually exists in the same time (1976, for the original production, looking back at events) as the audience and on the same plane (sharing the space of the theater), he is clearly not of the audience. He is a member of the society represented on stage; when he says "we," "us," or "our," he means the Japanese, and he is counting himself a part of that group. When he refers to the Americans, he calls them "Westerners," "they," or "them." This rhetorical distinction between "us" and "them" is particularly important because of the expectation that the Broadway audience for this show in 1976 would be primarily Caucasian Americans.[25] That the Reciter doesn't include the audience in his rhetorical "us," but rather considers them to be part of the outsiders, the "them," is clear from his last line: "There was a time when foreigners were not welcome here. But that was long ago. One hundred and twenty years. Welcome to Japan" (138). The use of the Reciter as storyteller, then, does two things. First, it foregrounds the notion of a narrative standpoint to frame the events of the past. Second, by putting an American audience in the position of the Other, the "them" in the "us/them" binary, and asking them to look at the past through the frame of another group, it contributes to the defamiliarizing effect of the play, unsettling the audience's expectations and their confidence in what they think they know.[26]

Further complicating our notions of what we know about the past and how we know about it is the song, often cited by Sondheim as his favorite of all the songs he has written, "Someone in a Tree." Placed near the end of the first act, this song is about the difficulty of knowing any event, in this case what happened between the Americans and the Japanese in the treaty house at Kanagawa. Instead of creating a scene that would dramatize the meeting, Sondheim and Weidman chose instead to write a scene showing various means of witnessing and representing the meeting. Thus the key historical event of the play is not presented directly; instead, it becomes a vehicle for the indirect, contingent, layered-by-representations way the past is known.

The Reciter introduces the scene with a straightforward statement of the problem of how narrative standpoint influences the historical narrative: "No one knows what was said behind the shutters of the Treaty House. The Shogun's Councilors kept their story secret, and though the Westerners have their own official version—I would not believe a word of it. What a shame that there is no authentic Japanese account of what took place on that historic day" (76). To offer a Japanese account, three characters come forward: an old man, dressed to suggest the turn of the twentieth century, who remembers as a boy having climbed a tree to watch the events from above; the boy the man was (a *Follies*-like fragmentation of the individual into old and young selves), who obligingly takes his place in the tree; and a warrior, who is hidden beneath the treaty house as a precaution against American treachery. These three represent the process by which the lost event of the past is narratized and the limitations of that process. The old man, although he claims, "I saw everything!" (*F* 321), cannot remember everything. Memory is fallible. At one point, his younger self corrects and excuses a memory lapse:

OLD MAN: Some of them have gold on their coats.
BOY: One of them has gold—
He was younger then. (*F* 321)

Immediately after, the old man laughingly points out the limitations of a little boy's perspective:

OLD MAN: Someone crawls around passing notes—
BOY: Someone very old—
OLD MAN: He was only ten. (*F* 321)

A bigger limitation is that the old man and his younger self can see everything but hear nothing. The hidden warrior, conversely, can hear everything but see nothing. In relating what he hears, however, the warrior exemplifies another limitation:

> First I hear a creak and a thump.
> Now I hear a clink.
> Then they talk a bit . . . (*F* 322)

Having been ordered to crash up through the floorboards at the signal of two knocks, the warrior is focused completely on listening for the knocks; the talking, which is what the Reciter and the audience are interested in, passes by him in another example of a limited perspective. As the three characters collaborate to tell the Reciter their stories of what happened, the song reveals both that the *pure* truth of what happened in the past can never be known and that the commingled memories, perceptions, and representations of what happened are inseparable from the *available* truth of the past.

Beyond contributing to the play's problematization and defamiliarization of history as a means of knowing the past, "Someone in a Tree" uses attitudes toward history to focus the theme of colliding worldviews. In a television program about the writing of this song, which aired shortly after *Pacific Overtures* opened, Sondheim spoke about his intentions for the music. He began with an accompaniment figure—five notes set to a basic rhythm—and repeated it with small and gradual variations, breaking up the notes in different ways, modulating up or down, introducing new tones. His idea here was to capture what he calls the relentlessness of Asian music and connect it to the movement of history, time's arrow. The effect, as he says, "stretched out the time" and created "the musical equivalent of the philosophical idea of the song, which is history."[27] He also draws attention to detail, how small changes in the music have important effects on the song as a whole, just as the details of this historical incident—the someone in a tree and the listener underneath—have repercussions for how the event is known. The song, then, becomes a statement of an aspect of the traditional Japanese worldview: attention to and understanding of the part is vital to an appreciation of the whole. The characters sing of their experience of this key historical moment,

> It's the fragment, not the day.
> It's the pebble, not the stream.
> It's the ripple, not the sea
> That is happening. (*F* 323)

This worldview clashes mightily with that of the Americans who have come to shore. Perry, in an excerpt from his journal quoted by the Reciter just before this song, reveals his reliance on the big picture and the sweep of history:

> As I supervise the final preparations for this afternoon's historic land-ing at Kanagawa, I am moved to hope the Japanese will voluntarily accept the reasonable and pacific overtures embodied in our friendly letter. Should I hope in vain, however, should these backward, semibarbarous people be reluctant to forsake their policy of isola-tion, then I stand prepared to introduce them into the community of civilized nations by whatever means are necessary. It is my under-standing that this preposterous empire has been closed to foreigners for over two hundred and fifty years, and I for one feel that that has been more than long enough! (75)

The collision of worldviews is narratively, thematically, and aestheti-cally at the heart of *Pacific Overtures*. To begin to explore this, we can turn to Sondheim's description of the process by which he and Weidman conceived the play: "What we actually did was to create a mythical Japa-nese playwright in our heads, who has come to New York, seen a couple of Broadway shows, and then goes back home and writes a musical about Commodore Perry's visit to Japan. It's this premise that helped give us tone and style for the show."[28] This rich explanation helps us see that the play's ideological themes are mirrored in and augmented by its self-ref-erential experiments in the style and the form of the musical theater. The result is a complex exploration of how different cultures encounter one another, how the power dynamics between them are played out, and how cultural identity and the forms for its expression can be transformed.

The concepts of mimicry and pastiche will be useful for us to understand how the play conducts its exploration. I am thinking of mimicry in postcolonial theorist Homi Bhabha's sense of "the desire for a reformed, recognizable Other, as *a subject of difference that is almost the same, but not quite*. Which is to say, that the discourse of mimicry is constructed around an *ambivalence*; in order to be effective, mimicry must continually produce its slippage, its excess, its difference."[29] That is, the colonizing power seeks to place its own systems—religious, linguistic, economic, social, cultural—over the systems of the indigenous population; the colonizers, of course, are convinced of the superiority of their own systems, and the colonizers' power over the colonized people depends to a great extent on their accepting the superiority of these systems too. The colonized subject is urged to desire to become like the colonizers—to speak their language, to worship their god, to participate in their economy, to live under their laws, to prefer their social practices and cultural products. At the same time, however, the colonizers' power is also dependent on maintaining the binary opposition of colonizer/colonized, Us/Other. Should the colonized subject actually become identical to the colonizers, all the colonizers' pretense to superiority would disappear, as would the rationalization that supports the colonial enterprise. Thus the colonized subject can never be allowed to fulfill his desire to become identical to the colonizer; at least a sliver of difference must remain, and that sliver turns the colonized's attempts to be like the colonizers to imitation, mimicry. Similarly, pastiche, as a musical-theater technique, is imitation with a difference; pastiche imitates other musical or artistic styles, not with the exaggeration leading to laughter that characterizes parody, but with a self-consciousness that creates a space for the audience to recall the sociocultural and ideological contexts of the stylistic source. In our discussions of *Anyone Can Whistle* and *Follies* we saw how Sondheim pastiched earlier musical-theater styles in order to comment on character or to juxtapose the past and present. The pastiche becomes about its subject, its own styles, and the ideological worldviews implied by its styles.[30]

The theme of mimicry is introduced and developed in the relationship between Manjiro and Kayama. Manjiro is a Japanese fisherman who became lost in a storm, was picked up by an American ship and taken to Massachusetts, where he went to school, and who has returned to Japan to warn of the impending arrival of Perry's fleet. He first appears in Western dress, the clothes of an American sailor, and, in his appearance before the shogun's court, he is voiceless—the Reciter speaks his lines. This is significant, because when Manjiro does speak, accompanying Kayama in a small boat to confront the American ships, he speaks as an American: he interrupts, he gives orders, he demands obeisance. As he explains to Kayama, "Americans are easy. They shout. You shout louder" (43). Manjiro's clothes, a Western sailor outfit, in contrast to the Japanese garments everyone else wears, draw attention to themselves as costume, and his taking on of the American voice is self-consciously performance, but as Kayama and the audience get to know him better, it's clear that during his time in America, he has internalized American values. He says to Kayama, "It is not the Americans who are barbarians. It is us!" (57). The desire engendered by this internalization to become American (the desire manifested in the mimicry of his clothes and speech) is most evident in the song "Poems," in which Kayama's love song to his wife is interwoven with Manjiro's love song to America. This desire and this internalization are disrupted when Manjiro is rewarded for his role in dealing with the Americans with promotion to the rank of samurai; this unexpected reconnection with the traditions of his own country overcomes the cultural self-loathing evident in his earlier conversations with Kayama. As a result of this disruption, in act 2 Manjiro becomes one of those seeking to purify Japan of Western influences.

In contrast, Kayama, the naive, minor bureaucrat who rises to the governorship of Uraga, begins the play so well socialized into his culture that he is easily manipulated into taking on the seemingly impossible task of ordering Perry's fleet away and accepts unquestioningly that failure will signify a dishonor for which only suicide can atone. His subsequent transformation is best seen in the second-act song "A Bowler Hat." While on one part of the stage Manjiro conducts the traditional tea ceremony in silence (once again Manjiro is out of step with his culture and so has no voice) and on another the Reciter reads excerpts from Kayama's official letters to the shogun documenting the growing influence of the Westerners in Uraga, on yet another part of the stage, Kayama sits at a table and sings of his life. As time passes (in the original production, stagehands aged Kayama and Manjiro with makeup between verses), we see Kayama gradually Westernized, in dress—he puts on a bowler hat, a pocket watch, a monocle, a cutaway—in language—he learns English and, apparently, French—and in habits—putting milk in his tea, going to a Christian church, smoking American cigars, reading Western philosophy, taking imported pills, building a Western-style house. He also internalizes Western-style condescension toward things Japanese. He sings, "I killed a spider on the wall. / One of the servants thought it was a lucky sign" (*F* 328). Concomitant with this self-loathing is a confidence growing to a sense of superiority in dealing with the Westerners. This is seen in his evolving relationship with the Dutch ambassador: he begins intimidated by the ambassador but over time moves to where he judges the man a fool because "He wears a bowler hat" (*F* 328), an item apparently hopelessly out of fashion. That this superiority is mimicked rather than genuine is underscored both by Kayama's ridiculous appearance, as he dons Western clothing over his Japanese garb, and by the Reciter's quotation of Kayama's letters, which make clear that economic, military, and social power is held by the Westerners.[31]

The growing influence of America and the European countries over Japan is further suggested by Sondheim's pastiche techniques. While the music in act 1, in style and orchestration, recalls Japanese musical forms, the music in act 2 becomes more familiarly Western in style. The change is announced with a bang in the first song of the second act, "Please Hello," in which admirals from America, Great Britain, Holland, Russia, and France present their demands for increased trade, a permanent consular presence, rights of extraterritoriality, and, finally, in the broadest wink to its original Kissinger-era audience, detente, all under the threat of their warships' guns. The rapid increase of Western power in and over Japan and the helplessness with which the new shogun, Abe, responds to it are signaled by the pastiched styles in which the admirals sing: the American admiral in a Sousa-style march, the British admiral in a Gilbert and Sullivan–style patter song, the French admiral in a cancan. After each admiral's solo, the previous admirals protest in their own musical styles, leading, by the end of the song, to a hectic cacophony that suggests the chaos descending on Japan in the guise of colonial order.

"Please Hello": Original cast of *Pacific Overtures*. Credit Line: Photo by Martha Swope/©The New York Public Library for the Performing Arts

"Please Hello" also adds another layer to the play's use of mimicry, a formal, self-referential layer. The practice has been for Asian actors to play the admirals in a self-consciously performative manner. They dress in exaggerated costume and makeup that draw attention to themselves as costume and makeup, and they exaggerate the style of standing and moving associated with a stereotyped view of each nation—the American marching, the Dutchman skating, the Frenchman prancing; in the original production, the British admiral had the bottom half of a wooden leg sticking out from one knee, so that he could walk normally on two legs, but when standing still, bend his knee and prop himself on the wooden leg. This mimicry has a quality of self-conscious performance that makes it quite different from either Manjiro's act 1 or Kayama's act 2 mimicry. The latter is born from a desire to become like the Westerners, a desire that the very terms of the Westerners' colonization of Japan will perpetually thwart; the former is born from a desire to use the Westerners' own form of appearance, movement, and speech to mock, critique, and subvert not only the process of Westernization through which Japan is going but also the ideological assumptions that underlie that process: binary oppositions (Us/Other), hierarchy (We and everything associated with Us are superior to Them), and difference (They can and should seek to become like Us, but, of course, as Other, They never can). The admirals' mimicry is not a mimicry of subservience, but a mimicry that, through its mockery, attacks the fundamental assumptions behind Japan's colonization.

This same technique of performative mimicry occurs whenever the Asian actors take on the roles of Westerners. In the confrontation between Kayama and Manjiro and Commodore Perry's officers, the Japanese characters speak in what Sondheim calls "elegant, formalized King's English," while the American characters "speak a pidgin form" of English.[32] For example, one officer says, "Commodore Payry also say: If big arrangement not made to greet him on land, he turn all cannon on Uraga and blast it off face of earth!!" (43). This pidgin stylization does several interconnected things. First, it performatively presents and critiques the Americans' condescension toward the Japanese. Second, it mockingly reverses the Westerners' hierarchy: with their unsophisticated use of language, the Americans seem inferior to the Japanese. Finally, it suggests that the Americans' superiority is based on nothing but the brute force they can marshal, an idea that is made explicit in "Please Hello" when Western diplomacy is accompanied by ever more terrifying artillery blasts from warships. Nevertheless, despite this critique and what it reveals about America's colonizing process, the Americans emerge triumphant. Though performatively the Japanese mimic and mock, practically the Americans end up laughing. As Kayama paddles away from Perry's ship humiliated, he says, "Why do they laugh? I do not laugh" (37). Another example occurs in an act 2 scene that was in the original production but has been removed from revivals. In it, the Reciter takes on the persona of Jonathan Goble, a marine from Perry's expedition who has returned to Japan ten years later to market his new invention: the ricksha. The Reciter puts on a Stetson, the incongruity of the hat and his Japanese costume again drawing attention to the performative, and speaks in a broad Western accent. He says to a prospective local partner, as a series of old Japanese men pull the ricksha, each until he collapses from exhaustion, "My friend, you got yourself a partner! We gonna git ourselves a factory—mebbe two. We gonna turn these beauties out dirt cheap, and sell 'em all across Japan. Why, before you know it—" (121). Again, the mimicry provides a means of critiquing American attitudes toward the Japanese and American business practices, in this case turning old Japanese men into a disposable resource. But again, despite the pointedness of the critique, the scene ends in frustration over Japanese powerlessness. As the Reciter drops the Goble character, he says,

> —before you know it, every city in our country will be overrun by
> rickshas. Invented, manufactured, marketed by Westerners—
>   (*He looks at the line of* OLD MEN, *then hurls away his Stetson hat*)
> —but pulled by Japanese. (121)

The Reciter's ineffectual gesture mirrors the result of his mimicry: the practice may critique the assumptions behind the colonizing power and it may reveal the workings of that power, but it can't in any real way challenge that power. It is still caught in the epistemology of the binary opposition, the ideology of difference.

In order to subvert the ideology of difference, the play moves beyond mimicry's mocking critique to the implications of its own technique of self-referentiality. The violation of the Us/Other binary opposition and the blurring of difference are foregrounded from the very beginning of the play by the play's very form. It is useful for us here to think about the play's form as well as its subject matter in terms of Mary Louise Pratt's concept of the contact zone, "the space of colonial encounters, the space in which peoples geographically and historically separated come into contact with each other and establish ongoing relations." Pratt argues that our binary assumptions about Us/Other, colonizer/colonized, victimizer/victimized frequently oversimplify the complexities of intercultural contact. She says, "A 'contact' perspective emphasizes how subjects are constituted in and by their relations to each other. It treats the relations among colonizers and colonized, or travelers and 'travelees,' not in terms of separateness or apartheid, but in terms of copresence, interaction, interlocking understandings and practices, often within radically asymmetrical relations of power." One manifestation of the copresence within the contact perspective is what she calls *autoethnography*, "instances in which colonized subjects undertake to represent themselves in ways that engage with the colonizer's own terms. [. . .] [A]utoethnography involves partial collaboration with and appropriation of the idioms of the conqueror."[33] If we recall Sondheim's story of the imaginary Japanese playwright who, after seeing several Broadway musicals, has returned to Japan to write his own musical, we can see that *Pacific Overtures* can be thought of as a representation of an autoethnography. Sondheim and Weidman have imagined an artist from the colonized people dramatizing the cultural conflict between colonized and colonizer and using a hybrid combination of his own and the colonizer's dramatic forms.

In other words, *Pacific Overtures,* by making the audience constantly aware of its own merged or hybrid form—the formal elements of the Broadway musical combined with formal elements of kabuki—challenges the concept of completely separate cultures, the difference, at the heart of the colonial worldview. This idea of hybrid form supporting the show's thematic development is especially true of the score. While it's true that Sondheim's music moves from Japanese influences to a pastiche of European styles to signify the growing Western presence in Japan, at no point, not even the beginning of the play, is Western style completely absent. In his interview with Mark Eden Horowitz, Sondheim describes researching Japanese music but insists that he was not trying to re-create or imitate it: "I went and I studied for two weeks in Japan. I also got some records of the various Japanese instruments that I knew nothing about. [. . .] And I listened to them, and listened to the Japanese scales which are essentially pentatonic minor scales—as opposed to the Chinese which are major. And then I tried to devise music that essentially used those elements, but was, of course, tonal music—Western tonal music."[34] In another interview he is more specific about the European influences in his score: "I was searching for a Western equivalent, and one day I hit on the correlation between the Japanese scale and the music of Manuel de Falla, a composer whose work I admire a lot. So I just started to imitate him. I took the pentatonic scale and bunched the chords together until they resembled that terrific guitar sound. And I was able to relate to it because suddenly it had a Spanish Western feeling and at the same time an Eastern feeling."[35] Beyond de Falla, musicologist Stephen Banfield argues that Sondheim's musical voice for the show was also influenced by British composer Benjamin Britten and that the opening song, "The Advantages of Floating in the Middle of the Sea," echoes in music, lyrics, and presentation the opening of Gilbert and Sullivan's *The Mikado*, "We Are Gentlemen of Japan."[36]

The play's self-referential, autoethnographic form functions in at least two ways. The first is to create, for an American audience, a defamiliarizing and alienating effect. The combination of very different formal techniques keeps the American audience off-balance and, presumably, challenged to rethink the assumptions about Us/Them and difference the play seeks to subvert. Similarly, the play asks a Broadway audience, presumably predominately non-Asian, to identify with Japan—not necessarily Japanese characters, as the play de-emphasizes individual characters in favor of a focus on the culture as a whole—and to see America as the enemy, the intruder, the Other. This reversal not only critiques American imperialism but also uses the audience members' confused sympathies to further blur the idea of difference, so seminal to the colonial process.

Sweeney Todd, the Demon Barber of Fleet Street, the crowning achievement of the Sondheim-Prince collaboration, is something of a hybrid musical as well, though in a different way from *Pacific Overtures. Sweeney Todd,* which opened at the Uris (now Gershwin) Theatre on 1 March 1979, is a daring play in many ways, not least in its subject matter.[37] It is an adaptation of a British legend of a mad barber who murders his customers for their money with the help of a neighbor, who bakes the bodies into meat pies. Having seen a new stage version of this story by Christopher Bond in London, Sondheim began musicalizing it, initially working alone with Bond's play, but eventually bringing in Hugh Wheeler to help shape the libretto.[38] The hybridity of the play comes from the different approaches that Sondheim and Prince took to the subject matter. For Sondheim, the play is about what happens when a person becomes obsessed with revenge. In an essay published shortly after the original production opened he writes, "*Sweeney Todd* is a play about obsession, and when a person is totally obsessed, everything else becomes irrelevant. In this sense, Sweeney is detached; the only interest from which he is not detached is his obsession: his revenge."[39] Interestingly, Prince reveals how he was able to bring his own ideas to the play:

I wanted it to have some social significance, and I realized the story takes place during the beginning of the Industrial Age in England, and that all of these people [. . .] [share] one thing. They never breathe clean air. They never see sunlight. From the day they're born to the day they die, they're victims. So I said to [scenic designer] Eugene Lee, "Let's do it in a factory, and let's put a glass roof on it that makes it claustrophobic, and let's tell all of these people that they are in the same spot really as the two leading characters in the play, that they're all victims of the Industrial Age." [40]

While it might seem that the play would have suffered from these two different approaches, from the composer and director being interested in what are essentially two different shows, Sondheim suggests how the two approaches came together: "Now Hal firmly believes that [*Sweeney Todd*] is a story about how society makes you impotent, and impotence leads to rage, and rage leads to murder—and, in fact, to the breaking down of society. Fine. In order to make the point, he had to show the society in action. When he grew excited about that idea, I started not so much to make reference to it but to soak it into the score." [41] Prince, however, concludes, "I suppose people who are collaborating should be after the same thing, but Steve and I were obviously not with respect to *Sweeney*." [42]

I think the two approaches work together because they intersect in the emotion of desire. Sweeney's desires are for completion—to be restored to Lucy and Johanna (the dream of home and family again), to achieve justice, to have revenge—completions that will provide narrative closure for the story he tells Anthony in "The Barber and His Wife." Mrs. Lovett represents the consumer capitalism arising out of the Victorian industrial age, a system that depends on the generation of desire—for products, as we saw in our discussion of *Evening Primrose*, or, as we saw in our discussion of *Anyone Can Whistle*, an improved identity—and the perpetual deferring of the completion of that desire so that more products can be sold. The tension between these two notions of desire and their relation to completion provides the context for the play's development of its ideas.

Compared to *Company, Follies,* and *Pacific Overtures, Sweeney Todd,* while dark, seems at first to be less narratively experimental. Yet this is not to say that the play is stylistically realistic. Sondheim set out to write a musical melodrama, *melodrama* not in the sense of campy over-the-topness contemporary audiences usually associate with the word but in the sense of exaggerated reality. In his essay on *Sweeney Todd* and melodrama Sondheim writes, "For me, melodrama is theater that is larger than life—in emotion, in subject, and in complication of plot."[43] Thus *Sweeney Todd* foregrounds and makes part of its subject matter its own dramatic style. The original production called attention to its own status as melodrama through its larger-than-life performances and exaggerated makeup. It also borrowed techniques from such theatrical forms as Grand Guignol and music hall. Most obviously, it set its action within a nineteenth-century Rhode Island iron foundry, which was taken apart and then reconstructed in the Uris Theatre.

More important than these factors in the play's calling attention to itself as a representation, however, is its play-within-a-play structure. In the original production, after the first factory whistle, almost the entire cast appeared onstage to sing the opening song, the first words of which are, "Attend the tale of Sweeney Todd" (*F* 333).[44] These words immediately establish that what we are to see over the next two and a half hours is not the story of Sweeney Todd but the narration of the story of Sweeney Todd, presumably by the actors assembled on the stage.[45] That we are watching a narration, a performance, is reinforced by the periodic reprises of "The Ballad of Sweeney Todd" that assist the transitions between scenes and comment on the action. This emphasis of the storytelling aspect of the play, its narrativity, gains importance if we recall some of the connections between narrative and time discussed in the section on *Company*. Narratives, because of their connection to time's arrow, move toward death. The desire for completed narrative-epistemological structures implies specifically a desire for death and, more generally, a desire for the transcendent, the ideal, absolutes that exist outside the completed structures and, implicitly, outside of time.

When the prologue ends and the narration we have been promised begins, the Sweeney we meet retuning to London after serving fifteen years of a life sentence believes in transcendent ideals and narrative closure. His bitterness is based in a disappointment that human systems—the legal system, organized religion—fall short of the ideals they are meant to represent—justice, Christianity. When pressed, Sweeney tries to explain his disappointment in the world:

> There's a hole in the world
> Like a great black pit
> And the vermin of the world
> Inhabit it [. . . .]

> At the top of the hole
> Sit the privileged few,
> Making mock of the vermin
> In the lower zoo,
> Turning beauty into filth and greed. (*F* 338)

Not only are the ideals of justice and Christianity perverted in the social system that is London, but another ideal, beauty, is degraded as well. As he goes on, we see that Sweeney has invested his wife Lucy with ideal qualities ("she was beautiful. / And she was virtuous" [*F* 338]) and blames his losing her on the corruption of human institutions (he was snatched away from her by "A pious vulture of the law" [*F* 338]). In his worldview, goodness, beauty, justice, and all the other virtues are lost because of the cruelty, selfishness, venality, and, most important, the hypocrisy of people. When he tells Anthony that he was naive, he means that he did not understand how the world works, not that he was foolish to believe in absolute qualities that exist outside of social contexts.[46]

Sweeney has no conclusion for the story he tells Anthony in "The Barber and His Wife," and when he tells the sailor, "There's somewhere I must go, something I must find out,"[47] he means that he wants to find out the end of the story. Despite his bitterness and cynicism, he is still naive and optimistic enough to hope for a happy ending to his story, an end in keeping with the dream of home and family. After Mrs. Lovett advances the story, telling him that Lucy was raped by Judge Turpin and subsequently poisoned herself and that Turpin adopted Sweeney and Lucy's child Johanna, the disappointed Sweeney says, "Fifteen years sweating in a living hell on a trumped up charge. Fifteen years dreaming that, perhaps, I might come home to a loving wife and child" (18). A reunion with his family and a happily-ever-after ending denied him, Sweeney immediately latches on to another conclusion to his story: "Let them quake in their boots—Judge Turpin and the Beadle—for their hour has come" (18). He now imagines an ending resulting from his bypassing corrupt human systems of justice and personally achieving perfect justice. The ends that Sweeney desires—happily-ever-after, ideal Christianity, absolute justice— are all transcendent ends, things that can be known only outside of time. Sweeney's desires are all for things that cannot be attained, at least not in the messy, far-from-ideal social world he lives in.

Contrast Sweeney's desire for transcendent ideals with the desires generated by the play's industrial-age setting. The set is a constant reminder, as Prince suggested, that all the people in this society are victims, living in a newly mechanized world that hides the sun, pollutes the air, and turns people into objects, all for the sake of increased production.[48] Increased production, of course, is connected to increased desire. A capitalist economy needs constantly to generate desire in consumers so that they will be motivated to buy products. For the system to keep growing, fulfillment of desire must be perpetually deferred. Slavoj Žižek argues that "desire's *raison d'être* is not to realize its goal, but to reproduce itself as desire."[49] Thus, while Sweeney's desires are totally end-based, the capitalist society that Sweeney finds on his return to London is focused on generated desires for deferred ends. The ends themselves are less important than keeping the consumer desiring.

In many ways Mrs. Lovett represents capitalism in the play. As Sondheim puts it, "While she is womanly and sexual, she is not vulnerable— she is venal. All she cares about is money."[50] For her, religious and ethical considerations are mere rhetorical positions to be brushed aside when the acquisition of money becomes an issue. In general, Mrs. Lovett is characterized by an amoral, ends-justify-the-means philosophy—she thinks nothing of lying to Sweeney, suggesting that he murder Anthony, or, when the time comes, preparing to kill Toby. The end that governs these means is making money, which, of course, is never really an end, because there is always more money to be made. This is not to say that Mrs. Lovett does not love Sweeney in her way, but it is a love that is subordinated to attaining security, wealth, and status.[51] Yes, when he first comes to her pie shop on his return to London, she lies to him about his wife being alive, presumably so as not to lose him, and in "My Friends" she admits, "Always had a fondness for you, / I did" (*F* 340). Her wanting to hold on to Sweeney, however, stems as much from wanting a man for economic security as from love. In "By the Sea" she creates a picture of their married life together, her own version of the dream of home and family, but it is as much about acquiring the signs of middle-class social status as about love. After all, she associates the seaside with her "rich Aunt Nettie" (127), and her main interest in getting married seems to be getting over the social stigma of living in sin.[52] In short, where Sweeney is obsessed with attaining justice for things done in the past, Mrs. Lovett is focused on the future, attaining more wealth and upward social mobility, ends that will always be deferred because, we imagine, she will always want more.

The play develops this theme of desire and capitalism in three songs, all of them titled "Johanna." Anthony sings his version of the song just after meeting Johanna and falling in love with her at first sight. Knowing nothing about her, he has fallen in love, like Dante with Beatrice, with an ideal he sees through her. Anthony associates Johanna, her beauty and her virtue, with a transcendent ideal. He sings, "I was half convinced I'd waken, / Satisfied enough to dream you" (*F* 342). In a conventional turn of this kind of love plot, just after meeting, the two lovers are separated. Judge Turpin and the Beadle threaten Anthony and order him away from Johanna. Anthony now has a narrative goal: to overcome this interposition and rescue Johanna so as to attain a happily-ever-after conclusion. Like young, naive Sweeney, Anthony directs his desires to ideals and imagines a narrative conclusion where his desires are fulfilled outside of time.[53] Anthony's narrative arc, then, is traditional and straightforward; it becomes complicated, however, when put into dialogue with the narrative arcs implied in the other "Johanna" songs.

In Judge Turpin's "Johanna" the desire for transcendent ideals is put into conflict with the desires of the body. The stage directions tell us that "The JUDGE is in his judicial clothes, a Bible in his hand" (179), symbolizing both the authority of his position and his reliance on the ideals of justice and Christianity. He is on his knees, praying to God for help in resisting temptation and, simultaneously, peeking through the keyhole at Johanna, lusting after her young body. His hypocrisy is the result of his desiring something that his belief system tells him he shouldn't. In beating himself with the scourge, he attempts to direct his desires away from the flesh and toward the transcendent, but the tension between the two drives him to an insane reconciliation of the two: he resolves to marry Johanna, a plan that Johanna and even the obsequious Beadle see as wildly inappropriate, so as to satisfy both his lust and the demands of church and state. When that plan fails (he learns of Johanna's plot to elope with Anthony), he swings between two extremes. Embracing the role of a righteous judge and father punishing an unruly child, he commits Johanna to Fogg's Asylum. Yet when Sweeney tricks him into thinking Johanna is ready to accept his proposal, he quickly submits once again to his lust.

Sweeney's "Johanna," like the Judge's, is contradictory. Singing calmly and lyrically while he slashes customers' throats and sends their bodies plummeting down the chute to the bakehouse, Sweeney sees Johanna as a symbol of the dream of home and family that he recognizes can now never be attained. Having found a new mission embodied in a new narrative desire, he seems reconciled and almost content with her loss. He sings that "The way ahead is clear" and that he has learned to say "Goodbye" (*F* 366, 367). At the same time he claims to be putting Johanna and the past behind him, however, he is conjuring an ideal version of her that he insists on believing in. He sings,

> And are you beautiful and pale,
> With yellow hair, like her?
> I'd want you beautiful and pale,
> The way I've dreamed you were [. . . .] (*F* 366)

That this dream version of Johanna is similar to the romanticized ideal Anthony has created is emphasized by Anthony singing parts of his "Johanna" during Sweeny's song as he wanders the streets of London looking for his lost love. Sweeney again reveals his obsession with ideals as he demands that his romanticized vision of Johanna be frozen, to exist eternally outside time: "You stay, Johanna— / The way I've dreamed you are" (*F* 366–67). This song is an important transition moment for Sweeney. The past, his wife and daughter, which has provided the main motivation for his narrative of achieving justice, is becoming remote, less real, more idealized, and his revenge, represented here by the anonymous men he is murdering, is becoming more abstract.

Clearly, each man, in singing of Johanna, has created a version of the girl and projected it onto the real Johanna, thus turning her into an object of desire. This process of objectification is also a process of dehumanization as a living human being is turned into an ideal to be desired and, less romantically, a product to be consumed. The real-life result is her forced immersion into the capitalist system, the machinery of which grinds individuals down into the only roles the system values: labor, products, or consumers. In "Green Finch and Linnet Bird" Johanna sings of escaping the cage she is trapped in. Most immediately, this cage is the Judge's house. Figuratively, however, the cage is the web of expectations created by the way society, represented by the men in her life, projects its desires onto her. Johanna's main goal is to escape from the efforts to objectify her. Indeed, the dramatic thrust of almost all her scenes is directed toward escape: escape from the Judge's house, escape from Fogg's Asylum, escape from Sweeney's razor. Her means to reach her goal vary, depending on whom she is dealing with; that is, she finds ways to use the idealizations projected onto her to her advantage. With Anthony, Johanna becomes the helpless maiden in a tower who needs a hero to rescue her. Although she has initiated the rescue attempt by stealing the key to her room and tossing it to Anthony from her window, when he comes to her, she grants him all agency, appearing too demure and, well, stupid to take charge herself. Much of the humor in "Kiss Me" comes from her silly babbling:

> I think I heard a click.
> It was a gate.
> It's the gate!
> We don't have a gate.
> Still there was a—wait! (*F* 351)

She even plays into Anthony's romantic ideal of love at first sight:

> Sir, I did
> Love you even as I
> Saw you, even as it

Did not matter that I
Did not know your name . . . (*F* 351)

With Judge Turpin, there is no babbling or stupidity. When he asks if
she has been near the window, Johanna replies with irony, "Hardly, dear
father, when it has been shuttered and barred these last three days" (182).
Intuiting the Judge's conflict, she plays to his sense of righteousness so
as to protect herself from his lust. She reminds him that she is a "maid
trained from the cradle to find in modesty and obedience the greatest
of all virtues" (183). She also repeatedly addresses him as "father" to try
to keep their relationship on a parent-child footing. In act 2, as her need
to escape becomes more desperate, she claims more agency. She shoots
Fogg when Anthony cannot bring himself to, and, trapped in the barber
chair with her life in the balance, she becomes the only one of Sweeney's
intended victims to elude him and escape.

The play's complications of its themes of desire—desire for completion
versus perpetual desire for an ever-deferred end—come together at the
end of the first act. Quite unexpectedly, Judge Turpin has come to Sweeney's barbershop for a shave. Sweeney has the chance to write an ending
to the story of "The Barber and His Wife" and achieve justice (not to mention end the play early) by killing the Judge, but, heeding Mrs. Lovett's
advice in "Wait," he chooses to enhance the pleasure of completion by
delaying slashing the Judge's throat. Of course, he waits too long: Anthony
bursts in babbling about his plan to elope with Johanna; the Judge is out-
raged and walks out, never to return. Sweeney, seeing the narrative end
to which he has been plotting snatched away from him and realizing that
he is unlikely ever to have another chance at the Judge, goes mad. Up until
now, there has been, as we have seen, a narrative-driven logic governing
his actions and his plans: they were all aimed at achieving pure justice and
narrative closure. Now, in his insanity, his desire for revenge as a means of
achieving justice becomes an obsession with revenge directed not specifically at Judge Turpin but at the world at large. Any man coming into the
barbershop can substitute for the Judge in a presumably infinite series of
slashed throats. In "Epiphany" Sweeney submerges into the capitalist notion of desire. He vows to act on his desire for revenge while deferring its
fulfillment. He sings to imaginary customers,

You, sir—anybody! [. . .]
Not one man, no,
Nor ten men,
Nor a hundred
Can assuage me—
I will have you! (*F* 355)

Nevertheless, he still kindles a hope that he will have another chance at the Judge ("And I will get him back / Even as he gloats" [*F* 355]), but it is unclear whether he can hold together his two conceptions of desire and revenge.

In "A Little Priest," the first-act finale, Sweeney's new desire for acting out an infinitely deferred revenge by means of anonymous victims is joined with the capitalist notions of desire the play has established. Sweeney's plans are grandly and madly philosophical, linking his own victimization and thwarted attempts at revenge to the larger operations of power in the social system, the British Beehive, as the drop depicting the nineteenth-century class system was titled in the original production. Mrs. Lovett, however, as always, is devoted to the practical, the material, and the economic. She sees the potentially infinite series of Sweeney's victims as raw material for her capitalist enterprise—meat for her pies. The venture that follows is a literalization of the process we saw at work in objectifying and dehumanizing Johanna. Capitalism values people not as people but as labor, products, or consumers. In "A Little Priest" Mrs. Lovett and Sweeney imagine a variety of people, most of them identified by their status as labor (priest, poet, lawyer, grocer, clerk, sweep, financier, and so on), turned into products (pies, each with its own qualities comically derived from their professions) to be consumed by still other people in a cycle of victimization that parodies and critiques the capitalist system all the characters are trapped in. The barber and the baker sum this up at the end of the song:

TODD: We'll not discriminate great from small.
No, we'll serve anyone—
Meaning anyone—

BOTH: And to anyone
At all! (*F* 361)

"God, That's Good!," the second-act opener, further brings home the play's points about desire and victimization. The number has many parts. It begins with Toby as a barker, generating desire for Mrs. Lovett's pies. The pies are so appealing (people cannot get enough of a product made from other people) that the customers are clamoring for more, to the

"A Little Priest": Angela Lansbury (Mrs. Lovett) and Len Cariou (Sweeney Todd) in *Sweeney Todd*. Credit Line: Photo by Martha Swope/©The New York Public Library for the Performing Arts

point that Mrs. Lovett and Toby nearly have to fight them off, cautioning them,

> Eat them slow, 'cos
> That's the lot and now we've sold it!
> Come again tomorrow—! (*F* 365)

Again, the fulfillment of desire is deferred, and business booms. Mrs. Lovett appears, the stage directions tell us, "in a 'fancy' gown, a sign of her upward mobility" (101). The success of the business has granted a part of her desires—for money and status—but, as we see in the upcoming parlor scene, she still desires more. Sweeney, meanwhile, during this number, welcomes the delivery of his new barber chair and tests with Mrs. Lovett his new system for delivering freshly slashed bodies from his shop to the bakehouse. At the end of the song, a new victim arrives (greedy Mrs. Lovett sings, "Bless my eyes—! / Fresh supplies!" [*F* 365]), evidence that Sweeney is acting on his never-to-be-satisfied desire for revenge. The song shows that all these various desires are supported by a cycle of victimization. We see a customer arrive and anticipate his murder. We see the meat pies, made, we know, from the bodies of previous customers. We see the enthusiasm with which Mrs. Lovett's customers consume the pies. We assume that some of these customers will eventually become Sweeney's customers and begin the cycle over again. Everyone is a victim of desire, his or her own and others', as desire keeps the cycle spinning. As a result, where the first act began with an unfinished narrative, "The Barber and His Wife," in search of closure, the second act begins with a cycle, which offers no closure, only growing desire.

Sweeney now contains within himself the conflict that in the first act existed in the tension between him and Mrs. Lovett. On the one hand, Sweeney is letting go of the past, becoming able, like Mrs. Lovett, to concentrate on the future, his grand plan of revenge. On the other hand, he still obsesses over the Judge and the Beadle, imagining a fulfillment of his desires should he be able to work his revenge on them. One result of this conflict, as we saw in the discussion of Sweeney's "Johanna," is that, as Sweeney kills more and more men, the motivation for his revenge, the loss of his wife and daughter, becomes less vivid to him, more idealized and more abstract. Another result is that the deaths that would have marked the narrative completion that was his major goal in act 1 now become just a part of the series as revenge for its own sake replaces revenge as a means of achieving ideal justice. After killing the Beadle, who, unluckily for him, had come to investigate complaints about the bakehouse, Sweeney shouts triumphantly about the completion of one of his goals, "It's done," to which Mrs. Lovett immediately replies, "Not yet it isn't!" (151). She knows that Toby has learned the secret of the bakehouse, and now he must be eliminated. Not long after, Sweeney, having lured the Judge to the barbershop, slashes his throat, an act that would have fulfilled his sense of justice and provided narrative closure had it happened in act 1. Even now, for a moment, Sweeney thinks he will finally be satisfied. To the melody of "My Friends," he sets down his razor and sings,

> Rest now, my friend,
> Rest now forever.
> Sleep now the untroubled
> Sleep of the angels . . . (*F* 374)

This almost holy moment of closure is interrupted by the thought of the still-at-large Toby, "The boy," and then, after starting from the shop, he remembers, "My razor!" (167). There can be no rest for the razor after all: the desire to kill now exists independently of the motivation for revenge.

Sweeney's story, the tale to which we have been told to attend, similarly resists closure. Sweeney, too late, finally recognizes his wife Lucy; the whole time he had been wreaking vengeance for her death, she was always nearby as the Beggar Woman. Worse, since he had recklessly slit her throat to get her out of the way before the Judge arrived at the barbershop, he, more than the Judge and the Beadle, bears responsibility for her death. The story he had been acting on was a lie (Mrs. Lovett pays for that lie with a fiery death in the bakehouse oven), and his moment of recognition consists both of seeing that the Beggar Woman is Lucy and of realizing that he has been imagining himself in the wrong story.[54] Holding dead Lucy in his arms, he returns to the beginning of the story, singing again "The Barber and His Wife," and admitting that he is still "Naïve" (*F* 374). Sweeney's efforts for most of the play were directed at revenge on those he imagined responsible for Lucy's death; that had been his goal and his desired narrative closure. Instead of reaching closure, his story circles back on itself as Sweeney becomes both antagonist and protagonist, the object and agent of revenge, the motivation for his own weird, perverted crusade for justice.

Sweeney dies, but his death points up the narrative's lack of closure. Toby, driven mad by his experiences in the bakehouse and the sewers, comes upon Sweeney with his dead Lucy in his arms. Finding Sweeney's discarded razor, he says, "Pat him and prick him and mark him with a B, and put him in the oven for baby and me!" (174) and then slits Sweeney's throat. As Johanna, Anthony, and the Officers of the Guard enter, Toby moves to the meat grinder and continues the work of making pies that Mrs. Lovett taught him: "Three times. That's the secret. Three times through for them to be tender and juicy" (174). Toby here performs the actions of both Sweeney and Mrs. Lovett, killing Sweeney in preparation, he imagines, for making him a pie and grinding the meat from previous customers. The symbolic child of Sweeney and Mrs. Lovett, Toby is bequeathed their work—murder and the making of people into objects—but stripped of their desires—for revenge and money. Sweeney's story ends with the suggestion that his and Mrs. Lovett's enterprise will continue, even without its principals, their desires, and their goals.

This lack of closure and this sense of the ongoing enterprise are further emphasized in the play's finale. Toby's last speech is punctuated by the slamming of a trapdoor, the lights coming up full for the only time in the show, and the actors stepping out of the roles they have been playing to address the audience directly, returning us to the storytelling frame that was established at the beginning of the play. Only now the story they ask us to hear is not a completed story about events in the past. The tense has changed to the present ("His needs are few, his room is bare" and so on [*F* 375]), indicating that Sweeney's story is not over. Indeed, Sweeney is present in all the quotidian areas of our lives and is even with us in the theater:

Sweeney waits in the parlor hall,
Sweeney leans on the office wall,
No one can help, nothing can hide you—
Isn't that Sweeney there beside you? (*F* 375)

Harold Prince and Stephen Sondheim at the first day of rehearsal for *Merrily We Roll Along*. Credit Line: Photo by Martha Swope/©The New York Public Library for the Performing Arts

The actors point him out in various areas of the theater until indicating him again rising from the grave, again eluding closure. In its complex presentation the play calls into question the reliance on completed narrative structure as a means of organizing knowledge and warns of the dangers of generating desires for infinitely deferred goals. These means of grasping identity and making sense of the world are likely instead to distort whatever truth might be available to us.

* * *

In looking at the Sondheim-Prince collaborations of the 1970s, I have argued that the various ways in which they challenge narrative as a meaning-providing structure connect to their questioning of conventional notions of identity and knowledge. *Merrily We Roll Along,* the sixth and
final musical in this phase of Sondheim and Prince's working together, addresses the connections among narrative structure, identity, and knowledge most directly and thus serves as a good summation for this part of
Sondheim's career.

In his biography, Sondheim is quoted as saying of his work, "I realize
that I am trying to recreate *Allegro* all the time."[55] Elsewhere, he recognizes "that *Merrily We Roll Along* is nothing more nor less than an updated version of *Allegro*."[56] *Allegro,* the 1947 Rodgers and Hammerstein
musical that followed the successes of *Oklahoma!* and *Carousel,* traces
the life story, from birth to a midlife epiphany, of Joseph Taylor Jr., the son
of a small-town doctor, who himself becomes a doctor but loses his ideals
when his ambitious wife persuades him to take a remunerative but empty
job at a Chicago clinic for wealthy hypochondriacs. His epiphany comes
at the end of the play when he summons the courage to reject a promotion and return to his hometown to help his father establish and run a
modest hospital. The play was self-consciously and determinedly groundbreaking. Read today, the script seems akin to the screenplay-like scripts
Prince asked librettists James Goldman and Hugh Wheeler to write for
him. Scenes are presented with only suggestions of settings, and they flow
into one another cinematically. A Greek chorus narrates and comments
on the action and, further, expresses to the audience the inner thoughts
of the characters. It also expresses the thoughts of the main character,
Joseph Taylor Jr., while he is an infant, a child, and a teenager. The actor
playing Joe doesn't actually appear onstage until he arrives at college; up
until then, the other characters directly address the audience when they
speak to Joe.

Although it ran a respectable 315 performances, *Allegro* was, by Rodgers and Hammerstein standards, a failure. Deeply disappointed, Hammerstein would never be so daring again; the next two Rodgers and Hammerstein shows, *South Pacific* and *The King and I,* while incorporating
some of the staging innovations of *Allegro,* were dramatically and narratively firmly in the aesthetic of musical-theater realism established by

Oklahoma! [57] Sondheim argues that Hammerstein's disappointment was personal as well as artistic:

> Oscar meant it as a metaphor for what had happened to him. He had become so successful with the results of *Oklahoma!* and *Carousel* that he was suddenly in demand all over the place. What he was talking about was the trappings, not so much of success, but of losing sight of what your goal is. [. . .] [A]ll the critics pounced on it as being a corny story, the doctor who gets corrupted by money. That's not what he meant. . . . It wasn't about money; it was about losing sight of your goal. On the highest level it's about—an artist has to be selfish. That's not what Oscar meant, but that's what I think it's about. [58]

Clearly, Sondheim is also describing one of the things *Merrily We Roll Along* is about.

Based on a 1934 play by George S. Kaufman and Moss Hart, *Merrily We Roll Along* tells the story of three friends—Franklin Shepard, a composer; Charley Kringas, a playwright and lyricist; and Mary Flynn, a novelist—who meet in the enthusiasm of youth, when everything seems possible. The play traces what happens to their dreams and goals as time passes and they are faced with life's surprises, travails, successes, and disappointments. The trick here is that the play moves chronologically backward. It begins on an evening in 1976 at a party for the opening of a movie Frank has produced. The movie is apparently a hit, but Frank's personal life is a mess. His second wife, Gussie, formerly a Broadway star, was supposed to have starred in the movie but was deemed too old; she resents being in the shadows and suspects, correctly, that Frank is having an affair with the young actress who took over her part. Frank is estranged from his son from his first marriage. He is also estranged from Charley, his former writing partner—so estranged, in fact, that the very mention of his name brings the party to an uncomfortable standstill. Mary, unable to re-create the success of her one and only novel and suffering from a longtime unreciprocated love for Frank, has become a critic and a drunk; the disturbance she causes at the party results in a permanent break with Frank. The opening scene reaches its climax when Gussie throws iodine in the eyes of Frank's mistress. The ensemble, commenting on the action much like the Greek chorus in *Allegro,* reprises the title song, asking, "How did you get to be here? / What was the moment?" (*F* 387). The play then moves backward in time as it looks for the turning points, the places where multiple possibilities morphed into narrative necessity.

Ironically, given its concern with success and failure, *Merrily We Roll Along* had a rocky reception on Broadway. The producers chose to follow the model of *Sweeney Todd* and preview in New York rather than trying out the show out of town, and so Prince, Sondheim, and librettist George Furth were faced with trying to solve the production's problems amid theater-district word of mouth and tabloid-item gossip. The opening was postponed twice while the actor playing Frank was replaced and choreographer Larry Fuller was brought in to replace Ron Field. When the play finally opened at the Alvin (now Neil Simon) Theatre on 16 November 1981, the critical community was prepared to see a show in trouble, and the reviews reflected their expectations. *Merrily We Roll Along* closed after only sixteen performances, the shortest Broadway run for any Sondheim musical except *Anyone Can Whistle.*[59]

No other Sondheim show has been revised as much as this one after its Broadway premiere. Sondheim and Furth, in several productions over twenty-two years, worked to refine the storytelling and to calibrate the most effective tension between what the audience needs to know and what they need to wait to find out.[60] For the sake of clarity, the following is the scene breakdown and chronology of the licensed version of the script:

Act 1
Scene 1: 1976, Frank's Bel Air, California, house—the opening party for Frank's film, *Darkness before Dawn*; Frank breaks permanently with drunken Mary; Gussie throws iodine in the eyes of Frank's mistress.
Scene 2: 1973, NBC Studio, New York City—Charley criticizes Frank during a television interview, thus ending their partnership and friendship.
Scene 3: 1968, Frank's New York apartment—Frank has returned from his around-the-world cruise extremely impressed by the lifestyles-of-the-rich-and-famous experience; Gussie leaves her husband, the producer Joe Josephson, for Frank.

Scene 4: 1967, outside the Manhattan Courthouse—Beth is divorcing
Frank over his affair with Gussie; Charley, Mary, and other friends
convince Frank to discontinue contesting the divorce because of the
potentially scandalous publicity and, instead, to get away from it all
with an around-the-world cruise.

Act 2

Scene 1: 1964, outside the Alvin Theatre—the opening of Frank and
Charley's first show, *Musical Husbands*; Beth goes with Charley
to the hospital where his wife is in labor, leaving Frank to go to the
opening-night party with Gussie.

Scene 2: 1962, Gussie and Joe's brownstone—Frank and Charley
perform "Good Thing Going" for Gussie, Joe, and their guests; Gussie
makes clear that she is hitching herself to Frank's star.

Scene 3: 1960, the Downtown Club—Joe and his fiancée Gussie attend a performance of the revue *Frankly Frank*; afterward, Frank and
Beth are married while heartbroken Mary watches.

Scene 4: 1957–1959, New York City—a montage in which Frank,
Charley, and Mary balance the excitement of their writing with the
necessity to earn money, in which they become despondent over
the rejection they face, and in which they decide to put on their own
revue; Beth auditions for and is cast in the revue.

Scene 5: 1957, a rooftop on 110th Street—Frank, just out of the army,
has moved in with Charley; each is inspired by the other's work and
they decide to collaborate on a musical play, *Take a Left*, that might,
they hope, change the world; waiting to see *Sputnik* pass overhead,
they meet Mary, another tenant, and in this hopeful and almost
sacred moment, the three pledge undying friendship.

The drama and the development of the play's ideas arise from a triangular tension implied in the above structure. The fundamental conflict of
the play, even more important than the conflicts among the characters, is
among the three organizational paradigms at work in the play's structure.
The first paradigm is the reversed chronology of the plot or the play's basic, backward-moving narrative structure. The second is directly opposed
to the first: the implied, ineluctable forward movement of time. The third

overlays the other two: a cyclical structure based in the play's method of repetition and variation.

The backward-moving narrative structure emphasizes two ideas we have already seen elsewhere. The first is a more elaborate development of the life-is-a-journey metaphor that Ben Stone employed in "The Road You Didn't Take." The second is the idea of a life's meaning being governed by the anticipated completion of a goal, the point of narrative closure that makes a complete, meaning-providing structure for a life story. Both ideas are established in the opening number, "Merrily We Roll Along," which is reprised throughout the show as a means of segueing from scene to scene and year to year. The song introduces the image of the dream as the goal one's life is aiming for, the end of the journey and, more than that, the thing that gives the journey its purpose and meaning. The ensemble sings:

> Dreams don't die,
> So keep an eye on your dream [. . . .]
> Time goes by
> And hopes go dry,
> But you still can try
> For your dream. (*F* 383)

Like Ben, the ensemble has conflicting feelings about life's journey. In a counterpoint section, one half of the ensemble sings "Plenty of roads to try," while the other half sings,

> One
> Trip, all you get is
> One quick ride [. . . .] (*F* 383)

Similarly, the admonition "Never look back" conflicts with the question "Why don't you turn around / And go back?" (*F* 383). The implication here is that there is a disjunction between the dream that was to be the destination of the life journey and the actual destination. Thus the ensemble asks the question that provides the motivation for the play: "How did you get to be here? / What was the moment?" (*F* 384). The next scene, the last scene chronologically and essentially the end of the story, establishes the corruption of Frank's dream and the hollowness of what he has actually achieved. The play, we understand, will be engaged in a search for the story that led to this ending instead of to the goal Frank started out with.

In this sense the play's impulse is essentially an (auto)biographical one. Remember, creating a life narrative involves establishing a narrative standpoint (an endpoint toward which the life events will move), selecting the key events of the life, and finding the cause-and-effect-based pattern of events that lead to the endpoint. Note that this process is governed by the premise of before and after. Each selected life event can be seen as a cause of some subsequent effect and thus can be considered as a turning point, a dividing line between before and after. In telling the story in reverse order, however, *Merrily We Roll Along* shatters the illusion of narrative coherence. The pattern of events, the cause and effect, and the significance of turning points lose their naturalness, their impression of inevitability, when regarded backward instead of forward. The play's backward structure, like the ghosts in *Follies,* fragments the coherence of individual identity.

Frank's life narrative, being the play's central concern, provides the clearest example. In act 1, scene 1, the final scene chronologically, Frank is celebrating his greatest success to date, the opening of *Darkness before Dawn,* the film he produced. Yet he says to Gussie, "I swear, if I could go back to the beginning, if I could somehow be starting over with Charley, writing shows, trying to change the world, I'd give all this up like that. [. . .] Do you really not see that I'm ashamed of all this? That I am as sick of myself as you are? That I just try to keep acting like it all matters. To not let people see how much I hate my life, how much I wish the God damn thing was over—"[61] Earlier, during "That Frank," when a guest asks if he misses writing music, Frank replies, "That was the *old* Franklin Shepard" (11). When we get to act 2, scene 5, the first scene chronologically, twenty-year-old Frank says that "writing music is not about words. It's about sounds and feelings and . . . To me, music is about everything. [. . .] If I didn't have music, I'd die" (158). When he proposes a writing partnership to Charley, he explains, "Musicals are popular. They're a great way to state important ideas. Ideas that could make a difference. Charley, we can change the world" (154). The opening number tells us to watch this story and look for the moment, the Faustian—or Joe Hardy–like—decision where Frank sold his soul to the devil. The play as it unfolds makes clear, however, that the path of a life is too complex to be reduced to a narrative device: there are too many moments, too many decisions that contribute to the seeming inevitability of a life.

Frank tries to reduce it all to an essential problem: "I've made only one mistake in my life. But I made it over and over and over. That was saying 'yes' when I meant 'no'" (26). Frank's notion of success is transformed from creating work of artistic integrity that contains the potential to change the world (act 2, scene 5) to the kind of worldly success that is marked by money, possessions, and status (act 1, scene 1), a transformation that occurs gradually through his relationship with Gussie. Gussie represents the worldly idea of success, and she positions herself with men who she thinks can help her get it. She moves from being Joe's secretary to being his wife so as to have a producer to cast her in shows. After five flops, she desperately needs a hit that will establish her as a star, and so she initiates her seduction of Frank. This begins a triangular tug-of-war with Frank in the middle: Mary (not the oblivious Beth) trying to pull Frank back from Gussie's sexual seduction; and Charley trying to pull Frank back from her idea of worldly success. This tug-of-war plays out through many decisions, some big, some small, not all of them Frank's: Frank and Charley's decision to do *Musical Husbands* as a vehicle for Gussie and then to do one more fluff musical, *Sweet Sorrow,* for Joe; Beth's decision to leave Frank with Gussie on the opening night of *Musical Husbands*; Charley and Mary's miscalculated decision to encourage Frank to go on the cruise; Gussie's decision to leave Joe; Frank's decision, seemingly a small one, not to join Charley and Mary at the Downtown Club on the night he returns from the cruise. Where exactly Frank could have or should have said no so as to have changed his life story is not clear. Rather, the cumulative effect of his and others' decisions is described by the ensemble in the title song:

How does it start to go?
Does it slip away slow,
So you never even notice it's happening? (*F* 383)

The backward-moving structure of the play is similarly complex in

Charley's case. Act 1, scene 1 encourages us to see Frank and Charley as opposites: Frank, his dream corrupted, has achieved a worldly success that he knows is worthless; Charley has stuck to his dream, resisted the worldly seductions Frank could not, and has achieved artistic success, the Pulitzer Prize. Charley's success seems to be an implicit condemnation of Frank's compromises. As the play takes us back in time, however, we see that Charley compromises too, by fighting, grumbling about, but finally going along with Frank's compromises. This allows him to believe in his own virtue while blaming Frank for his weakness. Still, in "Franklin Shepard, Inc.," Charley admits that Frank "makes a ton of money, / And a lot of it for me" (*F* 392). Frank's compromises, we see, have allowed Charley an entrée into Broadway and given him a more-than-comfortable income. Without these, who knows whether he would have been able to write his Pulitzer Prize–winning play or to get it produced? We see that Charley's journey to his goal is not as straightforward nor as pure as he would no doubt like to believe.

Directly opposed to the backward-moving structure of the play is the implied forward movement of time, time's arrow. Narrative, by its connections to time's arrow, implies a progressivism, an evolutionary moving forward. By divorcing its narrative structure from time's arrow, *Merrily We Roll Along* calls into question and frees itself from the expectation that narrative be progressive, that when we reach the endpoint, the point of narrative closure, conditions will have improved or new knowledge will have been gained or a lesson will have been learned. Instead, *Merrily We Roll Along* presents an entropic version of time: as time goes on, instead of getting better, things fall apart; instead of narrative closure providing an ordered and potentially meaningful structure, events tend toward chaos. We can see this idea in its most compact form in the first-act finale, "Now You Know." Here, Mary, Charley, and other friends try to convince Frank to quit contesting Beth's divorce action, put the mess behind him, and go on a cruise to relax and prepare for the rest of his life. The message they want to get across to him is essentially progressive. Charley and Mary explicitly cast the divorce in terms of a narrative. They sing, "Feels like an ending, / But it's really a beginning [. . .]" (*F* 397). Thus it promises the chance to move forward, to improve, or, as Mary sings, "Now you grow" (*F* 397). Various friends repeatedly sing out the cliché "Best thing that ever could have happened" (*F* 397), suggesting that as time passes and Frank gets to a future narrative spot, the divorce will seem retrospectively to have been a good narrative turning point, not the disaster it seems to be now. Contained within this articulation of the progressivism of the life narrative, however, are indications of the entropic nature of time. While explaining that "Life is crummy," Mary sings, "It's called flowers wilt, / It's called apples rot [...]" (*F* 397). This reminder undercuts the optimism of Frank's friends' advice and reveals the twofold desperation behind it: the specific desperation of the friends in trying to steer Frank away from the self-destructive divorce contestation; and the more general desperation with which people try to see their time-linked lives as always moving forward, always improving, always nearing the achievement of their dream.

Over and over, the play's score offers songs that begin with the promise of a better future only to fall victim to the entropic movement of time. The effect is perhaps most immediate in "Bobby and Jackie and Jack," the number from the *Frankly Frank* revue that Charley, Beth, and Frank perform at the Downtown Club in 1960. This affectionate satire of the newly elected president and his family communicates an optimism about the future inspired by the charismatic JFK. We in the audience, however, know where this optimism leads: by the end of the decade both brothers will have been assassinated. Audiences for the 1994 York Theatre production were aware that Jacqueline Kennedy had died only a few days before the opening. Thus, while viewing this number, audiences feel nostalgia for a time of innocent hope, feel the loss of what has been, and are also aware that the characters know nothing of these feelings. Their innocence and their optimism are heartbreaking.

In the play's central song, "Good Thing Going," promise is again betrayed by time. The song's first two verses establish the promise of a love relationship, the good thing that is "going" in the sense of moving forward. By the last verse, however, entropy has set in:

And while it's going along,
You take for granted some love
Will wear away.
We took for granted a lot,

But still I say:
It could have kept on growing,
Instead of just kept on.
We had a good thing going,
Going,
Gone. (*F* 403, 408)

Over time, love wears away, forward movement gives way to stasis, stasis gives way to loss. "Going" now implies a running down, and the vocal score indicates that the last word, "Gone," is to be sung pianissimo, a soft falling away rather than a more definite closure. After Frank and Charley finish the song, Gussie leads her guests' applause and says, "Wouldn't you all just like to live your entire life to that music?" (115). The irony, of course, is that they do. The song's use in the play reflects its theme. In "Opening Doors" we see Frank gradually developing the melody and harmonic structure for the song. At Gussie's party we hear the finished song in its simplicity and beauty. Then begins a process of vulgarization and commercialization. At the beginning of act 2, we see it adapted for Gussie in *Musical Husbands,* with a brassy Broadway arrangement and a clichéd verse. Finally (or, rather, first, since this is our initial exposure to the song in the show), in the television-studio scene we hear it sung by Frank Sinatra; it has apparently become a pop hit.[62]

An exclamation mark is put to the connection of time's arrow with the descent into chaos at Frank's party, the first scene of the play and the last scene of the plot. As we saw earlier, although the party celebrates the success of Frank's movie, his personal life is falling apart. After Gussie throws iodine into his mistress's eyes, she says to Frank, "You said we were finished, Frank? Well, now we're finished. You and her and me and every God damn thing is finished!" (28). In a sense this is the finish of the play, the endpoint of its chronology. Yet it is not an endpoint that provides closure or restores order or completes a structure or offers meaning. Instead, Frank is left at the end of the scene screaming the one-word question "Why?" (29). This ending offers no answers. Thus the play begins by calling into question the progressivism narrative brings to time's arrow. Removing the narrative form from the passing of time reveals the entropic tendency of time and the illusions we create for ourselves when we insist on looking for patterns of progress in our life stories.

Connected to this general notion of entropy as a movement from states of organization to states of chaos is communication entropy, which has to do with the disruption of communication or the loss of information due to noise, distraction, ambiguity, or predictability. In "Opening Doors" Frank, Charley, and Mary need more time for all the composing, writing, performing, and conversing they have bursting out of them. The possibilities for communication seem infinite and everything seems possible. Compare this to Gussie's "Blob," referring to the packs of partygoers who appear periodically throughout the show. They make noise but communicate nothing. Here is a typical example from the act 2 scene at Joe and Gussie's brownstone:

> It's the first—!
> It's the finest—!
> It's the latest—!
> It's the least—!
> It's the worst—!
> It's the absolutely lowest—!
> It's the greatest—!
> It's the single—!
> It's the only—!
> It's the perfect—! (*F* 402)

In a prefiguring of what is to come for Frank, when Gussie insists that Frank and Charley do an encore performance of "Good Thing Going," the babble of the "Blob" creeps in and then eventually drowns them out. Part of Frank's problem is that the more he is pulled into Gussie's world, the more he becomes swept up into the world of the "Blob," with its inanity, vapidity, confusion, and noise. He rarely has a moment of silence in which to reflect and regroup, and when he does, as in act 1, scene 3, where he sits alone at his piano and sings "Growing Up," really his most sympathetic moment, his words about adjusting one's dreams over time are betrayed by the melody: a slow-tempo version of Gussie's solo in "The Blob." When we meet Frank, in act 1, scene 1, the "Blob" is singing his praises, and he is right in step with their moronic babble: he has been absorbed into the "Blob."

The third structural paradigm at work here is based in repetition and variation. The other two paradigms—the backward-moving narrative and the forward-moving time's arrow—though in tension, are both nevertheless linear. This other aspect of the show's structure, which operates principally in the score, makes connections across time and narrative lines through repeating melodies, harmonies, lyrics, and dialogue or presenting variations on them, as in the previous example of "The Blob" and "Growing Up." The result is a layering effect wherein incidents disconnected in time are brought into resonating proximity. Sondheim says, "The idea of the score was that it was built in modular blocks, and the blocks were shifted around [. . . .] You take a release from one song and you make that a verse for a different song, and then you take a chorus from a song and make that a release for another song. [. . .] It's like modular furniture that you rearrange in a room: two chairs become a couch, two couches at an angle become a banquette."[63]

This modular technique is the basis for the connections across time that create possibilities for meaning beyond the other, linear structures. Sondheim establishes the score's method early on. When the prologue segues into the California-house scene, the brassy, Latin-inflected accompaniment for "That Frank" is taken from a melody we have just heard in the title song setting the lyrics "Dreams don't die, / So keep an eye on your dream—" (*F* 383). Before a single lyric is sung, the music establishes that Frank has failed to care for his dream. Later, the melody we first hear in "Franklin Shepard, Inc.," where Charley is complaining about Frank's moving away from his music to become a businessman, is used again as the verse to "Now You Know," where Charley and the others are convincing Frank to drop his contestation of the divorce and go on a cruise. The connection is important because, while on the cruise, Frank develops his desire to have the privilege, wealth, and power of the truly rich, thus leading to the transformation Charley deplores in the first song. Repeating the melody reveals Charley's implication in Frank's transformation: as much as he hates it, he is one of the ones who contributed to it and, as we saw earlier, profited from it. Another example can be seen in the connections between "Like It Was" and "Old Friends." If the score were moving chronologically instead of backward, the verse of "Like It Was" would be a straight reprise of "Old Friends." It then moves into the main song, Mary's lament for the lost past, a variation of the melody of which is the bridge in "Old Friends," where Frank and Charley begin fighting over Charley's disapproval of Frank's priorities and Mary tries to make peace. This connection is important because it shows the fragility of Frank, Charley, and Mary's friendship. The characters like to appeal to their friendship as if it were ideal, pure, and inviolable. Yet we see in the bridge of "Old Friends" that the conflicts among the characters are not resolved; as the music and lyrics (segueing into dialogue) reach a cacophonous climax, the characters return to the main theme. The appeal to the long-standing friendship covers over the disagreement but does not solve anything. In "Like It Was," Mary's appeal to the "Old Friends" theme in the verse is desperate and pathetic. What was in the other song the bridge, where conflict threatened the relationships, is here the main theme, a lament for the camaraderie of the past now seemingly lost. The overlay of these two songs, separated narratively and in time, helps us understand that the characters place more faith in the ideal of their friendship than work to make the actual friendship survive.

The first sung words in *Merrily We Roll Along* are "Yesterday is done" (*F* 383) and they are echoed in the opening stanza of the final song in the show, "Our Time" (*F* 419), but everything else in the play works to demonstrate that yesterday is not done, the past is never over. The tension created by the three structural paradigms the play employs reveals an increasingly complex relationship between the past and the present and an increasingly complex sense of how we perceive the past, how we make sense of it, how we relate to it, and how we use it to govern our sense of our lives.

We see, then, that the musicals Sondheim wrote in his collaboration with director Harold Prince—*Company, Follies, A Little Night Music, Pacific Overtures, Sweeney Todd,* and *Merrily We Roll Along*—are all engaged in an exploration of the ways we know, how those ways have been linked to narrative in its various forms, and what happens when narrative as a meaning-providing structure is undermined. In his subsequent plays, Sondheim and his collaborators continue these explorations, but, in keeping with the maturing postmodern culture around them, they also begin to explore how—given the postmodern problematicization of representation, the narrative construction of knowledge, and meaning-making—art can point beyond itself to say something about the world at large.

Four

Take Me to the World

I n the previous two chapters we studied the ways in which the plays
created by Stephen Sondheim and his collaborators in the 1950s,
1960s, and 1970s incorporated such postmodern-inflected ideas as
Foucauldian theories of the operations of power, Althusserian notions of
identity construction, the linking of identity and performance, and the
overall deconstruction of narrative as a meaning-providing structure. In
the plays of the 1980s, 1990s, and 2000s, Sondheim and his collaborators
continued to develop these ideas in new and interesting ways and also
began to address the implications of a postmodern backlash—the desire
to find a way out of the network of discourse, narrative, and representation that postmodernism has placed between the human consciousness
and the world and, to go further, into which human consciousness and the
world have been absorbed. In other words, while acknowledging the primary place of discourse, narrative, and representation in knowledge and
identity, can we nevertheless find a way to something beyond language?

Merrily We Roll Along marked an ending for Sondheim. It was the last
show in his remarkable eleven-season collaboration with Harold Prince;
he would not work with Prince again until the 2003 Chicago and Washington, DC, productions of *Bounce*. It was also the last show he would
write in the commercial practice of the Broadway theater in which he had
been trained. This practice was really not much different from the process
that composers and playwrights of earlier generations went through: get a
producer to commit to a play; raise money through individual investors;
try out the play in one or more cities before bringing it to New York; open
on Broadway and hope for good reviews. Sondheim was fortunate that,
with the exception of *Sweeney Todd*, Prince produced all their collaborations. During the 1970s, Prince had a reliable cadre of investors who were
willing to follow his lead, even on such dicey propositions as *Follies* and

Pacific Overtures. With the exception of *Sweeny Todd* and *Merrily We Roll Along* eschewing out-of-town tryouts, all the Sondheim shows to this point were produced in the traditional commercial manner.

However, none of the post-*Merrily* shows followed the traditional path to Broadway; in fact two of them did not, in their initial productions, arrive on Broadway—*Assassins* didn't play in a Broadway theater for thirteen years after its initial production, and *Road Show* has not yet had a Broadway production. These plays of the 1980s, 1990s, and 2000s all, at some point in their development, were associated with nonprofit theaters, either Off-Broadway theaters or regional theaters. These non-profits, which are funded by governmental and private foundation grants, by corporate and individual donations, and sometimes by enhancement money from commercial producers, provide time and a space where playwrights can develop their plays through workshops, informal and usually private productions that give an opportunity to assess a work-in-progress, and main-stage productions that are not required to be commercially successful.

Sondheim's transition into the nonprofit theater world is significant in two ways. First, it highlights a sea change in the nature of the Broadway musical. As producing a musical on Broadway became more and more expensive and as ticket prices rose higher and higher, it became harder to mount on Broadway a musical without obvious commercial appeal. As Broadway moved into the twenty-first century, the musical scene was dominated by stage versions of popular movies and evenings built around popular composers' and vocalists' songbooks. When a musical with serious intent that challenged audiences did appear on Broadway, it was almost always something that had been developed in the nonprofit world. For Sondheim to continue doing the kind of work he had always done, a move into the nonprofit world was inevitable.

The second way in which Sondheim's transition to the nonprofit world is significant is the more congenial process it offers for writing his shows. Sondheim famously wrote major parts of some of his scores only after the shows were in rehearsal. At the first read-through of *Follies,* the Loveland sequence had not yet been written, and when *A Little Night Music* began rehearsals, only ten of the sixteen songs were ready.[1] In fact, it was only after Prince, in frustration, staged *Night Music*'s first-act finale that

Sondheim was inspired to write "A Weekend in the Country." In his autobiography Prince relates, "'A Weekend in the Country' is such an accom-
plishment that Steve was prompted to suggest that next time we should
stage our libretto without any music, show it to him, then let him go away
for six months to write the score."[2] At its best, this is what the nonprofit-
theater process can offer: the chance to see and hear a work-in-progress
and then go away to write, rewrite, rethink, and revise. In the process
of developing *Sunday in the Park with George*, Playwrights Horizons, a
nonprofit Off-Broadway theater, held a staged reading of the first act of
James Lapine's book before Sondheim had written any songs and then
another reading of both acts and the five songs that had been written to
that point.[3] The readings led to a fully staged workshop production. The
luxury to experiment that this process offers is rare in the commercial-
theater world. Sondheim also notes the ways working in the nonprofit
theater has changed his work: "I found myself writing with more formal looseness than I had before, allowing songs to become fragmentary,
like musicalized snatches of dialogue, but avoiding the static verbosity of
recitative. I worried less about punctuating the piece with applause and
concentrated more on the flow of the story itself."[4]

As unconventional as the Sondheim-Prince plays had been, they seem
practically mainstream when compared to the daring and startling *Sunday in the Park with George*. Although *Sunday in the Park* moved from its
Playwrights Horizons workshop to a commercial production on Broadway, opening 2 May 1984 at the Booth Theatre and starring Mandy Patinkin and Bernadette Peters, it is hard to imagine the play being created
in the commercial-theater milieu. The first act fictionalizes the creation
of pointillist painter Georges Seurat's masterpiece *A Sunday Afternoon on
the Island of La Grande Jatte*, imagining lives for Seurat and the figures
in the painting as well as meditating on the process of artistic creation,
the nature and purpose of art, and how artists live. The second act moves
one hundred years into the future to focus on an American artist, another
George, possibly descended from Seurat, and his struggle to create art
and connect with others in an age when all possibilities for artistic and
personal expression seem to have been exhausted. (For the sake of clarity,
I shall refer to the first-act George as George 1 and the second-act George
as George 2.) The play ends with George 2 taking his latest creation, a

chromolume—apparently a combination of sculpture and light show—to La Grande Jatte, where in a surreal moment he meets Dot, George 1's mistress, and the other figures in the painting and comes to a new understanding of art and life.

In the end, *Sunday in the Park* is as intentionally plotless as *Company* and *Follies*. Granted, it offers the story of the creation of the painting and the story of George 1 and Dot's love relationship as well as fragments of the stories of other figures in the painting, but none of these dominates and none is the point. Rather, Sondheim and Lapine have created onstage a metaphorical canvas on which can be depicted an exploration of ideas about the relationship between art and the world.

Just as it does not have a foregrounded plot, the play does not develop its ideas in a sequential, thesis-like way. Rather, we as viewers must relate ideas across scenes and the two acts; like the Georges, we must connect. The first point we need to understand is that it is overly simplistic to think of art as merely representational. Art does not simply hold a mirror up to nature and reflect back to us what we see around us. (Also, representation is anything but a simple process, but more on that later.) We cannot understand art or the world by putting an equal sign between them. In a way this seems obvious. To judge a work of art by how accurately it replicates reality is naive, but even sophisticated characters in the play, perhaps unconsciously, bring this expectation to art and to the world. When George 2 arrives on La Grande Jatte, he is disappointed that, in 1984, modern buildings crowd the scene, that it does not look like the landscape in Seurat's painting. Finding a solitary tree that may be one of the trees in the painting, he has his picture taken standing in front of it and concludes, "At least something is recognizable."[5] Shortly afterward, in "Lesson #8," reflecting on his loneliness, his inability to connect with others, and his loss of faith in his work, George again reveals his expectation that the park would look like the painting: "George would have liked to see / People out strolling on Sunday . . ." (*L* 51). In act 1, George's friend Jules, a more successful artist, is appalled by his first viewing of the painting, saying, "You cannot even see these faces!" (79). We do not know what kind of painting Jules does, but he brings to George's the expectation that it will replicate its subject. Clearly, these responses to the painting, judging the world by what we see in art and judging art by what we see in the

"Beautiful": Barbara Byrne (Old Lady) and Mandy Patinkin (George) in *Sunday in the Park with George*. Credit Line: Photo by Martha Swope/©The New York Public Library for the Performing Arts

world, are inadequate to the complexity of Seurat's painting and, more generally, to any art.

A variation on the equal-sign attitude toward art is exhibited by the Old Lady, George 1's mother. In "Beautiful," near the end of the first act, she laments the loss of the past, which, to her mind, was always beautiful compared to the degraded present. She sings,

> Sundays
> Disappearing
> All the time,
> When things were beautiful . . . (*L* 31)

She implores her artist son, "Quick, draw it all [. . .]" (*L* 31). For her, art is a means of preserving a world that would otherwise be lost to time. She might imagine George's painting as a vintage photograph, showing people in the future what life was like in Paris in 1884. Of course, in some ways

Seurat's painting does just that, but to limit its purpose to that would reduce art to sociology and overlook the ways the painting is not realistic in style. Again, to insist on art as preserving a sociohistoric moment is an inadequate response.

The play's most direct comment on the absurdity of equating the world and art comes in the opening number of the second act, "It's Hot Up Here." The song imagines the figures in the painting as real people trapped, like bugs in amber, within the frame of the artist's work. They complain about the physical discomfort of being stuck in one place and one position, like Dot in the first-act song "Sunday in the Park with George," but here, as if by some sort of curse, they are forced to pose forever. There is also the suggestion of interrupted lives, the desire for what might have occurred had they not been frozen at this moment in this pose. The Soldier wistfully desires the Celestes, "I like the one in the light hat" (*L* 36), and Jules pursues his outdoor fetish, asking Dot, "Do you like tall grass?" (*L* 33). The humor here is based in the paradox, central to the play, of time passing within a frozen moment. On the one hand, the figures lament the discomfort and boredom that come from being stuck in this one pose, singing, "No change up here / Forever" (*L* 33). On the other hand, the figures have an awareness of time passing entropically, running down. They sing, "I'll rot up here [. . .]" (*L* 33) and

> Finding you're
> Fading
> Is very degrading [. . . .] (*L* 36)

Generally speaking, paintings do not represent time, unlike music and drama, for which time is seminal to our experience of them. The paradox played for laughs in this song is, as we shall see, at the heart of the conclusions this musical play about a painting comes to regarding the relationship between art and the world.

The figures in "It's Hot Up Here" also localize a connected paradoxical notion that is central to the play's form and style. The figures bring together two different things. The first is the characters, existing in time, who are the models for the figures in the painting; these are the parts of the figures who complain about their physical discomfort and their interrupted lives. The second is the representations of the characters created by paint on canvas; these are the parts of the figures that are subject to the passing of time, fading and "disappear- / Ing dot by dot" (*L* 36).[6] The figures in "It's Hot Up Here" are simultaneously people and representations of people, simultaneously inside and outside the painting. I shall shortly have more to say about this as it functions in the play as a whole, but for now we can conclude that the play goes beyond questioning the equal sign between the world and art to breaking down the distinction between the world and art. From the moment George 1 invites us, at the very beginning of the play, to enter his blank canvas as he proceeds to create his painting, we realize that the figures, George, and we, the audience, are always both inside and outside the painting.

Having breached the boundary between art and the world, the play proceeds to problematize both. Just as the play will not let us take a simplistic view of art as holding a mirror up to nature, neither will it let us see art as an object of wonder, the meaning of which transcends era and culture. It resists the worship of art as a quasi-religious object, product of an act of creation akin to God's creation of the world, to be housed in museums, placed on pedestals or on walls, illuminated by track lighting.[7] Rather, in *Sunday on the Park with George,* art, even great art, is produced and received within a tangle of social practices and relations. Art is a part of the dirty, political world. This notion is illustrated best in the second-act reception scene. Here, Seurat's painting hangs center stage, the prize of the museum's collection, received uncritically and unreflectively by the partygoers as Great Art. When one of George 2's cranky artist friends dares to criticize the painting, another dismisses him by saying, "It's a masterpiece!" (*L* 42). Beyond this exchange, the painting serves as background to social, commercial, and political squabbles associated with contemporary art. Harriet Pawling has no real love for or understanding of art; she collects it and supports it and serves as a member of the board of the museum as ways of establishing her own social position. Museum administrators Bob Greenberg and Charles Redmond maneuver to collect the trendiest art so as to keep their institutions in the spotlight. Fellow artists Alex, Betty, and Naomi Eisen bicker pettily about their and George 2's art, always aware of who is moving up and down in the pecking order. Blair Daniels is an art critic who thinks her reviews are more important than the works she writes about. In "Putting It Together" George 2 reveals himself to be a master of the politics of making art:

Link by link,
Making the connections.
Drink by drink,
Fixing and perfecting the design.
Adding just a dab of politician
(Always knowing where to draw the line),
Lining up the funds, but in addition
Lining up a prominent commission,
Otherwise your perfect composition
Isn't going to get much exhibition. (*L* 39)

George 2 is more than willing to schmooze so as to make the contacts and get the funding and exhibition opportunities to the point that creating the art becomes an afterthought. He understands that art is not created or consumed in a vacuum. He sings, "If no one gets to see it, / It's as good as dead" (*L* 39).

Of course, by the time we see the reception scene in act 2, any temptation to view the economic, social, and political squabbling as unique to the contemporary art scene has been dispelled by what we saw in act 1. Although Seurat's *A Sunday Afternoon* hangs untouchably over the reception in 1984, act 1 has shown us how it was created amid the noise of the social and political discourses of its own time. George 1 confronts these discourses primarily through his interactions with Jules, apparently a well-known, successful, conventional artist. Jules criticizes George's choice of subject matter. After seeing George's *Bathers at Asnières* at an exhibition, Jules says to his face, "Boys bathing—what a curious subject" (23) and behind his back, "*I* must paint a factory next!" (20). Later, he tut-tuts when he spies George sketching his servants: "Certainly, George, you could find more colorful subjects" (57). Dot reports that café denizens have been mocking George after someone spotted him at the zoo drawing monkeys. To these conventional minds, art must reproduce not just the world but only certain parts of the world; other parts are off-limits as inappropriate for artistic treatment. This judgment is based, not in something inherent in the subjects or in art, but in the trends, the fashions, and the aesthetics of the moment. In challenging these conventions, George invites the mockery and the enmity of those who have cast their artistic lot with the mainstream. George further challenges conventional aesthetics with his technique, scientifically plotted dots, as he explains to Jules, "Only eleven colors—no black—divided, not mixed on the palette [. . .]" (79). In "No Life" Jules and his wife Yvonne reject George's technical experiments:

YVONNE: It's so mechanical.
JULES: Methodical. [. . .]
YVONNE: So drab, so cold.
JULES: And so controlled. (*L* 12)

Later, Jules loses his temper with George for "Always changing" his technique (58). Not appreciating George's choice of subjects and not understanding his technique, Jules and Yvonne conclude, "All mind, no heart. / No life in his art" (*L* 12), a conclusion that art critic Blair echoes about George 2's *Chromolume #7* when she suggests that only the presence of Marie, George's grandmother, contributes "a certain humanity to the proceedings" (146).

As might be suspected from the aggressive way in which George 1 refuses to conform to the aesthetic expectations of his time, he is as inept at playing politics on behalf of his painting as George 2 is adept. He ignores Jules's advice to schmooze: "Your life needs spice, George. Go to some parties. That is where you'll meet prospective buyers" (58). When it comes time to exhibit *A Sunday Afternoon*, he turns for help to Jules, whom he knows to be an ambiguous friend at best. Moments after rejecting Jules's standards ("Why should I paint like you or anybody else? I am trying to get through to something new. Something that is my own" [79–80]), George is almost pathetic in admitting that he needs Jules's influence: "It will be finished soon. I want it to be seen" (80). Further evidence of George 1's failure to negotiate the artistic politics of his time is furnished in George 2's introductory material before the chromolume premiere. We are told that, although *A Sunday Afternoon* was shown at the Eighth Impressionist Exhibition, "Monet, Renoir, and Sisley withdrew their submissions [. . .]" in protest (122). Even more damning is the conclusion, "He never sold a painting in his lifetime" (122). The creation of art is a social practice bound up in social relations charged with social discourse. These relations and their concomitant discourses influence what opportunities to create art exist, what counts as art, how art is disseminated, and how art is received. In trying to isolate himself from these relations and discourses, George 1 creates great art, but it is not recognized as such in his own short lifetime. In immersing himself in the art game, George 2 has painted himself into an artistic corner, unable to create art that surprises him or anyone else.

In addition to exploring the real social conditions within which art is created, the play further problematizes art's relationship to the world by stressing the techniques or craft that serve as a means of representation, the conduit through which the world is reimagined as art. We best see the foregrounding of representation in George 2's *Chromolume #7*. Just as it is about to project its images, the 1980s version of Seurat's color and light, the mechanical aspect of the art reasserts itself by shorting out. George explains to the audience the technicalities of the mechanical failure and then apologizes, "Unfortunately, no electricity, no art" (124). George 1 similarly but privately reveals some of the technique that creates the illusion of reality in his painting. In "Color and Light," while he works on his painting, he occasionally mentions the techniques he uses to create certain effects. One is the effect of directing a figure's gaze by the use of certain color combinations:

No, look over there, miss—
That's done with green . . .
Conjoined with orange . . . (*L* 15)

Further on, he suggests how colors create the impression of air temperature:

It's getting hot. . . .
It's getting orange. . . .
(*Dabbing intensely*)
Hotter . . . (*L* 16)

This device of referring to the figures in the painting simultaneously as people ("miss") and as paint applied to the canvas by means of particular artistic techniques reinforces the idea discussed earlier of the figures being both inside and outside the painting. In the first-act finale, "Sunday," where the painting takes its final form, this idea is expanded so that the painting is inside the world and the world is inside the painting. As the figures are arranged into their places, they sing both of the scene and the technique that has created the scene:

> Sunday,
> By the blue
> Purple yellow red water
> On the green
> Purple yellow red grass,
> Let us pass
> Through our perfect park,
>
> Pausing on a Sunday
> By the cool
> Blue triangular water
> On the soft
> Green elliptical grass
> As we pass
> Through arrangements of shadows
> Toward the verticals of trees [. . . .] (*L* 32)

The idea is cemented near the end of the song, where George and the ensemble speak of the components of this perfect park:

> GEORGE: Made of flecks of light
> And dark,
> MEN: And parasols [. . . .] (*L* 32)

The painting is both real—a park and parasols—and a representation—flecks of light and dark. The painting is both a picture of the world and a picture of a picture of the world.

In so stressing the technique by which the process of representation is accomplished, the play also calls attention to the role of the viewer in the creation of art. The viewer's role is especially overt in the case of *A Sunday Afternoon*. George 2 explains Seurat's technique in his introduction to the chromolume: "Having studied scientific findings on color, [Seurat] developed a new style of painting. He found by painting tiny particles, color next to color, that at a certain distance the eye would fuse the specks optically, giving them greater intensity than any mixed pigments" (122). In other words, the viewer's eye does the work of mixing the colors and, in effect, creates the painting and makes the world the painting seeks to represent. This idea can be extended to all art—painting, sculpture, music, drama, literature: what each individual viewer, listener, audience member, or reader brings to it and what the individual does with it are central to the experience of the art. Art isn't easy for the artist, but neither is it—nor should it be—easy for the one experiencing the art. Experiencing art is easy only when the art is formulaic and lacking surprise, only when the audience has experienced something like it many times before. To experience something different, new, and confusing, one must be willing to work. George 1 accuses Jules of being a lazy viewer after he fails to appreciate *A Sunday Afternoon*. Addressing the painting, George says, "He does not like you. He does not understand or appreciate you. He can only see you as everyone else does. Afraid to take you apart and put you back together again for himself" (81). Similarly, we see in act 2 that most of the characters are unable or unwilling to do the work necessary to engage with George 2's *Chromolume #7*. Harriet and Billy let it go over their heads. Greenberg and Redmond see it not as art but as cultural capital for their institutions. Blair and Alex slap easy judgments on it to aggrandize their own positions. The only genuine response comes from Marie in "Children and Art":

I don't understand what it was,
But, Mama, the things that he does—!
They twinkle and shimmer and buzz.
You would have liked them . . . (*L* 49)

The only way we can think of art holding a mirror up to nature, then, is if we think of the mirror as dynamic, subjective, individualized—a mirror, in short, that creates nature as much as, if not more than, it reflects it.

The dynamic manner in which the viewer engages art connects to the play's problematization of the other part of the art-world equation—the world. The holding-a-mirror-up-to-nature notion of art presupposes a stable, objectively knowable world for art to reproduce. The world is not a stable, easy-to-pin-down thing. Reality, because it is experienced in time, is fluid and protean, not a still life that can be easily captured in a mirror or within the frames of a painting. In "Beautiful," while the Old Lady laments the passing of time and the loss of the past and calls on George 1 to preserve it in his art, George celebrates the fluidity of the world:

> Pretty isn't beautiful, Mother,
> Pretty is what changes.
> What the eye arranges
> Is what is beautiful. (*L* 31)

George's second sentence here suggests a further complication. Our understanding of the world, of reality, of what is, is inextricably bound up in our engagement with that world. Just as we bring our experiences, advantages, and limitations to our engagement with a work of art, to take it apart and put it back together for ourselves, so too do we experience reality through the frames of our experience and the ideological systems into which we have been interpellated. We saw in the last chapter how we seek to know the past and our lives through the narratives we can conjure from them. Our experience of what we call reality is similarly mediated through the narratives and discourses we have available to make sense of it.

Later in "Beautiful," George makes a further significant claim about art and reality. Countering his mother's view of art as preserving an objectively knowable but receding reality, he offers, "You watch / While I revise the world" (*L* 31). This idea of art as not imitating or reproducing the world but revising, re-creating it is central to the play's presentation of art. In act 1, just as the figures are both inside and outside the painting, so is there a tension between the disorder of the characters' lives and the structure the painting provides. The park scenes are often interrupted by or descend into chaos—the noisy swimming boys who intrude into

the opening scene and are transformed by George into his first major painting; the gossipy murmuring at the end of "The Day Off" sequence, which rises to a climax when Dot reveals to George that she is pregnant; the cacophony just before the finale when fractured relationships bring the characters to the brink of violence. It is at this last point that George, intoning the principles of "Order. Design. Tension. Balance. Harmony" (101), finishes the painting, moving the figures out of chaos into an arrangement that makes them and their world structured and potentially meaningful. This is what art does, and this is most clearly why art is not a straightforward replication of the world: the world is random, fluid, entropic, chaotic; art takes that world and gives it structure, order, and meaning. Like the narrative structure explored in chapters 2 and 3, art is a means of representation by which the unknowable is made knowable. One signal that George 2 is failing as an artist is that at the end of "Putting It Together," when the characters' overlapping voices and his attempts to deal with them all are approaching chaos, he tries to freeze everyone into a tableau, as George 1 had at the end of "Sunday," but after a brief hold for applause, the scene collapses. He cannot mine order and meaning out of this scene.

Sunday in the Park with George, then, presents a complex interrelationship between art and the world. There is no clear, inviolable boundary between the two. Each is dynamic and unstable. While something we call reality may be the source for art, art, at least in act 1, is the means by which reality becomes knowable, purposeful, and potentially meaningful. While developing these ideas about art and the world, the play is also interested in the artist and the role he plays in all this. Both Georges reveal the difficulty of negotiating the interrelationship of art and the world. Two songs in the first act concentrate on this negotiation. In one section of "The Day Off" George 1 sketches two dogs for the painting. In this process, however, he so identifies with the dogs as his subjects that he imagines them speaking to him and each other, he creates background for what each of their lives is like, and he even joins them in sniffing around at the trash on the ground. His method here explains other parts of this scene where George sings along with statements from the characters he is observing. He is immersing himself in the world he seeks to represent, hoping to understand every aspect of it in all its complexity. Sondheim describes this as George's "inhabiting, as Seurat did, the interior lives of the major figures in his painting."[8] Later in the same scene, however, George sings another song, "Finishing the Hat," that reveals the loneliness he feels. Absorbed in his painting, he feels separated from others. He sings of his disappointment that Dot does not understand

> How you watch the rest of the world
> From a window
> While you finish the hat. (*L* 27)

This separation from the world, paradoxically, is as necessary as immersion in the world for the creation of art. The artist needs to understand as much as possible the world he wants to depict, but in order to re-create it as art, he also needs to maintain a critical distance. George sings,

> Studying a face,
> Stepping back to look at a face
> Leaves a little space in the way like a window,
> But to see—
> It's the only way to see. (*L* 27)

In their confrontation in the studio when Dot comes to tell George she is going to America, she accuses him of hiding behind his painting, to which he responds, "[. . .] I am not hiding behind my canvas—I am living in it" (83). Both characters are correct. The version of the world he is creating in his painting overlaps and supersedes the world outside the painting. As we have seen, he talks to it. He identifies with the figures in it to the point that he speaks for them. He cannot leave it behind when he stops working on it. At the same time, however, when things in his life trouble him, he tries to repress them, but they come out in his dissatisfaction with his work. When he tells Dot he cannot go to the Follies because he has to finish the hat, she stalks off, and he wonders, as he returns to the painting, if she will leave him:

> Too green . . .

Do I care?
Too blue . . .
Yes . . .
Too soft . . . (*L* 17)

Near the end of the act, after he refuses to let Dot show him the newborn Marie, his child, and she leaves him for the last time, George continues sketching his mother, but now finds much wrong with his work: "Shadows are too heavy. [. . .] Softer light" (93–94). He then says, "Connect, George. Connect . . ." (94). This statement is both an admission of his failure in his relationship with Dot, his inability to connect with her as a human being, and an assertion of the connection with his subject, a connection made through the artistic imagination, that he employs as the painting takes its final shape.

All these ideas about the world, art, and the artist come together in the second act. The second act proper begins after the transitional material of "It's Hot Up Here" and the figures' dialogue that follows it. During the dialogue, the figures drift off, and the park scenery disappears until, as the stage directions explain, "the set is returned to its original white configuration" (115). Just as at the beginning of the show, the stage is a blank canvas, and we are to be invited into a work of art. Since in the first act we are invited into George 1's *A Sunday Afternoon,* we might expect in the second act to be invited into George 2's chromolume, but that is not the case: we are as much outside that work (which is really not representable—the chromolume stands in for a kind of art that has not been created yet) as the spectators onstage. Rather, we are invited into something of a portrait of the artist, a work of art with George 2 as the subject, the artist, and the resulting art. Here, the boundaries among world, art, and artist are collapsed even more completely than they were in act 1. "Putting It Together" sends the clearest signals that George himself is the work of art comparable to the first act's *A Sunday Afternoon.* While singing, George strives to be the center of attention of each of several conversations by conjuring representations of himself. In the original production these were life-size cut-out photographs of Mandy Patinkin that recalled the cut-outs used in act 1 for many of the figures in the painting: the dogs, the deaf-mute soldier, and so on. In the 2008 Broadway revival, video of

163

Daniel Evans was projected onto the set, so the several representations of George were able to converse, drink, and interact with the other actors. With these multiple George-representations seemingly as real as George, it is no wonder he becomes confused: "So that you can go on exhibit— / So that your *work* can go on exhibition" (*L* 39). The folding of artist into art is complete.

George 2, then, is both inside and outside his art and inside and outside his life. His problem, we come to see, is that he is disconnected from both. In his life, as we see in "Putting It Together," he feels fragmented, a fragmentation that is literalized in the several representations of him he shares the stage with. He is divorced and childless. Dennis, his longtime technical collaborator on the chromolumes, is leaving him. Between the reception scene and George's arrival on La Grande Jatte, Marie has died. In "Lesson #8," he keenly feels how alone he is. This aloneness, however, is different from the kind George 1 sang about in "Finishing the Hat." George 1 was able to imaginatively immerse himself in the world around him so as to create his art. George 2, between the mess of his personal relations and the distractions caused by his constantly raising money, arranging exhibitions, and promoting himself, has lost a connection with the world, a connection that ought to be the source of the inspiration for his art. Further, he has become so swept up in the swirling discourses about art—conversations with funders, museum directors, competing artists, critics—that he has become exhausted: both mentally and physically fatigued from the art-of-making-art runaround and, as an artist, run dry. He cannot create new art because he has lost his sense of vision. He tells Dot, "I've nothing to say. [. . .] / Well, nothing that's not been said" (*L* 52). He echoes George 1 when he says, "Connect, George. Connect" (159), but his need is even more desperate.

"Lesson #8" is the barest expression of George's artistic and personal despair, but it is also the beginning of his redemption. Just as George 2's being thirty-two years old suggests a passing of the torch from George 1, who died at age thirty-one, so too is it significant that *Chromolume #7* initiates George 2's crises and "Lesson #8" offers a way to move past them. At this point the red grammar book that Marie inherited from her mother becomes a conduit between the act 2 portrait of an artist in which George is floundering and the act 1 painting. Dot, both the figure from the painting and the person it was based on, appears to George and offers him a way past his despair. She sees that he fears the future—what he should do, what his art should be, how his art will be received. In "Move On," echoing George 1's words to Jules, he sings,

I want to know how to get through,
Through to something new,
Something of my own— (*L* 52)

Dot's lesson is that to live and to create art, one must be, not in the past or the future, but immersed completely in the moment. Dot explains what she learned from George 1 while modeling for him: "At first I thought [concentration] meant just being still, but I was to understand it meant much more. You meant to tell me to be where I was—not some place in the past or future" (165). Understanding the complex, fluid, dynamic moment opens up the possibilities for moving into the future. In "Move On" Dot sings,

Look at what you want,
Not at where you are,
Not at what you'll be. (*L* 52)

Think of the characters in *Follies* and *Merrily We Roll Along* who become lost because they are obsessed with their life stories, anticipated goals in the future and failures in the past. Dot suggests that the past is transformed into the future in the now, the present moment.

George learns this lesson by listening to Dot's words and by looking at her as the figure in the painting. He truly engages the painting here, taking it apart and putting it back together for himself, and using it as a means of structuring and making sense of his own moment. As he looks, really looks, at Dot, he becomes able to see his surroundings more clearly:

Something in the light,
Something in the sky,
In the grass,
Up behind the trees . . .

Things I hadn't looked at
Till now:
Flower in your hat.
And your smile.
And the color of your hair,
And the way you catch the light.
And the care,
And the feeling.
And the life
Moving on! (*L* 52)

Earlier, as we saw, George was disappointed that the park did not look like the painting. However, when the Old Lady appears and asks if the park is as he expected it, he answers, "Well, the greens are a little darker. The sky a little grayer. Mud tones in the water. [. . .] But the air is rich and full of light" (171). George now understands how to engage a dynamic work of art and how that art provides a possibility for meaning in the world and for his life.

Sondheim's several previous plays, as we have seen, can be interpreted as criticizing the human desire to impose narrative on life events or history so as to create an ordered, meaning-providing structure, yet here, using art as a means to structure the world seems to be the lesson with which we are left. The difference, I think, is that in those earlier plays the characters did not recognize their narratives as artificial structures being placed over the events of the past; rather, they thought the narrative elements rested implicitly in the events, waiting to be discovered. As a result, the narrative becomes more real than the reality it was supposed to help interpret, in effect replacing it. In *Sunday in the Park with George* the characters who want to see art as synonymous with the world are presented as naive. Instead, as both Georges help us see, art is a means of representing a dynamic, fluid, chaotic world, an attempt to capture the uncapturable, to perfect the imperfect. Art's very artificiality, which we perceive at the same time we perceive its subject, reminds us that, while it can offer order, structure, and potential meaning for the world, it does so contingently, not absolutely. Each work of art provides a window through which we can engage a way of understanding the world. Fittingly, then, the play ends with a return to the blank canvas, ready to receive a new window to the world, as George 2, quoting George 1's words, concludes, "So many possibilities . . ." (173).

Like *Sunday in the Park with George, Into the Woods* was a collaboration with James Lapine, who wrote the book and provided the direction, and, like *Sunday*, it was developed through nonprofit theaters, Playwrights Horizons and the Old Globe theater in San Diego. It opened on Broadway on 5 November 1987 at the Martin Beck Theatre (now the Al Hirschfeld), with a cast headed by Bernadette Peters, Joanna Gleason, and Chip Zien.[9] Also like *Sunday in the Park, Into the Woods* draws overtly on familiar source material, in this case fairy tales. The first act interweaves several well-known fairy tales—Cinderella, Little Red Ridinghood, Jack and the Beanstalk, Rapunzel—with a new one about a Baker and his Wife who, at the direction of the Witch next door, go into the woods on a quest for the several objects the Witch needs to restore her beauty; if they are successful, the Witch will remove the curse that has kept them childless. In the second act the perpetual happiness the characters thought they had achieved at the end of act 1 is shattered by the arrival of a Giant, the widow of the giant Jack slew, who tramples much of the kingdom and kills several of the characters in her quest for revenge. She is finally killed when four of the survivors, the Baker, Cinderella, Red Ridinghood, and Jack, learn to work together in a common cause. They also learn the bittersweet nature of communities: acts have far-reaching and unpredictable consequences; through our acts, we are connected to countless others; and through our stories, we are connected to the past and future.

The familiarity of the source fairy tales and the onstage presence of a Narrator foreground the narrativity of the play. Like Sondheim's musicals of the 1970s, *Into the Woods* uses and subverts audiences' expectations for how narrative functions and employs and explodes narrative's potential as a meaning-providing structure. The dramatic tension in the show is the product of two conflicting narrative desires, a conflict that is especially central to the first act. The first desire is expressed in terms of the conventional narrative structure discussed previously, the structure based in beginning and end and the cause-and-effect sequence that connects them, the structure that is both necessarily time-bound and implicitly closed off from time by means of a projected, anticipated end. This structure is invoked in the very first words of the show: "Once upon a time—."[10] Through prior experience with the fairy-tale genre, theatergoers glean from these words that, yes, they are about to experience a fairy tale and that, having begun with "Once upon a time," the narrative will ineluctably conclude with "Happily ever after." The prologue establishes the three desires that will fuel the narrative and generate the events linking "Once upon a time" to "Happily ever after," and it does so with the repeated words "I wish" (*L* 59). Cinderella wishes to go to the king's festival, which is a manifestation of a larger wish to escape the drudgery in which she languishes and to be noticed and appreciated. Jack wishes to keep his pet cow rather than sell her, which is a manifestation of a larger wish to escape the poverty he and his mother live in. The Baker and his Wife wish for a child. These wishes establish the motivations for the narratives, and the narratives are set in motion when the characters all go into the woods so as to make their wishes come true. There, their stories become tangled, each with the others, as well as with the stories of other characters who are pursuing their own wishes: one Prince desires Cinderella, the other desires Rapunzel; the Witch desires youth and beauty; Red Ridinghood desires to visit her Granny; the Wolf desires to consume Red Ridinghood and her Granny; Cinderella's Stepmother and Stepsisters desire an advantageous match with the Prince; the Mysterious Man desires to set right the misstep he made in the past that resulted in the curse of childlessness on his son, the Baker.

The woods is a place of narrative complication and confusion where obstacles interdict beginning and end, desire and fulfillment. As in *Merrily We Roll Along*, *Into the Woods* makes use of a title song that connects narrative to the metaphor of the journey. The ensemble makes clear the connection between the woods and the middle part of a narrative: "Into the woods to get the thing / That makes it worth the journeying" (*L* 64). This lyric suggests a point about narrative that we have seen before: the projected endpoint for a narrative becomes the thing that governs how the sequence of events leading up to the endpoint is understood. In this case the narrative expectations are fulfilled: Cinderella weds the Price and escapes her drudgery; Jack and his Mother become wealthy from the things Jack has stolen from the giants; the Baker's Wife becomes pregnant. The other characters have their wishes fulfilled or not depending on their worth, or as the Narrator sums up, "And it came to pass, all that seemed wrong was now right, the kingdoms were filled with joy, and those who deserved to were certain to live a long and happy life. Ever after . . ." (74). Here, at the end of the first act, we have reached the "Happily ever after" implied by the opening line of the play. The narrative journey is finished and the narrative structure is completed, closed, detached from the movement of time's arrow, immutable and immoveable forever, or, as the Narrator sings,

> Journey over, all is mended,
> And it's not just for today,
> But tomorrow, and extended
> Ever after! (*L* 82)

Thus, in a manner that is perhaps surprising in a Sondheim musical, given how his earlier plays deconstructed narrative structure and subverted the expectations for it, in the first act of *Into the Woods* the first kind of narrative desire invoked by the play is fulfilled.

This forward-moving narrative structure, however, is put into conflict with a contrary, psychological narrative desire to move backward in time to recover a sense of wholeness and unity that has been lost as time passes. In writing *Into the Woods,* Lapine was reportedly influenced by Bruno Bettelheim's psychological study of fairy tales, *The Uses of Enchantment,*[11] but another psychological theorist, Jacques Lacan, can help us understand how the play creates tension between the two contradictory narrative desires. Lacan proposes that as children psychologically develop, they move from a sense of identity based in a unity with their mother and environment to a more fragmented sense of self when their notion of identity becomes placed in an image outside of the self and then to an even more fragmented sense of self when they are hurled into the domain of language, which then becomes the basis for identity. This last stage is marked by the introduction of the Law of the Father: children's relationships with the mother is interrupted by the presence of the father, who brings rules and codes that they must learn to live by, limiting freedom and encouraging social conformity.[12]

In "Giants in the Sky" Jack describes a Lacanian progression. He climbs the beanstalk acting on his narrative desire to escape poverty, but in the kingdom in the sky, instead of moving forward in a time-bound, narrative manner, he finds himself returned to infancy. As he climbs, he perceives himself as regressing in size; referring to himself in the second person, he knows "just how small you are" (L 71). Further, in the giants' home, he is no longer bound by social codes and rules and laws, just like an infant. He sings, "You're free to do / Whatever pleases you [. . .]" (L 71). Most important, in the lady giant he finds a mother substitute with whom he can recover the unified sense of identity that he has lost as he has grown toward adulthood. Notice the details that suggest a mother-infant relationship:

> And she gives you food
> And she gives you rest,
> And she draws you close
> To her giant breast [. . . .] (L 71)

This return to infantile holism, however, is interrupted by the arrival of the male giant, who disrupts the mother-infant relationship and threatens the individuality (and life) of the infant. Jack is threatened by the substitute father and betrayed by the substitute mother, yanked from his sense of unity and left "really scared being all alone" (L 71). He reacts to this threat and betrayal by moving forward narratively—stealing things that will lead toward his narrative desire for wealth—and by backward-looking yearning again for his lost mother-infant relationship. As he climbs down the beanstalk, the first details he notices are, "The roof, the house, and your mother at the door" (L 72). Jack is left ambivalent, wishing he "could live in between" (L 72) the realm of the giants and home, childhood and adulthood, the backward-looking narrative of desire for past holistic unity and the forward-moving narrative desire for the future.

More broadly, we see that motivating many of the characters' backward-looking narrative desires are childhoods with variously fractured families. The Baker's mother died shortly after the birth of his sister Rapunzel, and, although the Baker thinks his father died in a baking accident, he is in fact the Mysterious Man, alone and lonely, estranged from any human community. Jack and his Mother (and the cow) live alone, his father apparently having abandoned them. Cinderella's Mother has died, and her Father has remarried. Her Father has become withdrawn and ineffectual, while her Stepmother and Stepsisters cruelly resent Cinderella, essentially redefining her from a family member to a servant. Red Riding-hood has a mother and her Granny but apparently no father. The only family Rapunzel knows is the Witch, who wants to fill the role of mother to her but does so by imprisoning her in a tower, hoping to stop time and keep her permanently a child.

We see that at the same time the characters are moving narratively forward in pursuit of their wishes, many of them are motivated by a contrary desire to move narratively backward so as to repair their damaged, fractured families and reclaim their prefragmented, presocialized, pre-adulthood selves, selves that are marked by a peaceful, contented, holistic unity. The unity here is connected not just to an infant's relationship with the mother but also to a complete family unit: mother, father, child, and home. While the desires motivating the forward-moving narratives in act 1 are fulfilled, the desires motivating the backward-looking narratives mostly fail. Cinderella is most successful in that her Mother's spirit provides means to fulfill her broader wish to escape drudgery and receive loving attention. However, this success marks less a return to infantile unity with the Mother than a passing of the torch. As the Mother gives her benediction to her daughter and the Prince, she recognizes Cinderella's passing into adulthood, where her sense of self will be bound up in her husband, not her mother, and formally withdraws from her life. The desire to return to the past and repair a ruptured family is defeated by the inevitability of time's arrow. The Baker suffers a similar defeat. His forward- and backward-looking goals are intertwined: in completing the Witch's quest, he anticipates fulfilling his narrative desire, having a child, and repairing the family that was devastated when he was a child. The Witch speaks of *reversing*, not removing, the curse, which suggests a moving back in time to fix a mistake or take a different fork in the road. Ironically, because he does not realize that the Mysterious Man is his father, he rebuffs his attempts, like Cinderella's Mother's, to provide guidance and assistance in the quest. Only as the quest is fulfilled and the conception of a child is guaranteed does he learn that his father is not dead, that he might have had a reunion with him, but at that moment, the Mysterious Man dies. His last words are "All is repaired" (70), but for the Baker, his death marks not repair but an opportunity lost.

The tyranny of time is most evident in the relationship of the Witch and her erstwhile daughter Rapunzel. To preserve the mother-child-home relationship, the Witch has ensconced Rapunzel in a doorless tower to which she is the only visitor. She hopes to keep Rapunzel a child forever, protected and nourished and loved only by her. In "Our Little World," a song added to the 1990 London production for the scene when the tower first appears, the Witch sings,

> Children need protection
> Just the way they need affection
> Or they wonder, and they wander, and they run
> From your little world . . . (*L* 68)

Her desire to stop time so as to save Rapunzel motivates the urgency with which she seeks the potion that will make her young and beautiful again: reversing time in her own case will make her a better companion for Rapunzel and will delay the inevitable end to their special relationship.

This, then, is the result in the first act of the tension between the two different narrative desires: the fulfillment of the desires and the structural completion of the forward-moving narratives are mitigated by the failure of the backward-looking desires and narratives. The holistically unified family units of the past remain irrecoverable and irreparable. The same time's arrow that implicitly makes possible the achievement of the first kind of desire is viewed regretfully by the Baker and the Witch because it closes off possibilities and necessitates change. Some of the other characters, like Jack in "Giants in the Sky," at least sense the double-sided fulfillment/failure of their desires and are left ambivalent. In "I Know Things Now" and "On the Steps of the Palace" Red Ridinghood and Cinderella both embrace and resist the temporally forward movement toward adulthood. Thus the happily ever after celebrated in the first-act finale is to a certain extent colored by regret for things lost—lost opportunities, lost youth, lost innocence, but mostly lost family units.

Deceptively, act 2 opens as act 1 did; its structure echoes that of the act 1 prologue, and the music offers repetitions of and variations on the prologue's music. This use of familiar material, however, prepares a trap for audience expectations, as the generic conventions of the fairy tale are invoked, only to break down. The Narrator's first words, "Once upon a time—later [. . .]" (83), are a good example. "Once upon a time," as we saw earlier, implies an ineluctable movement to "Happy ever after," narrative closure that completes the story and removes it from time. In act 2 the Narrator again gestures toward that narrative expectation but then adds the word *later,* which reintroduces time to the narrative. The word ends up being an important fulcrum in the play. It takes the happy-ever-after conclusion of act 1 and returns it to time—what happens after happily ever after?—and it undercuts the promise of a completed, happy-ever-after ending for act 2. The act's next words, "I wish . . ." (*L* 86), repeat the way in which the first act introduced the desires that would fuel each of the main characters' narratives throughout the act. Here, however, the wishes—Cinderella's for another festival, Jack's for a return to the kingdom in the sky, the Baker and his Wife's for more room—are false leads: the violent arrival of the Giant, the widow of the giant Jack killed, derails these narrative desires before they can even get started, leaving the audience confused about where the act is going.

Even after the Giant's interruption of act 2's narrative desires, the opening echoes the structure of the act 1 opening. The Witch visits the Baker and his Wife, once again with a concern about her garden. Red Ridinghood comes to the Baker and his Wife, once again preparing to go visit her Granny. Cinderella again resolves to visit her Mother's grave. Finally, the characters all go into the woods, reprising the now familiar melody, although the opening phrase is now flattened at the end, signaling a twist in the journey and the narrative. As Cinderella sings,

Into the woods,
But not too long:
The skies are strange,
The winds are strong. (*L* 88)

Indeed, the stage directions describe a change in the wood from act 1: "Something is wrong. The natural order has been broken. Trees have fallen. The birds no longer chirp" (95). The woods in act 1 were a place where the characters' narratives were complicated. Now in the second act the woods become a place of total narrative confusion: the characters lose their sense of direction and, more important, their anticipated destination, just as they lose the sense of the story they are trying to work themselves through. Because they have no clear goal for their journey or their narrative, they have no idea to govern a structure for the things that are happening to them.

The play makes a connection between being physically lost and narratively lost when a group including the Witch, the Baker and his Wife, Red Ridinghood, Cinderella's Stepmother and Stepsisters, and the Prince's Steward decide to sacrifice the Narrator to the Giant. Just as he is lecturing the audience on the "finality of stories" (102), the conclusions that govern their structure and provide their meaning, the group becomes aware of his presence, breaking the narrative frame and confusing the boundaries of the story. As the one looking back at the narrative events from or beyond their endpoint, the Narrator knows where the events are heading, why they are significant, how they add up, and how they are meaningful. He warns, "If you drag me into this mess, you'll never know how your story ends. You'll be lost!" (102). His logic convinces everyone but the Witch, who shoves him into the Giant's arms. With the death of the Narrator, narrative confusion reigns. Ideas of what to do are offered and rejected, plans are made and revised, then abandoned. The characters even comment on the failure of narrative. When the Baker's Wife is being seduced by the Prince, she sings an aside to the audience,

This is ridiculous,
What am I doing here?
I'm in the wrong story. (*L* 91)

In this general context of the failure of narrative structure, three second-act songs explore more specifically the dangers and possibilities of narrative as a vehicle for providing meaning. In the reprise of "Agony" the two Princes, each having overcome barriers and complications to wed his beloved at the end of act 1, have surreptitiously returned to the woods in pursuit of new damsels. The Princes are committed to the paradox of narrative and time. They need a goal that gives the events of their lives meaning, yet they cannot achieve the goal lest their life narratives become completed structures, robbed of purpose. They need to live narratively, in time, with a goal governing their life events, but, to maintain the meaning, they must constantly approach but continually avoid the goal. As they sing,

Not forgetting
The tasks unachievable,
Mountains unscalable—
If it's conceivable
But unavailable [. . . .] (*L* 89)

At this point, as if succumbing to the paradox, words fail them. The princes want the pursuit of the goal and the goal, they want to be in process and completed, they want to be in time and out of time.

Something of the opposite approach to narrative is articulated in "Moments in the Woods." In the song just before this, "Any Moment," Cinderella's Prince has seduced the Baker's Wife by asking her to think of their chance encounter in the woods as a moment divorced from any larger narrative arc. He sings, "Best to take the moment present / As a present for the moment" (*L* 91). After he leaves, the Baker's Wife reflects on the advantages of thinking of life, not as narratively linked events, but as individual, disconnected moments, each to be experienced and understood for itself. She quickly sees, however, the impossibility of such a way of thinking:

Oh, if life were made of moments,
Even now and then a bad one—!
But if life were only moments,
Then you'd never know you had one. (*L* 92)

Life events, moments, take their meaning from their relation to other life events. Narrative structure, as a means of organizing and providing a meaning for one's life events is, as we have seen, problematic for many reasons, but some kind of story seems necessary.

This complication of narrative is resolved to a certain extent in "No More," a song in three movements. The first movement is sung by the Baker at his lowest point, after he has learned of his Wife's death, after the surviving characters have tried to blame each other for their predicament, after the Witch has cursed and left them, and after he has abandoned the others—and his child—to go into the woods alone. He does not go far before he comes across the Mysterious Man, his father, who it turns out is not "completely" dead (123). The seed for the song comes in the first act, when the Baker imagines the quest being over: "And then we can just go about our life. No more hunting about in the woods for strange objects. No more witches and dimwitted boys and hungry little girls" (46). He wishes here to be removed from the narrative complications, the middle of his story, and to be at the endpoint. By the middle of act 2, however, the Baker rejects narrative and the possibility of meaning. His "no more" is a cry against the impulse to try to find meaning by telling stories. Rejecting meaning, he sings, "Comes the day you say, 'What for?'" (*L* 100), and rejecting narrative beginnings, middles, and ends, he sings,

No more curses you can't undo
Left by fathers you never knew,
No more quests. (*L* 100)

In the second movement the Mysterious Man gently makes the case for narrative as a way of making a kind of meaning. He first agrees that "Running away" (*L* 100), as the Baker proposes to do, is appealing, suggesting a return to the kind of infantile freedom Jack sang about in "Giants in the Sky":

[. . .] Free from the ties that bind.
No more despair
Or burdens to bear
Out there in the yonder. (*L* 100)

He then points out, however, that that kind of freedom lacks a purpose and thus a meaning. Some kind of destination or narrative endpoint is necessary:

Have to take care:
Unless there's a "where,"
You'll only be wandering blind.
Just more questions,
Different kind. (*L* 100)

The twist here is that the destination is not in and of itself important; rather, some kind of contingent goal is needed to provide a structure for the middle of our stories. Without such a destination, the Mysterious Man suggests, we will always be lost, not in terms of where we are headed in the future, but in terms of our own present and past:

[. . .] The farther you run,
The more you feel undefined
For what you have left undone
And, more, what you've left behind. (*L* 100)

In the final movement, the Baker, left alone after the Mysterious Man disappears, comes to understand that the middle parts of journeys and the middle parts of stories are not irrelevant things to be gotten through so that one can reach and enjoy the end. Rather, the middle parts are the point. The end is not a necessary absolute that governs the journey or story preceding it. The end is a changeable and useful fiction that we can employ to provide a contingent sense of a path, a story, a structure to orient ourselves in an otherwise chaotic series of events. The emphasis here is on *contingent*: we can never know absolutely where we are going, and we can never have a completely secure sense of the structure of our lives. We might think of ourselves as being picaresque Candides, using narrative to make at least temporary sense of the always-changing journey we find ourselves on. The Baker, as he resolves to return to the others and his son, finally recognizes the importance of middles:

[. . .] How do you ignore
All the witches,
All the curses,
All the wolves, all the lies,

The false hopes, the goodbyes,
The reverses,
All the wondering what even worse is
Still in store? (*L* 100)

In a similar manner, the second act complicates the characters' backward-looking narrative desires. Here, these desires, which, at the end of the first act, were left unfulfilled, are completely dashed as each of the major characters loses the family member on whom he or she was most dependent. The Giant smashes the tree that is home to Cinderella's Mother's spirit. Jack's Mother is killed by the Steward. Red Ridinghood's mother and Granny are both apparently killed when the Giant steps on their houses. These deaths end absolutely any possibility of moving into the past to repair and restore family units. Time's arrow and its necessary end, death, have trumped the characters' desires to resist it. The Baker, as we have seen, has one last chance when he encounters his father (or, perhaps, his father's lingering memory) in the woods, but, by this point, he seeks neither reunion nor reconciliation, and the two part with only a guarded understanding. The second act of the play is emphatic in denying the possibility of moving into the past. The characters, in their present, are left alone to make their way through the woods without a path.

The second act, then, in effectively exploding both forward-looking and backward-looking narrative desires, leaves the surviving characters alone and lost. Their situation is bleak, grim even by Brothers Grimm standards, and they are tempted to slide into the despair of aloneness, a choice the Witch articulates in her song "Last Midnight." Faced with the loss of a clear narrative structure, the Witch attempts to make of their situation a new, larger, perhaps universal narrative with the Giant destroying them all as the endpoint. This is, in effect, an apocalyptic narrative leading inevitably to the end of the world, a final stoppage of time, signaled by the last midnight ever. Her song is full of apocalyptic imagery:

It's the last midnight.
It's the last wish.
It's the last midnight,

Soon it will be boom—
Squish! [. . .]
Nothing but a vast midnight,
Everybody smashed flat! (*L* 98)

The Witch condemns the others' vacillation in the face of apocalypse. On the one hand, the others simultaneously try each to remove himself or herself from the situation and to find a scapegoat. On the other hand, they refuse to follow the Witch's pragmatic advice to sacrifice Jack to the Giant and thus end the destruction. They are lost in terms of direction, in terms of moral sense, in terms of the extent to which they are independent from and responsible to each other. The Witch sneers at them in what she thinks is the inevitable outcome of their lost, narrativeless state:

I'm leaving you alone.
You can tend the garden, it's yours.
Separate and alone,
Everybody down on all fours. (*L* 98)

In the face of her apocalyptic narrative, with all other narratives, forward-looking and backward-looking, lost, the Witch chooses aloneness. Having thrown away her beans, she is again punished by her mother with ugliness, but she regains her powers and disappears, leaving the others.

The others, especially the Baker, almost fulfill the Witch's curse and succumb to the despair of loneliness, but in the end they make a different choice based in what they learn about the possibilities for meaning in contingent narratives and in the possibilities for new communities growing out of failed families. Rejecting the Witch's apocalyptic narrative, the four surviving characters come together, drawing on the experiences of their first-act narratives—Cinderella making use of her bird friends and finding a new way to use the pitch that the Prince had used to trap her; Jack drawing on the confidence he earned by besting the first giant—to try to create a different conclusion. This coming together marks both a new sense of community beyond family and a more sophisticated sense of connectedness. The characters come to this new understanding while they are waiting to spring their trap on the Giant, in the song "No One Is Alone." Cinderella begins by closing the door on the desire to restore and repair lost families, yet claiming that the resulting aloneness is different from the despair the Witch wished upon them:

> Mother cannot guide you.
> Now you're on your own.
> Only me beside you.
> Still, you're not alone.
> No one is alone [. . . .] (*L* 101)

The aloneness Cinderella and then the Baker are imagining is marked by two things. The first is an independence resulting from the loss of one's parental figures, the bittersweet movement into adulthood. The second is the loss of the totalized narratives that might have provided direction and guidance at times of difficult decision. Cinderella emphasizes, "You decide alone" (*L* 101), and the Baker notes that moral decisions, in the absence of absolutes, must be made individually and situationally: "Wrong things, right things . . . / Who can say what's true?" (*L* 101). The aloneness and the difficulty of deciding and acting in a state of aloneness are mitigated by the potential for new connections, new community. Cinderella and the Baker sing, "Someone is on your side" (*L* 102). However, we must see that the potential for connection goes far beyond "our side." Cinderella and the Baker continue,

> While we're seeing our side— [. . .]
> Maybe we forgot:
> They are not alone. (*L* 102)

The characters are wrestling here with an awareness that who we are and what we do cannot be cast as a binary opposition—Us/Them—that everyone is connected in a giant web of relations.

This notion of interdependence becomes the context within which moral decisions must be made. In the dialogue leading in to the song, Red Ridinghood and Cinderella in the clearing and Jack and the Baker in the tree discuss the morality of killing. When Cinderella tries to explain away Red Ridinghood's qualms about killing the Giant, Red responds, "But the giant's a person. Aren't we to show forgiveness?" (128). Jack, having just learned that his mother was killed, vows revenge on the Steward, and the Baker has trouble explaining why this would be wrong. The song further explores these moral dilemmas. The characters, seeming to have learned from the ways their first-act actions have contributed to the second-act disaster they find themselves in, realize that, although moral decisions are made individually and situationally, acts have consequences far beyond what any of us might expect. As the Baker and Cinderella sing,

> You move just a finger,
> Say the slightest word,
> Something's bound to linger,
> Be heard. (*L* 101)

A truly moral action is one that is made with an awareness of the potential consequences throughout the web of relations of which each one of us is a part. Killing the Giant is necessary for self-preservation, but it is not something to be celebrated. In an interesting change from the original production, the 2002 Broadway revival offered a solemn tolling bell after the Giant's death.

The play's final sequence brings together its ideas about community, narrative, and morality. Having worked together to save themselves from the Giant and, more important, to work past the despair of aloneness to an adult independence and a sense of morality based in interrelation, the four surviving characters form an ad hoc community, based neither in family nor romantic relationships, to build a new life from the ruins the Giant left. This larger sense of community is celebrated in the final iteration of the title song. Where in the original Broadway production's first-act finale the characters' dancing was segregated into class, here, at the end of the play, the characters are integrated, dancing together across class and family lines, while singing,

> The way is dark,

The light is dim,
But now there's you,
Me, her and him. (*L* 103)

The song becomes a celebration of connection.

Also in the final sequence, narrative becomes a means by which we are able to make connections. The Baker, uncertain of how to be a parent to his infant son, is advised by the spirit of his dead Wife, "Look, tell him the story / Of how it all happened" (*L* 102). And, beginning with "Once upon a time," the Baker uses the words of the Narrator at the opening of the show to pass on the story to his son (136).[13] Narrative here, as we saw in "No More," serves as a means of orientation in a chaotic world. The danger of narratives comes when our focus moves from narratives as a means (of understanding our lives and our actions in the world) to an end (a totalized structure that in effect supersedes reality for us). We slide easily into this latter sense of narrative, as we see throughout much of the play and then at the very end, when Cinderella's final words are "I wish . . ." (*L* 105): as she did at the beginning, she here invokes a narrative desire. The necessary danger of narrative for our lives is the subject of "Children Will Listen." The Witch sings,

Careful the things you say,
Children will listen. [. . .]
Children will look to you
For which way to turn,
To learn what to be. (*L* 102–3)

Narratives are powerful in their effects, and so we need to choose carefully what stories we tell. In this sense, storytelling is a moral act.

The play's sense of morality, individual and situational choices made in the context of a complex web of relations, is emphasized again in the final reprise of the title song. One quatrain brings together the importance of narrative and moral action. The ensemble sings:

You can't just act,
You have to listen.

You can't just act,
You have to think. (*L* 103)

We saw earlier the characters' recognition in this song of the multiple connections among individuals that make up potential communities. The song goes on to suggest that the larger our sense of community and the more complexly we are able to think about our place in a web of relations, the more fully and morally we will be able to act. One last list of reasons to go into the woods shows that one's community can grow large enough to include those who were once thought of as enemies or Other and that these connections can help us live more deeply:

Into the woods to mind the Wolf,
To heed the Witch,
To honor the Giant,
To mind,
To heed,
To find,
To think,
To teach,
To join [. . . .] (*L* 105)

The final "happy ever after" (*L* 105) offers a twist on the completed structure outside of time that was signaled by the first-act finale, "Ever After." Here, the happiness comes from an awareness of living in time, in process, making meaning by living with as deep and far-reaching an awareness as possible of our connections to others.

The exploration of social and interpersonal connections took a decidedly darker turn in Sondheim's next project, *Assassins*. Written with John Weidman, his *Pacific Overtures* collaborator, *Assassins* is an episodic exploration of nine historic figures who attempted or succeeded in assassinating US presidents. Like *Sunday in the Park* and *Into the Woods*, *Assassins* was developed in nonprofit theaters; unlike those previous plays, it did not, in its original production, transfer to Broadway. Indeed, it was the first of Sondheim's plays since *Saturday Night* in 1955 not to make it to Broadway.

Assassins, directed by Jerry Zaks, opened for a limited run Off Broadway at Playwrights Horizons on 27 January 1991, at the height of the patriotic fervor inspired by the first Persian Gulf War. Although in his preface to the published version of the play, André Bishop, the artistic director of Playwrights Horizons, argues that war fever was not responsible for the negative critical response to the play,[14] the play's exploding of the American Dream, its critical examination of the nature of American democracy, and its challenging of authority made it as much a misfit in that time of flag-waving and yellow ribbons as its characters are in their society. Reviewers responded with distaste for the subject matter, even such a Sondheim-sympathetic reviewer as the *New York Times's* Frank Rich: "The effect of this recurrent chorus line [of assassins], a striking image in a diffuse evening, is totally disorienting, as if someone had removed a huge boulder from the picturesque landscape of American history to expose to light all the mutant creatures that had been hiding in the dankness underneath."[15] Because of the pans in the popular press, tentative plans to transfer the show to a small Broadway house were canceled.[16]

Ten years after the initial production, the Roundabout Theatre made plans to mount the first Broadway production of *Assassins,* with Joe Mantello directing, but once again current events interfered. Rehearsals were scheduled to begin in the third week of September 2001; however, two days after 9/11, the production was postponed via an announcement by Sondheim and Weidman: "*Assassins* is a show which asks audiences to think critically about various aspects of the American experience. In light of Tuesday's murderous assault on our nation and on the most fundamental things in which we all believe, we, the Roundabout, and director Joe Mantello believe this is not an appropriate time to present a show which makes such a demand."[17] After a lapse of over two years, the Roundabout production finally opened at Studio 54 on 22 April 2004. The show received rapturous reviews, many of them by the same reviewers who had panned it in 1991,[18] and five Tony Awards, including Best Musical Revival.[19]

Assassins brings together ideas from many of the other plays we have discussed. Like *Follies, Merrily We Roll Along,* and others, it challenges narrative as a meaning-providing structure. Like *Pacific Overtures,* it examines the role of narrative in the presentation of history and offers a version of American history as perceived by outsiders. Like *Gypsy,* it critiques the master narrative of the American Dream. Like *West Side Story,* it is concerned with the transmission and possible disruption of the dominant ideology. *Assassins* is set in a nontime and nonspace, where historic incidents can be replayed while sharing the stage with other times and places, where characters from different times can meet and interact, and where cause-and-effect sequence, the basis for narrative history, can be abandoned. The play begins with the shooting-gallery Proprietor enticing the potential assassins to "C'mere and kill a president" (*L* 114). From there, in dialogue and song, the assassins' stories are told: what drove them to their acts and what they hoped to accomplish. The play climaxes with the assassins as a group tempting and goading Lee Harvey Oswald to shoot John F. Kennedy. The ahistorical structure of the show, however, encourages us to see it as more than a history lesson. *Assassins* is about contemporary America; more specifically, it is about our conception of America and the language, the narratives, the images—in short, the discourse in which this conception is expressed.

We can understand the presentation of discourse in the play with the help of Ernest Bormann's symbolic convergence communication theory and Mikhail Bakhtin's theory of dialogic discourse. Symbolic convergence theory begins with an idea we have already discussed: individuals' sense of reality is structured, organized, and given meaning through narratives. Bormann argues that all communication is made possible by speakers and listeners sharing certain narratives, what he calls *fantasy themes,* about themselves and their world. A given fantasy theme can be indicated in speaking or writing by a symbolic cue. Listeners or readers recognize a given cue, connect it to the appropriate fantasy theme, and consciously or unconsciously complete the meaning-providing narrative: fantasy chaining has occurred and communication has been successful. When listeners or readers are members of the same rhetorical community, they share a set of fantasy themes and the understanding of the world they construct. However, when listeners either do not recognize the symbolic cues or reject the associated fantasy theme, fantasy chaining does not occur, and communication fails.[20]

Bakhtin argues that meaning in art results from the dialogic interaction of multiple discourses, each discourse being a manifestation of a specific ideological belief system or worldview. He calls art that puts such a dialogic interaction into motion *heteroglottal,* or many-voiced. When discourses engage in dialogue, so too do their associated worldviews: some belief systems are seen to be identical; some are seen to be analogic; some are seen to be in conflict; and some, by being placed in each other's context, synthesize into something new. Monoglottal, or single-voiced, texts present only the official discourse of the dominant ideology; thus they serve only to reproduce the dominant ideology. Heteroglottal texts, by putting into dialogue multiple discourses and juxtaposing their associated ideological belief systems, challenge the dominant ideology and any belief system that claims totality. Thus the heteroglottal text is always subversive.[21]

In this context of discourse, communication, narrative, and ideology, *Assassins* is not so much about the assassins and their acts as it is about sharing or failing to share an idea of America, communicating or failing to communicate a construction of America. Discourse here not only is a vehicle for representation but also is one of the things the play is about. The first two scenes establish these ideas. As the play opens, the Proprietor and John Wilkes Booth try to convince the potential assassins to, as the shooting-gallery sign puts it, "HIT THE 'PREZ' AND WIN A PRIZE."[22] Singing to an upbeat melody, reminiscent of "Put on a Happy Face" from *Bye Bye Birdie* or "You're Never Fully Dressed without a Smile" from *Annie,* the Proprietor asserts:

> If you keep your goal in sight,
> You can climb to any height.
> Everybody's got the right
> To their dreams . . . (*L* 114)

He goes on to claim that living in a free country "Means your dreams can come true" (*L* 115). Eventually, all the assassins sing, "Rich man, poor man, black or white, / Pick your apple, take a bite" (*L* 115). The discourse here offers symbolic cues in both the words and music. The words cue numerous fantasy themes of the American experience: America as dedicated to equality of opportunity; America as a classless society; America as home to the self-made man; America as the setting for rags-to-riches

"Everybody's Got the Right": Original cast of *Assassins*. Credit Line: Photo by Martha Swope/©The New York Public Library for the Performing Arts

stories. Using these fantasy themes to encourage and justify the murder of a president shakes them loose from the contexts in which audiences are accustomed to placing them, in effect decentering them and bringing them forward for examination. The musical style also functions as a symbolic cue, recalling the Rodgers and Hammerstein Broadway musical tradition in which middle-class American fantasy themes are reaffirmed. Again, however, the characters and the subject matter inhibit the fantasy chaining that might normally result from this cue. The Broadway musical form itself, and, as we shall see, the other musical forms that have been associated with the expression of the American experience, are also brought forward for examination. The stage becomes a neutral territory, dissociated from comfortable narrative and dramatic assumptions (with all they imply about structure, cause-and-effect sequence, meaning, and ideology), in which this examination will take place.

The examination begins in the second scene, focusing on John Wilkes Booth and the assassination of Abraham Lincoln. Set in a Virginia barn just before Booth's death, it establishes a conflict between the discourse of mainstream America, represented by the Balladeer, singer of the American song, and the attempted communications of the assassins, who exist outside of the American mainstream. The Balladeer sings of the American experience (and implicitly the discourse through which it is expressed) as a "song," which may be temporarily affected by assassinations, those times when "a madman's / Bound to come along" (*L* 119), but which is too strong to be fundamentally changed. For him, Booth's act is inexplicable because Booth the actor had attained the American idea of success: fame and wealth, the dream of stardom. He sings that Booth was "handsome," wore "rings and fancy silks," "lived with a grace and glitter," and, in fact, "had everything" (*L* 119). He is as appalled that Booth would "Throw it all away" (*L* 119) as he is that a president is dead. To him, the murder makes sense only in terms of success lost: Booth must have had "A slew of bad / Reviews—" (*L* 119).[23]

Booth, on his side, intended the assassination of Lincoln to be a message to his country about his country, but, having abandoned the mainstream with his act, he still must rely on official history, represented by the Balladeer, as a vehicle of communication. He fumes at how his act is being interpreted in the press, the rough draft of history, shouting at his accomplice, "Have you seen these papers?! Do you know what they're calling me?! A common cutthroat! A hired assassin! This one says I'm mad!" (17). In a moment reminiscent of the fairy-tale characters attacking the Narrator in *Into the Woods*, narrative boundaries break down as Booth becomes aware of the Balladeer's interpretation of his motive and threatens him. After his accomplice gives himself up to the troops who have surrounded the barn, Booth pleads with the Balladeer, "I have given up my life for one act, you understand? Do not let history rob me of its meaning. Pass on the truth! You're the only one who can" (19). With the Balladeer's permission and help, Booth proceeds in a discourse that undercuts his meaning and reveals the hollowness behind his words. Cuing fantasy themes about democracy, equality, and self-determination, he argues that because of Lincoln, "the country is not what it was [. . .]" (*L* 120). In pursuing a war that set brother against brother, Lincoln destroyed the concept of the Union, and in the process he became a tyrant, revoking rights guaranteed by the Constitution. As a result, "the nation can never again / Be the hope that it was [. . .]" (*L* 120). In a moment of rising anger, however, Booth, in a discourse that betrays him, sings,

> the Union can never recover
> From that vulgar,
> High and mighty
> Nigger lover,
> Never—! (*L* 120)

Suddenly, a different and contradictory set of fantasy themes becomes clear: Lincoln was a backwoods bumpkin, a frontier lawyer who had gone beyond his class and station in becoming president; Lincoln supported freedom for America's black slaves. Booth's classist and racist reactions show that his claims for American democracy are limited to whites of a certain economic and educational background. His discourse of equality under the Constitution is shown to be a sham. His case against Lincoln collapses on itself.

Booth thinks that by explaining his action to the Balladeer, and through him to the audience, he has determined its historical presentation. He sings about those who attack him,

> Let them curse me to hell,
> Leave it to history to tell [. . . .]
>
> Let them cry, "Dirty traitor!"
> They will understand it later. (*L* 120)

However, after Booth's death, the Balladeer, the representative of official American history, presents an interpretation more in keeping with the mainstream notion of America. Booth, he concludes, "was off his head," a traitor who tried to turn "treason" and "butchery" into "a cause" (*L* 120). Booth's message about Lincoln and the death of democracy has been lost, for, the Balladeer sings, "[. . .] Lincoln, who got mixed reviews, / Because of you, John, now gets only raves" (*L* 120). The Balladeer rejects information and ideas that do not fit into the paradigm of officially promulgated

American narratives. As a result, Americans have not had to face the implications of Booth's act; rather, he and it are dismissed as aberrations, not a part of the narrative of the American experience.

The ideas introduced in scenes 1 and 2 become the focus for the rest of the play. Each of the assassins attempts to communicate with mainstream America. Each of these attempts problematizes the discourse of American democracy. This problematization highlights the conflict between official and alternative narratives about American history and the American experience. This logic reaches its climax in the twentieth-century repetition of and variation on the Lincoln assassination, the assassination of John F. Kennedy.

Like Booth, the other assassins are trying to communicate through their acts. Unlike Booth, they are not examples of American successes. They are people for whom the American Dream has failed. They speak from outside the established systems of mainstream America, trying, to varying degrees, to make mainstream America aware of them and the failure of the Dream. As John Weidman writes, "We live in a country whose most cherished national myths, at least as currently propagated, encourage us to believe that in America our dreams not only *can* come true, but *should* come true, and that if they don't someone or something is to blame."[24] Some of the assassins' messages arise out of an individual sense of desire and failure. John Hinckley hopes to send a message of love to Jodie Foster by shooting Ronald Reagan. Charles Guiteau, would-be ambassador to France, kills James Garfield to show "That I am not a man to overlook!" (*L* 127). Sara Jane Moore attempts to shoot Gerald Ford in order to fix and define an identity made unstable by a consumer economy. (Note Moore's obsession with consumer goods, everything from Kentucky Fried Chicken to the various items she pulls out of her purse in "Gun Song.") Others' messages of personal failure are self-consciously set in a larger context of the failure of America. Samuel Byck tries to crash a 747 into Richard Nixon's White House because he feels betrayed by a loss of principles in those around him and projects this loss onto the political system as a whole. Leon Czolgosz kills William McKinley to draw attention to the miserable treatment of the average worker and the inequalities of the capitalist economic system. Giuseppe Zangara attempts to shoot

Franklin Roosevelt after the many frustrations of second-class, natural-ized citizenship have ruined his health. "Squeaky" Fromme tries to kill Gerald Ford so that her trial will provide a forum for Charles Manson to "save the world" (80).

At heart, all these messages are, as Weidman suggests, about the fail-ure of the discourse that has constructed the sense of what America is. In each case, the assassins intentionally or unintentionally reveal the facti-tious nature of the American discourse. Some of the assassins, Hinckley and Guiteau, for instance, use the discourse sincerely, seeing their acts as ways of becoming a part of the American fantasy themes: gaining love, achieving success, earning a place in history. Most, however, see their acts as exposing the discourse of the American Dream as a fiction. For ex-ample, Zangara, like Booth, must share the stage with representatives of mainstream America in telling his story. Alone, strapped into the electric chair, he must compete for the audience's attention with the eyewitnesses to the shooting, reporters and photographers hovering around them. The bystanders' positive assertions, each claiming, "I saved Roosevelt!" (*L* 121), are countered by Zangara's negations. In his Italian-accented English he repeats "no" over and over as he tries to correct the bystanders' misun-derstandings:

> Zangara have nothing,
> No luck, no girl,
> Zangara no smart, no school,
> But Zangara no foreign tool,
> Zangara American!
> American nothing! (*L* 125)

Even his last word, sung as he is electrocuted, is "No" (*L* 125). In this con-text of negation the bystanders' song confirms Zangara's claims for the failure of democracy in his experience. Two men report with pride their refusal to let someone so obviously not a WASP in front of them. One sings,

> I say, "Listen, you runt,

You're not pulling that stunt—
No gentleman pushes their way to the front."
I say, "Move to the back!," which he does with a grunt— (*L* 121)

The same man later dismisses Zangara as "Some left wing foreigner" (*L* 125). The eyewitnesses, representative of the white middle and upper classes, are revealed to have a restricted and exclusionary notion of democracy. Immigrant Americans, even naturalized ones, are seen to be, at best, second-class citizens, at worst, not Americans at all.

The play's method of critically examining the discourse and its implied narratives that construct the official notion of America and the American Dream is augmented by the musical styles Sondheim brings to bear on the assassins' stories. We have already seen the ways in which he employs pastiche in *Anyone Can Whistle, Follies,* and *Pacific Overtures,* but *Assassins* offers the most complex entwining of pastiched musical styles and theme. Sondheim sets each of the songs to music not only appropriate to the historical period but also indicative of expressions of the American experience. Each song adopts a style of music mainstream Americans have used to tell their stories. As a result, the musical style and the stories associated with it become part of what each song is about. The previous example of "How I Saved Roosevelt" is the most obvious: major portions of the bystanders' song are set to John Philip Sousa's "El Capitan" and "Washington Post March." "Gun Song" incorporates a barbershop quartet. Hinckley's and Fromme's song to their respective loves, "Unworthy of Your Love," is a 1970s pop-rock number, inspired, reportedly, by the style of the Carpenters. Charles Guiteau's refrain is set to a cakewalk. "Another National Anthem" offers a group's self-celebration, as its title suggests. "The Ballad of Booth," "The Ballad of Czolgosz," and "The Ballad of Guiteau," all sung in part by the Balladeer, draw on the American folk-ballad tradition.[25] In fact, Sondheim's overall method here simultaneously adopts and pastiches the use of American themes by such composers as Charles Ives, Aaron Copland, and Antonín Dvořák. These pastiched musical styles, themselves symbolic cues with associated fantasy themes, make two points. First, they reinforce the disjunction between the rhetoric of American democracy and the actual experience of life in America. Second, they destabilize the certainty with which these rhetorical forms can be used by *anyone* to express the American experience. If the rhetorical forms that have traditionally celebrated America can with equal facility be used to justify murder, can we ignore the other atrocities—wars, imperialism, institutionalized racism and sexism, economic terrorism— they have justified?

In other words, the song styles Sondheim employs are manifestations, as Bakhtin argues all discourses are, of ideological belief systems. By using them as he does—by making their own styles and their implied worldviews part of what the songs are about and by placing them in the defamiliarizing context of telling the stories of assassins—Sondheim invokes and undercuts the ideological purpose they traditionally perform. The clearest examples of his technique here are the three ballads: "The Ballad of Booth," "The Ballad of Czolgosz," and "The Ballad of Guiteau." Sondheim draws on a tradition of folk ballads about presidential assassinations.[26] In fact, for "The Ballad of Czolgosz" and "The Ballad of Guiteau," he apparently was inspired by two traditional ballads. The traditional "Mister MacKinley" makes use of the refrain "In Buffalo, / in Buffalo," just as Sondheim's "The Ballad of Czolgosz" does. The traditional "Charles Guiteau" begins "Come all you Christian people, wherever you may be," which is recalled in the opening of Sondheim's "The Ballad of Guiteau," "Come all ye Christians [. . .]" (65).[27] In discussing these traditional ballads, folk-music specialist Alan Lomax connects them to the criminal's good-night tradition and reveals their ideological purpose:

> Whether or not he has confessed at his trial, [the criminal] often
> does so in his ballad, at the same time calling God to witness that he
> is sorry for his act. This formula, which at first glance may appear
> absurdly sentimental, is actually the key to the psychological function
> of these ballads. Such songs furnish the singers and their audience
> with outlets for strong aggressive emotions; in a word, they enable
> the folk to commit crimes in fantasy. Without the pious ending, a
> residue of guilty emotion would remain in the heart of the singer.
> Therefore a moralizing conclusion is essential to the ballad's effect
> within the framework of a culture where aggression and rebellion are
> considered wrong. The singer needs to reidentify himself with the
> "good people."

Neither the medieval ballad nor the American Negro murder ballads have such conclusions, for in these cultures individual acts of violence were simply a normal part of life. However, in the Anglo-American culture of the past three hundred years, where open aggression has been thoroughly repressed, the murder ballad had to assume the form of an apology for violence.[28]

That Lomax is able with a straight face to claim that ours is a culture where aggression and violence are considered wrong rather than the motivating forces behind much of our history demonstrates how successfully songs like these and other pop-cultural manifestations of the same worldview have served their purpose. Sondheim, in pastiching these ballads, both invokes their traditional ideological purpose and reveals the absurd contradiction at the heart of it: we live in a traditionally violent culture where history's good guys and bad guys have tried to shape the world to their liking by means of guns. In his attempts to dismiss the assassins as aberrations, the Balladeer contributes to the ideological purpose Lomax sees the assassins' ballads serving. That he is unable to silence the assassins' voices completely reveals the contradictions in his and the ballads' efforts.

However, the score's simultaneous assertion and subversion of American discourses and narratives contribute to the failure of the assassins' attempts to communicate. Although the assassins want to reveal the bankruptcy of the America constructed by the prevailing discourse, they are caught up in that discourse themselves. As a result, they are using the same words and gestures (symbolic cues) as mainstream America, but the fantasy themes intended and received are different. Fantasy chaining and communication fail. The play offers example after example of failed communication. Booth fails to persuade the Balladeer to pass on his motive for assassinating Lincoln. Guiteau cannot get Garfield to listen to him. Byck desperately sends cassette tapes of his ranting to celebrities. The characters cannot even communicate among themselves successfully. Sara Jane Moore greets each of Squeaky Fromme's statements of Charles Manson's social philosophy with a non sequitur from her consumerist conditioning ("I think there's a new perfume called Charlie" [42]). Emma Goldman, using a familiar symbolic cue, tells Czolgosz, "It's a free country," then must explain, "That was a joke" (39). Byck and Lee Harvey

Oswald reject attempts at communication with a conversation-ending "Fuck you" (25, 91, 93). "The Ballad of Czolgosz" hangs on a divergence of meaning of two associated fantasy themes: the notions that opportunity is distributed equally in the United States and that through hard work anyone can succeed. The Balladeer presents William McKinley as keying into the discourse supporting these fantasy themes in his speech at the Pan-American Exposition:

"Some men have everything and some have none,
But that's just fine:
In the U.S.A.
You can work your way
To the head of the line!" (*L* 130)

He presents Czolgosz, however, as using the same language to attack this fantasy theme:

"Nothin' wrong about what I done.
Some men have everything and some have none—
That's by design. [. . .]

In the U.S.A.
You can have your say,
You can set your goals
And seize the day,
You've been given the freedom
To work your way
To the head of the line—" (*L* 130)

Czolgosz's physical actions similarly belie the fantasy theme, since when he works his way to the head of the line of fairgoers waiting to shake hands with the president, he shoots this symbol of prosperity and success.

The disjunction of meaning caused by these conflicting uses of the same discourse allows mainstream America to reject the assassins and their attempts to communicate as insane or irrelevant, just as the Balladeer rejects Booth as an aberration of the American story (and just as

Times reviewer Frank Rich rejected them as mutants). The "Another National Anthem" sequence offers a final confrontation between the Balladeer and the assassins. Where previously the assassins had been sure that with their guns they could change the world, this sequence begins with them lamenting their acts' failure to communicate. The Balladeer confirms this sense of failure:

> But it didn't fix the stomach
> And you've drunk your final Bud,
> And it didn't help the workers
> And it didn't heal the country
> And it didn't make them listen
> And they never said, "We're sorry"— (*L* 135)

He tries to co-opt them into the mainstream American discourse of opportunity and success, assuring them "There are prizes all around you, / If you're wise enough to see [. . .]" (*L* 135). The assassins counter by reasserting the validity of their messages. Using the national pastime as a symbolic cue for the narrative of the American good life, they sing of an alternative national anthem for "The ones that can't get in / To the ball park," convinced that mainstream Americans

> may not want to hear it,
> But they listen,
> Once they think it's gonna stop the game. (*L* 136)

In a reversal of the play's failures of communication, now it is the Balladeer who is misunderstood: his discourse of perseverance and success is adopted by the assassins as they drive him from the stage: "You've got to keep on trying . . ."; "Mustn't give up hope . . ." (*L* 137). With new determination, they prepare for a final attempt to communicate, to "Spread the word . . ." (*L* 137).

This final attempt is the assassination of Kennedy. The assassins, led by Booth, gather on the sixth floor of the Texas School Book Depository to convince a suicidal Lee Harvey Oswald to shoot the president. Like the others, Oswald exists outside the American community, dispossessed of his share of the American Dream and unable, despite such unorthodox actions as defecting to the Soviet Union and distributing pro-Cuba literature, to have any impact on that community. Booth argues that assassinating the president will send a message that mainstream America will be unable to ignore. Further, in a new twist, Booth argues that Oswald can end his isolation and alienation by joining a different community, the community of assassins. Indicating the assassins, Booth says, "All your life you've wanted to be part of something, Lee. You're finally going to get your wish" (96). Czolgosz, representing the earlier assassins, tells Oswald, "You're going to bring us back"; Hinckley, representing the later assassins, adds, "And make us possible" (96). Oswald's act, the assassins argue, will remove *their* acts from the category of aberrations in the American narrative and will bring them together into a narrative sequence, an alternative narrative, telling the story of the dispossessed, the disappointed, the disenfranchised, in Michael Harrington's term, the Other America, which by its very existence gives the lie to the America constructed by the official narrative. Zangara offers a plea in Italian, which is translated by the others:

CZOLGOSZ: We are the hopeless ones. The lost ones . . .
GUITEAU: We live our lives in exile . . .
BYCK: Expatriates in our own country [. . .]
MOORE: Through you and your act we are revived and given meaning [. . .]
FROMME: Today we are reborn, through you . . . (100)

They continue,

MOORE: Without you, we're just footnotes in a history book. [. . .]
HINCKLEY: With you we're a force of history. (100)

Oswald is the assassin who can organize all the other assassins' acts into a narrative that mainstream American will have to recognize. This narrative, grounded in and expressed through its own discourse, will exist alongside the official, mainstream American narrative, destabilizing it and challenging its totality and its claims to exclusive truth. Thus destabilized, the American narrative will no longer be able to mask the reality of the American experience as the assassins have lived it. With the assassination of Kennedy, their message will finally be passed on.

We see the complex effect of this message in "Something Just Broke," in which ordinary Americans of various classes and occupations and from various historical periods respond to the news of the assassination of a president. In one sense the assassins have apparently succeeded in their mission to destabilize American certainties. The singers express a sense of loss, not just of a leader, but of a feeling of security in understanding their world. The discourses and narratives that explain the American experience have lost their confidence. One woman sings,

> Something just broke—
> —Only for a moment.
> Something got bent.
> Something just left a little mark.
> Something just went a little dark.
> Something just went. (*L* 141)

Later, all the citizens sing, "Something just spoke, / Something I wish I hadn't heard" (*L* 142). In this sense, the assassins' creation of a collective, alternative narrative and their final attempt to communicate have been successful. The effect of this communication, however, is not the kind of critical examination into the nature of the American experience or the sudden appreciation of the Other America they had hoped for. Rather, the ordinary citizens react to their shaken faith not by reaching out to the Other but by longing to move back to the time before the assassination when they felt secure in what they believe about themselves and their country. The assassinations, like all national disasters (Pearl Harbor, 9/11), have the effect of "Bringing us all together" (*L* 141), at least temporarily establishing a sense of community and common purpose, a retrenchment in the familiar rather than an openness to the unknown Other. Moreover, we see here the intellectual process, first exhibited by the Balladeer, by which the assassins' acts are rejected from the official American narratives and consigned to individual aberrations. The characters variously sing,

198

Fix it up fast,
Please—
Till it's just smoke,
Till it's only something just passed—
—Nothing that will last.
Nothing but the moment,
Just an awful moment . . . (*L* 142)

Faced with the horrific acts of the assassins and the disturbing truths they seek to communicate about America, the ordinary citizens instinctively dehistoricize, denarratize, the acts, reducing them again to only moments, separate and alone, storyless, mute.

The musical's finale similarly undercuts the successful narrative-making of the Oswald scene. On the one hand, the assassins have made a communion: as Oswald, joining them, sings, they have connected. On the other hand, the song they sing, a reprise of "Everybody's Got the Right," reveals them as still caught up in the discourse of the American Dream. Even in the neutral space of the stage, the assassins are not able to communicate their collective message without interference. Enough of the assassins either undercut their own discourse, as Booth did, or are clearly mad, as Guiteau and Byck are, that their narratives cannot be accepted without qualification. More significant, the play's structure refuses to give the assassins their narrative. Presented in a revue style, the play offers no consistent chronology or sequential logic. In his review of the original production, Frank Rich, missing the point, complained, "'Assassins' does not flow like a musical, but seems to start anew with each scene, and the scenes sit like clumps in isolation from the songs. The order of the numbers often seems arbitrary."[29] This lack of narrative flow is the clearest signal that the play does not intend to be the assassins' alternative narrative, that, while giving them the voice that official history has denied them, it is not trying to justify or approve of their acts. Rather, the play asks its audience to recognize the possibility of the assassins' alternative narrative and to hold it up against the official American narrative they know so well they take it for granted. Set side by side, put into Bakhtinian dialogue, the two narratives of America destabilize each other. The play leaves its audience without an American narrative to believe in, forcing them either to reject the examination of discourse they have been offered and return to what they have always believed or to question the assumptions that lie behind their construction of the idea of America and perhaps construct a new one.

Passion, Sondheim's next play, further complicates the issues of narrative and discourse as epistemological and ontological structures. Where the earlier plays made use of and critiqued narrative as an epistemological structure and discourse as means of reproducing ideologically charged subject positions, *Passion* looks at the postmodern discourse-infused world, the layers of language and multiple narratives, the signifiers perpetually pointing at more signifiers, as a potential trap and expresses a yearning after a transcendent reality beyond language.

Based on the 1981 film *Passione d'Amore,* by Ettore Scola, and an 1869 novel, *Fosca,* by I. U. Tarchetti,[30] *Passion* tells the story of a handsome Italian army officer, Giorgio, who is involved, as the play begins, in an intense affair with a married woman, Clara, and who, after being transferred to a remote army outpost, is pursued by his commanding officer's cousin, a sickly and ugly woman named Fosca. Driven to illness by Fosca's relentless attentions, Giorgio eventually comes to see the limitations of Clara's love and, in a gender reversal of the Beauty and the Beast fairy tale, comes to love Fosca. With book and direction by James Lapine, *Passion* was workshopped at the nonprofit Lincoln Center Theater and then, with a cast that included Donna Murphy, Jere Shea, and Marin Mazzie, opened at the Plymouth (now Gerald Schoenfeld) Theatre on 9 May 1994.[31]

Passion is often, unfairly, I think, characterized as no one's favorite Sondheim musical, possibly because of its nineteenth-century cultural sensibilities, its emotional intensity, and its seriousness of tone. (I once heard Sondheim in a question-and-answer session respond to someone who asked if *Passion* was groundbreaking by joking that it was the first totally humorless musical comedy.) *Passion* strikes me as being especially important because it marks a change, as I suggest earlier, in its attitude toward language, discourse, and narrative, a change that connects to a larger cultural disquiet regarding postmodernism. By the 1990s, many writers and theorists were beginning to suspect that postmodernism as a style had reached a point of exhaustion. Postmodernism's smashing the mirror art holds up to nature and cutting the cord connecting word and world had been seen as revolutionary, a way to disrupt narrative- and dis-coursed-based transmission of officially defined reality as the only reality, a way of understanding that no one society or organization or institution has claim to absolute truth and that what we think of as reality is the inter-section of multiple, often contradictory truths manifested in the world's multifarious narratives. Of course, to say that postmodernism smashed the mirror and cut the cord is, to my mind, overstating the case. While postmodernism, as we have seen in our discussions of Sondheim's plays, certainly complicated and problematized the process of representation, the process by which art claims to reflect the world and by which words claim to denote objects, it only rarely (and eccentrically) denies represen-tation altogether. Rather, in its self-reflexivity, in its critique of narrative structure, in its emphasis on the freeplay of language, postmodernism ups the ante on representation. Art, narrative, and language become always simultaneously about their subject matter and about themselves being about their subject matter. By the 1990s, however, the liberatory potential of postmodernism had been tempered by the suspicion that the move-ment had left us trapped in a cycle of language, an endless series of signi-fiers with perpetually deferred signifieds.[32]

Passion invokes this sense of language as a trap in multiple, themati-cally significant ways. The play begins with Giorgio and Clara having sex and then, in the postcoital song "Happiness,"[33] singing of their emotions and their love. In a way, this should be the last scene of a musical. The lovers, we learn, like the lovers in *West Side Story* and *Sweeney Todd,* have fallen in love at first sight. Now, their love is consummated, and, in the terms of conventional narrative, we would expect this to be an endpoint, the removal of the narrative from time, the closure of happily ever after. Like *Into the Woods,* however, *Passion* goes on to show us what happens after happily ever after, thus denying narrative containment and deny-ing closure—and meaning—outside of time. The scene offers a hint that not all is well: the afternoon light that streams into the room when Clara opens the curtains signals that this is an illicit affair. More important, the news that Giorgio is being transferred to an outpost away from Milan thrusts a complication into their relationship. In this first scene, Giorgio and Clara have been shown as being together with each other as closely, as intimately, as possible. This togetherness is disrupted by language, the orders Giorgio has presumably received, and his announcement of his impending departure. Clara at once recognizes that language has come between them: "All this happiness— / —Ended by a word in the dark" (*L* 149). Giorgio, however, offers a different take. He says that "after I leave, we'll write each other daily. We'll make love with our words. You'll be with me every day, Clara."[34] For Giorgio, the words of their letters, which imply an absence—that they are not together—can in fact be a presence: they will be present to each other through their words.

This first scene, then, introduces two important, interconnected formal and thematic elements of the play. The first is the narrative inversion signaled by beginning with an ending, a narrative inversion that will, as we will see, lead to narrative collapsing onto itself. The second is the attention drawn to the layers of language that mediate between us and our experience of the world and the tension between substituted presence and a desire for actual presence, knowledge beyond language.

These two elements come together in the play's form; Sondheim says that *Passion* "is the only epistolary musical ever written."[35] Letters—written, narrated, received—dominate the play. One result of this choice of form is the collapse of narrative or, perhaps more precisely, the folding in of narrative onto itself. Such distinctions as those among beginning, middle, and end, between character and narrator, and between action and narrative standpoint—distinctions, as we have seen, seminal to narrative structure's functioning—are collapsed and superimposed here. A clear example is scene 3, the garden scene in which Giorgio and Fosca, accompanied by the colonel and the doctor, take an excursion to the garden of a ruined castle. We see the action as it takes place, but Giorgio is simultaneously a character in the action and a narrator, as he writes about the action to Clara. Then, at the same time, we see Clara reading and responding to Giorgio's letter reporting on the action. Time's arrow is lost here as we take in as one moment what must be three distinct chronological moments. The result is something of a cubist effect wherein at least three perspectives on the same topic are apprehended simultaneously. This effect also emphasizes the impossibility of knowing an event separate from the narratives and discourses about it. As an overall result, the structure of this scene allows the audience to see that each of the three characters understands the action—what happened—differently, differences that tell us about the characters and that initiate important complications in the relationships among them. Giorgio turns the excursion into a reverie on Clara. Clara joins in Giorgio's celebration of their love but also is unnerved by and a bit suspicious of his interest in Fosca and in his equating Fosca with her. For her part, Fosca takes advantage of Giorgio's distraction to display the pretense of offense over his talking to her of love and to force him to accept her as a special friend, something of a soul mate. Interestingly, the lyrics with which she does this ("All the time I watched from my room" and so on [*L* 158]) are set to a variation of the music that accompanies Giorgio and Clara's statement of how love brings them together ("Love that fuses two into one" and so on [*L* 158]). This both establishes Fosca as a vampire—she frequently borrows others' music—and inserts a counternarrative in between Giorgio and Clara's narrative of love, another example of layers of language coming between them.

The flashback in scene 8 functions similarly. We see the events of Fosca's past—her being reared by her parents, her meeting and courting by Count Ludovic, her learning of his deception, his leaving her—but these events are being narrated to Giorgio by the colonel and, in a letter, by Fosca at the same time. As in the garden scene, we are given alternate perspectives on the events (Fosca describes her childhood as "happy," while the colonel describes it as "lonely" [*L* 165]), and the events, through the media of letter writing and storytelling, are textualized—we perceive the layers of language between the events and the characters' understanding of them. The scene presents this textualization as working in two interconnected ways. First, narratizing the past, as we saw earlier, gives the events of the past a structure and makes them interpretable. In the flashback scene, the two distinct narrations allow us to see Fosca and the colonel drawing different interpretations from their stories. For Fosca, the moral of her story is "Beauty is power . . . / Longing a disease . . ." (*L* 167). Thus, her betrayal by Ludovic, which, more than his squandering her parents' money and keeping mistresses, is marked by his admission that he used his handsome looks to take advantage of an ugly woman desperate to marry, is the etiology of her illness. For the colonel,

> The enemy was love—
> Selfishness really, but love.
> All of us blinded by love
> That makes everything seem possible.
>
> You have to pay a consequence
> For things that you've denied.
> This is the thorn in my side. (*L* 167)

The colonel feels inadequate both because he willfully let himself be fooled by Ludovic and because he was unable to attain revenge in an *affaire d'honneur*. The lesson he expresses here explains why, at the end of the play, he cannot believe that Giorgio truly loves his cousin and why he is so quick to demand reparation in a duel.

The thorn-in-my-side cliché at the end of the colonel's statement points to the second way in which the flashback is textualized. Just as Fosca and the colonel derive lessons based on interpretations of past events that influence their future actions, so too are the events of the past, simultaneously acted and narrated, influenced by previously received narratives and their lessons. Fosca's hyperconsciousness of her lack of physical beauty comes from the emphasis her parents, representing the culture at large, put on it. Fosca and the colonel sing,

> As long as you're a man,
> You still have opportunities.
> Whereas, if you're a woman,
> You either are a daughter or a wife. (*L* 165)

This lesson is a manifestation of a patriarchal ideology that finds limited value in women, that assumes women cannot care for themselves, and that defines women's identities in terms of their relations with men. The operations of this ideology motivate the events narrated in the flashback: the urgency with which Fosca needs to marry; the colonel's willingness to blind himself to the unlikelihood of Ludovic's attentions to Fosca; Ludovic's playing the conventions demanded by the ideology against themselves for his own profit. The motivating lessons are all summed up at the end of the flashback:

MISTRESS: As long as you're a man,
You're what the world will make of you.
MISTRESS, MOTHER: Whereas if you're a woman,
You're only what it sees.
COLONEL, FATHER, LUDOVIC: A woman is a flower
Whose purpose is to please. (*L* 167)

These lessons recall the watchcries of the interrogation scene in *Anyone Can Whistle,* the clichés learned in childhood that end up shaping character. Like those watchcries, the lessons here are received by various means from the culture at large, becoming the means by which subject positions are made and identity formed.

The flashback scene, then, shows us the ways in which ideology is reproduced via narrative. Ideology received through narratives and the lessons they offer shape identity and influence action; the action is subsequently turned into a narrative from which a lesson is learned, a lesson that essentially reiterates the ideology. The characters here are trapped in an ideological, narrative, and interpretive cycle. The intertwining of ideology, knowledge, and narrative makes escape from the cycle unlikely if not impossible.

Concomitant with this idea is a presentation of discourse similar to what we saw in *Assassins.* In discussing Bakhtin and Bormann, we saw that discourse implies narrative, which in turn implies an ideological belief system. Being set in a time and place very different from our own, mid-nineteenth-century Italy, *Passion* is able, through a few words, to imply a great deal about the ideology—the assumptions about power, the social system, the rules—within which the characters act. In the scene where Giorgio first meets and is appalled by Fosca, she tells him that she likes to visit the garden at the ruined castle and sings, "Perhaps you'll join me," but recognizing his discomfort at the inappropriateness of them going on an excursion unescorted, she quickly adds, "And my cousin" (*L*

154). This fear of breaking the rule about an unmarried man and woman being alone together recurs throughout the play: when Fosca accosts Giorgio as he departs on his first leave; when the doctor implores him to visit her in her bedroom; when she follows him to the bluff; when she shows up on the train as he goes on his sick leave. The reminders of this social stricture create an interesting tension between the generally accepted implausibility of Giorgio and Fosca being romantically involved and the culturally imbued suspicion that when a man and a woman are alone together some hanky-panky must be going on. Another example involves social expectations for gender roles. In "Soldiers' Gossip," when Giorgio politely refuses an invitation to join the other officers in playing pool, they respond cattily:

AUGENTI: Never trust a man who doesn't drink.
TORASSO: And he keeps a journal. (*L* 164)

In just a few words the men make clear that Giorgio does not fulfill their set's expectations for masculinity. To the officers' minds, real men drink and play pool, they do not write down their thoughts, and they do not read or do any of the things Giorgio does. His failure to fulfill these expectations helps us understand Fosca's claims for their affinity. In the garden of the ruined castle she sings to him of the other officers,

They hear drums,
You hear music,
As do I.
Don't you see?
We're the same.
We are different [. . . .] (*L* 158)

The more we see Giorgio failing in his interactions with the others, the more we see the sense of Fosca's point: although he is handsome and desirable and she is ugly and ill, neither fits in well with their community.[36]

On the one hand, then, language, discourse, and narratives are ideologically charged and thus vitally important in the way social systems, identities, and personal relations are constructed and enacted. On the other hand, language is socially situated and thus arbitrary, lacking no necessary connection to anything outside itself. This idea is most explicitly put by the doctor when he asks Giorgio to visit Fosca's sickbed: "she is dying, and you have only to give her words. Words that will make her well. What is the cost of a few words when a life hangs in the balance?" (55). For the doctor, words have no intrinsic value or meaning. They are something to be used in specific situations to obtain specific results. Beyond that, they are empty.

Looking at the play as a whole, we see the three main characters— Giorgio, Clara, and Fosca—trapped in an environment of ideologically determinant but self-reflexive language, seeking a way out. They desire something definite, absolute, something that transcends the circular, self-generating, and self-perpetuating linguistic world in which they find themselves, and for them that something is love. Love offers escape from who they are supposed to be. Thus Giorgio and Clara treasure their room, a sanctuary from the rest of the world and the roles—army officer, wife and mother—they must play there. Thus Fosca seeks in Giorgio a way out of the many undesirable roles—abandoned wife, invalid, ugly woman— she must play. And thus the three characters spend a great deal of their time thinking, talking, and writing about love. Here, however, lies the paradox. At the same time they want love to be something that transcends the linguistic trap, they insist on drawing it back into language—to define it and understand it in the terms of their linguistic world.

This paradox begins to be developed in the opening scene. I argued earlier that in this scene Giorgio and Clara are as physically close and emotionally intimate as possible until language begins to come between them. Looking more closely, however, we can see that even before the announcement of Giorgio's transfer, their love relationship is tied up in language. Both claim that they did not know what love was until meeting the other, but now they do. Still, they express this knowledge of love in synonyms: love is "happiness"; "a miracle"; the "pity" that leads to love; "what kindness became" (*L* 148). They express it in euphemism. Clara sings, "I'm so happy, / I'm afraid I'll die [. . .]" (*L* 148). They express it in terms of narrative structure. The love at first sight, the "glance in the park," makes their relationship, as Giorgio says, "inevitable" (*L* 148), destined, written, plotted. This sense of their love as a love story, a narrative, reveals the paradox at the heart of their idea of love. Together they sing,

> Just another love story,
> That's what they would claim.
> Another simple love story—
> Aren't all of them the same? (*L* 148)

Clara adds, "No, but this is more, / We feel more!" (*L* 148). This is their most explicit rejection of language as sufficient for explaining their love and their most explicit assertion that their love transcends language and the clichéd love stories usually employed to express it. In the very next line, however, they affectionately but sheepishly admit that this rejection and assertion are "Like every other love story" (*L* 148), drawing their love back into language and the conventions of the love story. Giorgio's announcement of his orders, then, certainly inserts language between the lovers, but it does not introduce language as an issue as they try to express a love beyond language with the only communicative means they have—language.

The tension of this paradox arises again and again, whenever the characters try to pin love down as something not to pin down. In the garden scene, Giorgio, speaking simultaneously to Fosca (in person) and Clara (through his letter), and Clara, reading his letter, sing of their love,

> Love that thinks
> Everything is pure,
> Everything is beautiful,
> Everything is possible. (*L* 157)

Love here is something that defies definition because it is "everything"; it signifies endlessly. Yet almost everywhere else Giorgio attempts to say what love is, he ends up saying what love is not, definition through negation. In his response to the final letter, in which Clara proposes waiting a few years before they run off together, Giorgio explodes, saying that Clara does not know what love is. In a variation of the melody with which Fosca first suggested the connection between her and Giorgio ("I've watched you from my window" and so on [L 158], which we later learn Fosca has appropriated from Ludovic's courting of her), Giorgio rants,

Love isn't so convenient.
Love isn't scheduled in advance [. . . .]
What's love unless it's unconditional? (L 174)

Interestingly, where before Giorgio saw his and Clara's love as encompass-ing everything, here he concludes "That what we have is nothing . . ." (L 174). Even after this, when he goes to Fosca's bedroom and at last declares his love, his revelation of what love really is is still expressed primarily in negatives:

Love without reason,
Love without mercy,
Love without pride or shame.
Love unconcerned
With being returned—
No wisdom, no judgment,
No caution, no blame. [. . .]

Not pretty or safe or easy,
But more than I ever knew.
Love within reason—that isn't love. (L 175)

In what becomes a real struggle for Giorgio to understand love, to under-stand the emotions he feels (he tells Fosca, "I feel so much . . ." [122]), he cannot get beyond the cycle of words pointing toward other words. He intuits that love is something that transcends language, but, as a being who exists in a world of words, he has no means of grasping it. He needs language more and more, even as it increasingly fails him.

Fosca faces a similar conundrum. As we saw earlier, the social situation that has been constructed for her by the ideologically charged discourse of her culture is intolerable. When we first meet her, she seeks escape from the oppressively determinate power of this discourse through immersion in another kind of discourse, the language of literature. Unhappy with her own life, she can construct happier, fantasy lives from the fiction she reads. She claims to recognize the distinction between these fantasy lives and her real situation:

> I know how painful dreams can be
> Unless you know
> They're merely dreams. (*L* 152)

She loses sight of this distinction, however, after she falls in love with Giorgio. She begins using her facility with language—the language of fiction—to construct a situation in which Giorgio will be in love with her. In the process she manipulates language and Giorgio. She begins her construction in the garden scene when she willfully misinterprets his words about his love with Clara as an improper declaration to herself. She huffs, "To speak to me of love—" (*L* 158). Her campaign continues when Giorgio comes to her room because she is supposedly dying. Giorgio suspects that this arrangement may itself be something of a fiction, managed with the collusion of the doctor. Nevertheless, thrust into this situation, he adopts a role to play in the little drama, telling Fosca of his heart, "Tonight it loves you as you wish" (58). Fosca is performer, playwright, and director of this scene, taking advantage of his willingness to act a part by providing him with dialogue:

> FOSCA: Call me by my name.
> GIORGIO: Fosca.
> FOSCA: Say "Giorgio and Fosca."
> GIORGIO: Giorgio and Fosca.
> FOSCA: "Fosca and Giorgio."
> GIORGIO: Fosca and Giorgio. (59)

Going further, she directs him to write her a love letter, which she dictates, putting words in his mouth, words that she will presumably read over and over, like one of her novels, to contribute to the construction of the fictional world in which she imagines Giorgio will love her. That the fantasy world increasingly impinges on the real one becomes clear late in the play when the colonel discovers this letter, and Giorgio realizes that the extent of its factitiousness is no longer clear. Even in their last scene together, when Giorgio declares his love for her, Fosca continues to direct his dialogue, asking, "Say it again" and "Once more" (123). Like Giorgio and Clara's love, Fosca's love for Giorgio and, eventually, his for Fosca, rather than being an escape from a world made of language, are themselves bound up in language.

This linguistic paradox, the desire to escape language being itself bound up in language, helps account for the play's linking of love and death. Death is a transcendent that eludes human linguistic and episte-mological systems, just as the characters want love to.[37] The absurdity of trying to make the experience of death explainable in human terms is suggested in the garden scene when Fosca apologizes to Giorgio for her fit in the previous scene: "I rather think I'd welcome dying. It's every-thing that follows that I dread: being shut up in a coffin, smothered in the earth, turning into dust. These images send me into a state of terror" (29). While these images are certainly macabre, the whole point, of course, is that she would not actually experience them: she would be dead. Death is connected to love in Fosca's clearest statement of her love for Giorgio. In "Loving You" she concludes by saying that her love gives her a purpose and a goal:

I will live,
And I would die
For you. (*L* 172)

The dialogue immediately following these lines is key to Giorgio's trans-formation:

GIORGIO: Die for me? What kind of love is that?
FOSCA: The truest love. Would Clara give her life for yours? Would she, Giorgio? (101)

Even now, he knows that she would not.

Thus Giorgio learns that love is irrational; it cannot be contained in the logic of an epistemological system. Fosca learns that love is selfless;

it demands a denial of the ego. At the end of the play, on their last night together and their only night as lovers, love as a desire for transcendence becomes a specific desire to get beyond their culture's linguistic-based epistemological and ontological systems. Like Tony and Maria in *West Side Story,* Fosca and Giorgio need a somewhere beyond ideology and the demands it makes on identity and social practice. However, unlike Tony and Maria's story, which ends in a death that offers hope that the reproduction of ideology can be disrupted and reconfigured by people of goodwill coming together, Fosca and Giorgio's story founders on the paradox of language and knowledge. In the discussion of *Follies* we saw the contradiction at the heart of Foucault's modern episteme: that knowledge exists in time but is made knowable by a narrative structure that cannot be complete until an endpoint is reached, until it is removed from time. A life story is not complete until the main character/narrator is dead. Thought about in this way, Fosca and Giorgio's somewhere is death. Their love beyond reason and self, beyond language and ideology, cannot be known or expressed in the terms of their culture's epistemological systems. Their coming together, their one act of sex, is performed with the knowledge that Fosca cannot survive it. Love and death are linked here, not in a metaphor, but as partners. What was a euphemism for Clara ("[. . .] I'm afraid I'll die / Here in your arms" [*L* 148]) is real for Fosca.

After this partnering of sex and death, after the practically dialogueless scene where Giorgio faces death in the duel with the colonel, and after Giorgio's wordless, senseless scream, language returns to the play in the last scene, but it returns in an unsettled form. Giorgio, at a hospital, recovering from a "nervous condition" (126) reminiscent of Fosca's illness, receives a letter from the doctor, explaining some of the aftermath of the duel and announcing Fosca's death "three days after the night you last saw one another" (126). This letter's attempt to re-rationalize and renarratize Giorgio's experience with Fosca is undone by the package of papers the doctor has sent along. When Giorgio opens it, language floods out, fragments of music and lyrics we have heard before, but unstructured, unorganized, a cacophony that recalls the falling apart of Loveland in *Follies.* Included in the package is a final letter from Fosca, written as she knew she was dying. As he reads the letter, her spirit appears. She tries to explain how loving and being loved have changed her, but, as in all the other attempts to bring love into language, she fails. She falls back on language that echoes Giorgio and Clara's claims for the overdetermination of the word *love*:

Everything seems right,
Everything seems possible,
Every moment bursts with feeling. (*L* 176)

The ghostly ensemble, Giorgio, and Fosca then segue into a reprise of "I Wish I Could Forget You," the letter Fosca dictated to Giorgio in her bedroom. We saw before how that letter blurred identities and developed a fluid sense of meaning as the relationship among its dictator, amanuensis, and auditor shifted. Here, as the ensemble fades away and the two lovers are left repeating and echoing the final lines, "Your love will live in me . . ." (*L* 176), who is speaking and who is listening, who is *you* and who is *me*, becomes hopelessly ambiguous. As Fosca fades away, Giorgio is left with a piece of paper with words on it, the play's ultimate comment on the pretense of language making the absent present: Fosca's words, ink on paper, cannot transcend the grave.

The desire to transcend the exhaustion of language and the dangers posed by a society drowned in language's used-upness are among the thematic interests of *The Frogs,* at this writing the most recent new play Sondheim has had on Broadway. Its newness, however, is qualified by its long production history. Burt Shevelove, one of Sondheim's *Forum* collaborators, adapted *The Frogs* from Aristophanes's 405 BC comedy in 1974 for a production at the Yale Repertory Theatre and invited Sondheim to contribute some songs. In 2000, at the Library of Congress's celebration of Sondheim's seventieth birthday, a concert version of *The Frogs,* adapted by Sondheim, was presented, with Nathan Lane, Brian Stokes Mitchell, and Davis Gaines as soloists supported by a chorus. Later that year, the same cast made a studio recording of the score. These experiences inspired Lane to revise and expand Shevelove's book, with Sondheim agreeing to write several new songs and Susan Stroman signing on as director and choreographer. This new version of *The Frogs* reached Broadway on 22 July 2004, produced by the nonprofit Lincoln Center Theater at the Vivian Beaumont Theater.[38]

Set simultaneously in the present and in ancient Greece, the story of *The Frogs* is a journey to hell and back. Dionysos, the god of the drama (and wine) travels with his comically whiney slave Xanthias to the underworld to bring George Bernard Shaw back to the world of the living. To the god's mind, Shaw's intellect and wit are needed to save a dying world. Dionysos argues that "if Shaw were to write again, he could show us the truth about ourselves and how we live," and he could "challenge our complacencies."[39] He finds Shaw, but before bringing him back to earth, he organizes a contest between longtime antagonists Shaw and Shakespeare in which each playwright comments on various topics, using words from his writings. For the last topic, death, Shaw recites Saint Joan's speech to her judges, and Shakespeare sings "Fear No More," a young man's reflection on death. Moved by the beauty of this poetry, Dionysos resolves to leave Shaw in the underworld and take Shakespeare with him. Presenting Shakespeare to the audience, Dionysos is confident we all can be shaken out of our complacencies.

In the liner notes for the Broadway cast recording, Nathan Lane writes that he was inspired to begin his revision of *The Frogs* while listening to the song "It's Only a Play." This song encapsulates the thematic conflict of the play and offers an important indication of the direction Lane and Sondheim took with their revision. In the song, the chorus, representing the complacent, narrow-minded, change-resisting frogs—and their human counterparts—dismiss Dionysos's plan to save the world with a playwright, and they do so through a series of clichés:

There's plenty of time—
There always is time.
You've got all the time in the world.
You know, time has a way of healing all things.
Things fix themselves.
Don't worry, relax.
Why not wait and see what happens?
It's only a play. (*F* 298)

The use of clichés here is significant, because the more familiar language becomes, the more frequently we have heard a term, phrase, or sentence, the less information it communicates. The chorus represents an entropic culture in which language has become degraded and deadened, and so has life. Accustomed to language that communicates nothing, the chorus cannot comprehend Dionysos's objections to the life they live or how language could change it. They sing:

> Well, words are merely chatter,
> And easy to say.
> It doesn't really matter,
> It's only a play.
>
> It's only so much natter
> Which somebody wrote. [. . .]
>
> It really doesn't matter
> What somebody writes. (*F* 298)

Recognizing that they live in language and recognizing the exhaustion of language, the chorus concludes that life, like language, is used up and pointless, not worth reforming because the reforms are only more language. Both ideas are established more hectically in "The Frogs," where the amphibians attack Dionysos as he crosses the River Styx on Charon's boat. Embracing the social and ideological status quo, the frogs sing,

> Whaddaya care the world's a wreck?
> Leave 'em alone, send 'em a check.
> Sit in the sun and what the heck,
> Whaddaya want to break your neck
> For? (*F* 293)

Emphasizing the exhaustion of language, the frogs rely on clichéd language here too, as well as on familiar music: in one section of overlapping voices, one group sings "Row, Row, Row Your Boat," while another sings "Ol' Man River," and another sings the Gershwins' "Who Cares?"

This attitude toward language and life is exactly what Dionysos wants to save the world from, and it is seminal to the play's form and style. The play is purposely and overwhelmingly intertextual in multiple ways. First, it is based on an existing text, Aristophanes's comedy, and its status as a play is foregrounded; both points are impressed upon the audience in "Invocation and Instructions to the Audience." Second, Sondheim has structured the choral numbers in accordance with the sections of a classical Greek comedy: prologos, parados, hymnos, parabasis, and exodos.[40] Third, much of the last section of the play is made up of the words of Shaw and Shakespeare. Building on this intertextual structure, Lane and Sondheim fill the play with pop-cultural catchphrases and allusions. From the opening of act 1, where Xanthias has trouble with his cell phone's signal and asks, "Can you hear me now?," to the first-act curtain line, "I think we're gonna need a bigger boat," the play makes the point that the characters continually express themselves in inherited language, the language of a culture drowning in language. Charon sings out for passengers to cross the river Styx,

If you fell off of the perch,
If you bought the farm,
Kicked the bucket,
Bit the dust,
All aboard! (*F* 292)

The characters even make reference to other musicals. When Dionysos parades in a lion skin Herakles has given him, the muscular hero critiques him as being "Too Fosse" (*F* 291), and Xanthias suggests that it looks "Like the circle of life has stopped." When Xanthias asks what is in Dionysos's luggage, the god replies, "Baubles, bangles, bright shiny beads." Later, in the underworld, when Dionysos finally meets Shaw, he announces the fact to the audience in a melody borrowed from *My Fair Lady*'s "You Did It":

I knew if I stuck to it,
I'd somehow get through it.

At times I thought, "Oh, screw it!"
But proceed I did [. . . .] (*F* 299)

There are many other examples, but the point is clear: contemporary society thinks and experiences life through layer upon layer of language, overused and clichéd.

To some thinkers, such a state is the inheritance of postmodernism's hyperconsciousness of language, an inheritance that can be ideologically reactionary in two interconnected ways. First, as novelist David Foster Wallace argues, postmodernism's consciousness of language, which in the 1950s and 1960s played an important role in exposing and debunking many long-held social conceits and hypocrisies, by the late 1980s and 1990s had devolved into an all-purpose irony, the rolling of the eyes and the nudging in the ribs that mock any assertion that eschews irony's game and aspires to sincerity.[41] Sondheim makes a similar point in *Look, I Made a Hat*: "Using irony gives you an excuse to say anything, no matter how crass or banal or pretentious, and get away with it. Irony is a made-to-order refuge from emotion or criticism; the author is asserting with a smile, 'You can't criticize what I'm saying, you can't even accuse me of believing it, because I'm fully aware of it and I'm making fun of it while I'm saying it; I'm making fun of it before you can.'"[42] While irony and sarcasm are excellent tools for criticizing what exists, they are useless for producing anything new. The more deeply a society becomes immersed in inherited language and the more self-conscious it becomes of that immersion, the less likely it is to reimagine itself.

Connected with this is a second problem: the multiplicity of discourses at work in contemporary society. We saw earlier that Bakhtin sees multiple discourses in dialogue with each other as a good thing; they offer a way of challenging the truth claims of the official discourse of a society and its associated dominant ideological belief system. In this sense, heteroglossia is subversive. However, Bakhtin never anticipated the potential for our media-saturated culture to produce and disseminate discourse. Each day we are bombarded with language from television, radio, smartphones, the Internet, and, more quaintly, books, magazines, and newspapers. Most of these language sources offer us increasingly intertwined combinations of information, entertainment, and advertising. The result is distraction: there is too much to take in, too much to sort, too much to think about, too many truth claims to assess. The result is also stagnation, and the dominant ideology is reified. Thus in our contemporary society the officially defined status quo may be viewed with cynicism, but the multifarious, media-supplied discourses leave the populace without a means of articulating other possible realities, and even if they did, the prevailing cynicism regarding attempts at sincere assertions would result in yet another failure to communicate. This state of affairs is manifested in the complacency represented by the frogs and represented in *The Frogs* by the mélange of clichés, allusions, and cultural references.

The Frogs proposes the possibility of action and change, the first step of which is climbing out of our language-bound complacencies. By the end of the contest, Dionysos realizes that Shaw, whatever his intellect and wit, cannot save the world, because his words, the volumes of which surround him during the debate, would just add to the already overwhelming sea of language in which society is drowning. His ideas may be valuable, but he is intolerant and overbearing, a better speaker than listener who would be at home among cable television's shouting pundits. Dionysos chooses to bring Shakespeare back because he is a poet who can touch his listeners' hearts as he reaches their minds. He is able to express the human experience in language that defamiliarizes it, that makes it simultaneously familiar and new. His poetry, if we really engage it, forces us to look, really look (as *Sunday in the Park*'s Georges Seurat would ask us to) at ourselves and our world and to see everything with new eyes. As Dionysos and Shakespeare leave the underworld, the Dionysians sing,

> Bring a sense of purpose,
> Bring the taste of words,
> Bring the sound of wit,
> Bring the feel of passion,
> Bring the glow of thought
> To the darkening earth. (*F* 300)

Then, in "Final Instructions to the Audience," Dionysos offers instructions, not on how to watch the play, but on how to be active in the world:

Don't just shrug,
Content to be a conscientious slug.
It's fine to feel contented, safe and snug,
But soon enough contented turns to smug.
Don't shovel what's uncomfortable underneath the rug.
Speak up! Get sore!
Do something more than just deplore. (*F* 300)

In a sense, *The Frogs* has taken advantage of the theater's position of marginalization in a digital-media world and of that world's condescension to the musical theater especially to place before us both a demonstration of the threat of ideological stagnation in a language-sodden society and the possibility of reinvigorating language to make it a vehicle for reimagining the possibilities for reality.

Sondheim's newest show as of this writing has had, like *The Frogs*, a long history, but a significantly more troubled one. Between 1999 and 2008, it had three major productions and underwent four titles and countless revisions.[43] Written with *Pacific Overtures* and *Assassins* collaborator John Weidman, *Road Show* is the story of Wilson and Addison Mizner, colorful brothers who cut a swath through the United States in the first third of the twentieth century. Their story was told by Alva Johnston in the 1950s in a series of articles for the *New Yorker* that were later collected in a book, *The Legendary Mizners*. Wilson was what Johnston calls a "conversational artist,"[44] reportedly the wittiest man of his time and something of a shady Renaissance man. During his life, he was involved in numerous pursuits—prospecting in the Yukon, running a New York hotel of ill repute, playwriting, managing prizefighters, marrying a wealthy widow, hawking real estate, screenwriting—and he almost always managed to turn his vocations into some kind of con game. Sondheim describes him as "someone with too many talents and too few principles."[45] Addison, in comparison with Wilson, was the respectable brother, but only in comparison. After some traveling and living as a hanger-on in New York's high society, Addison discovered a calling as an architect. His style, which was an amalgamation of other styles from around the world, especially Spain, became for a time the latest thing in Florida, where many of the buildings he designed in Palm Beach and Boca Raton still stand.[46] Both brothers became involved in the 1920s Florida land boom, and when the bubble burst, so did their fortunes.

Sondheim was first drawn to *The Legendary Mizners* as possible musical material in the 1950s, but at that time the stage rights to the book were controlled by Irving Berlin and S. N. Behrman for a show that was never completed. (Berlin had known the Mizners and was a stockholder in the Mizner Development Corporation in Boca Raton. Perhaps drawing on that experience, he had treated the Florida land boom years earlier, in the Marx Brothers musical *The Cocoanuts* [1926].) Forty years later, Sondheim returned to the subject with Weidman. Sondheim initially imagined the play to be about Wilson, but Weidman saw the potential of telling the stories of both brothers. They eventually saw the drama as being based in the conflict between the destructive (Wilson) and the productive (Addison) sides of the American Dream, or as Sondheim puts it, the "symbiotic relationship between the two visionaries, one a snake-oil entrepreneur, the other a creative dreamer."[47] After years of gestation, workshops, and regional theater productions, *Road Show* finally opened in New York on 18 November 2008 at the Off-Broadway nonprofit Public Theater. It was staged on and around a huge pile of apparently junked desks, file cabinets, and other office furniture, the detritus of failed entrepreneurship, set in an otherwise empty space bound by the dark, brick theater walls.

Road Show brings together themes from many of Sondheim's previous musicals. Like *Follies* and *Merrily We Roll Along,* it critiques the connection of life stories and journey metaphors as a means of finding meaning. Like *Assassins,* it explores the dark side of the American Dream. Like *Gypsy,* it depicts an entropic America, looping back onto itself and slowly running down. Like *Passion* and *The Frogs,* it shows a society drowning in exhausted and referentless language and the desperate need to break out of the consequent hyperreality. These themes are put in motion in its opening number, "Waste." The play begins with Addison on his deathbed, reaching out for something, and then, with a last gasp, dying. He has reached the final narrative standpoint of his life, the point where the life story moves out of time and stands as a completed, supposedly meaning-providing structure. What he finds, however, in this office-furniture-junk-pile of an afterlife, are the various people he knew in the times of his life, all pronouncing judgment on his life story, summing it up and interpreting it as a waste. We have seen this kind of life-narratizing critiqued before, and some of the same objections are presented here. One is that incidents can be narratized and interpreted in different ways, making the meaning of a life story contested or negotiated. Lives or parts of lives can mean multiply and thus resist being contained in a single story. This resistance to containment connects to a second objection to the narratized life. Life events are random, incidents occur by chance, events have many meanings or perhaps none. The narrative organization and containment of life events—governed by the principles of origin, end, and cause and effect—necessarily distort them. A life is altogether too messy to be contained in a well-structured, meaning-providing narrative. *Road Show* makes this clear as, after the first scene in the afterlife, Addison and Wilson revert to young men and we see their adventures played out chronologically until we end up with them again after their deaths. Their lives are packed with incidents, but the incidents don't cohere into a neat, well-made narrative, and cause and effect are supplanted by chance, surprise, and capriciousness. As the brothers, reunited in death, lie in bed and contemplate eternity, the set a junk pile and the stage littered with the $100 bills characters have thrown around all evening, their father announces, "I expected you'd make history, boys. Instead, you made a mess."[48]

Implied in the foregoing is another significance of the title "Waste": the movement from order to chaos—entropy. One of the ways the tension between order and chaos, progress and devolution, is established is through the metaphor of the journey. The brothers are brought from the afterlife to a flashback of their youths by their mother calling them to their father's deathbed. Papa Mizner leaves his sons not with an inheritance but with a charge. He says that "with the dawning of a new century, your work begins. The work of determining what type of nation we shall be" (16). As he sings of America as "a land of opportunity and more" (*L* 220), he seems, in his waistcoat and top hat, to represent the class of men who, following Manifest Destiny and enacting the frontier thesis, moved west, helped settle and define the territory that became the United States, and grew prosperous. (According to Johnston, Lansing Bond Mizner "was a lawyer, politician, railroad promoter, land speculator, and presiding officer of the

California Senate for many years, and was often suggested for Governor."[49] Unlike Papa Mizner in the play, he did not die broke.) Papa asks his sons to imagine "a road straight ahead" that will allow them to achieve "the very best / That you can be" (*L* 220). His philosophy clearly envisions history as linear and progressive. This, at any rate, is how he experienced history in the second half of the nineteenth century and how he imagines his sons will experience it in the first half of the twentieth. His faith is in an infinitely improvable world. This faith, however, introduces an interesting paradox. On the one hand, he urges his sons to have a destination for their journey, a goal for their lives. On the other hand, as he sings, the road "never ends" (*L* 220). Whatever one achieves, there is always "something better just around the corner" (*L* 220). This certainty recalls Mrs. Lovett's perpetually deferred desire and suggests an open-ended road, one with no definite destination or meaning-providing endpoint.

Papa's song contains the contradictions at the heart of Manifest Destiny. As a philosophy its goal was the conquering, settling, and civilizing of the continent for European-descended Americans. As a practice, its movement was a clear line from east to west. As a myth of America and Americans, however, it has no end. It remains a motivating force behind our national and personal ambitions. Papa Mizner's generation reached the westernmost point of the continent and in that sense closed the frontier, but they did not close the myth-generated desire for progress, achievement, and wealth. His bequest to his sons is this myth. The boys' response to this bequest makes up the main dramatic tension of the play. In a country with no remaining frontiers, where language is used up, and where hype takes precedence over reality, how does one escape from the closed system of the dying, entropic world and find what is beyond, the new?

Like *Gypsy*'s Rose, a pioneer woman without a frontier, the Mizner brothers, in their search for a new frontier in the new century, are forced by the dead end of the Pacific Ocean to abandon the progressive, vector-like movement west and instead circle back around the points of the compass. They go north to the Yukon, east to New York City, and south to Florida. Addison, on his own, loops around in the other direction, the Yukon to Honolulu to Bombay to Hong Kong to Guatemala and then to New York. Compared with the westward movement of the frontier thesis and their father's philosophy of Manifest Destiny, this circular movement suggests a lack of direction, goal, and purpose. As in *Gypsy*, it suggests movement for the sake of movement, a gradual but inevitable loss of energy, and the loss of meaning from the American mythos. The myth of purpose, opportunity, and success that the boys inherited from their father is now an empty story.

Earlier, we noted the authors' sense that Addison represents the productive aspect of the American Dream and Wilson the destructive aspect. However, as we examine the characters closely, we see that their relationship, positioned as it is in the context of a twentieth-century America collapsing in on itself, lacking direction and meaning, is not so rigidly dichotomous. Addison's creativity, his talent for design and ambition to build, is not so much an ability to discover the new as it is a knack for rearranging the old. At the end of "Addison's Trip," when each of his business ventures has resulted in failure and a boatload of souvenirs—desks, chairs, fans, tureens, screens, trunks—Addison has an epiphany: he can imagine how these pieces from Hawaii, India, China, and Central America can be satisfyingly arranged in relation to each other, and he can imagine the space, the building or house, in which this arrangement can be set. Addison's architectural and design style is, in fact, a bricolage of styles borrowed piecemeal from other cultures and combined. As he says, his designs have "Echoes of Guatemala, a touch of the British Raj, a little bit of everything I picked up while I was traveling" (43). He tells Hollis's aunt that "every house should have a history," and then he creates one for the house he is designing for her: he imagines a castle in Spain, hundreds of years old, beset first by Saracens, then by Goths, and finally by the Moors, "Raping and pillaging, and putting in cabanas and a tennis court" (61). Of course, this is an imagined history, not an actual one. (Johnston recounts how Addison would distress furniture, walls, and finishings to give the impression of age and how he would order his workers to march up and down staircases wearing hobnail shoes to make them appear worn with hundreds of years of use.[50]) Thus his combinations of architectural styles do not represent actual history so much as Baudrillardian hyperreal history, a history made into image. Seen in this way, Addison's designs arise from and participate in the exhaustion of discourse, referentless styles combining and recombining endlessly with other referentless styles.

Where Addison shows his immersion in the exhaustion of discourses through his architectural style, Wilson shows it through his ambiguous relation to language. On the one hand, he accepts his father's dying words as a watchcry, frequently quoting them and relying on them as he moves from scheme to scheme. In this case, for him, language points toward a truth about the world. But in every other case, his schemes rely on a conscious overuse of language—a hype—that, rather than pointing toward a truth about the world, creates a self-serving, con man's reality, temporary, but one, while it lasts, that Wilson can operate in and get others to believe in. We see this just after his father's death when he spins a narrative fantasy to persuade Addison to go to the Yukon. Once camping out on a claim, of course, he is the first one to become disillusioned by the actual conditions there—so different from the fantasy he created—and throw it over for another temporary fantasy, running a saloon. His use of language, like Addison's architecture, promotes image at the expense of content.

Wilson's ambivalent relation to language is responsible for the climactic disaster of the play: the collapse of the Florida land boom and the financial ruin of Addison's dream city, Boca Raton. In a sense we see both brothers as artists here, using the real estate of Boca Raton as a blank canvas on which to create—Addison with pen and ink on his drafting board, Wilson with words over the radio. He claims that a futuristic superhighway leads to the community, that buyers will find buried Spanish doubloons on the beachfront lots, that land values will climb infinitely (all claims that were actually made in land-boom advertising, according to Johnston[51]). When a nervous Hollis Bessemer, the main financial backer and Addison's lover, asks if one of the brothers' claims is true, if the Gulf Stream really touches each lot, Wilson dismissively responds, "Who knows? Is Maxwell House really good to the last drop?" (86). For Hollis, language points to something that is true. For Wilson, it is just language, playing endlessly, making the idea of an ultimate referent irrelevant.

In one sense, then, *Road Show* establishes as its setting an America suffering from the exhaustion of its national narratives, an exhaustion of its artistic discourses, an exhaustion of its language.[52] It is an America that has transformed into a Baudrillardian hyperreality, where image has superseded reality. It is an America with its frontiers closed and its boundaries rigid, a closed system entropically losing energy and meaning, a totalized system in which the possibilities for knowledge, truths, and ways of being are being inexorably stripped away.

In another sense, however, *Road Show* shows us the Mizner brothers, particularly Wilson, offering a response to the seemingly hopelessly determinate, meaning-deprived, and totalized twentieth-century American system. Wilson is adept at engendering narratives as a means of conjuring possibilities for the new in a system that tends to close down possibilities. He explains his philosophy while involved in a Yukon poker game: "The thing that really matters is the game" (*L* 221). Like Bobby in *Company*, Wilson finds the meaning of a narrative in the process of its being narrated, not in the finished structure of the completed narrative. The completed narrative, as we have seen, is equivalent to death, the ultimate closure of the system. A narrative in process offers, not determinate, inevitable death, but, like *Sunday in the Park*'s blank page or canvas, so many possibilities. Wilson tries to make Addison see this, singing, "Every card you're dealt opens new frontiers—" (*L* 221). He adds, near the end of the song,

> It's never really money that's at stake.
> That's nice, but it's just icing on the cake.
> It's your life, every pot,
> What you are, not what you've got.
> Compared to that, the world seems pretty tame. (*L* 222)

In other words, life is conjured not out of a totalized narrative with a meaning-providing endpoint but in the stories that are generated in the moment, stories that enliven an exhausted world.

After marrying wealthy widow Mrs. Myra Yerkes, Wilson acts out his philosophy in "That Was a Year." Finally financially independent, Wilson manages prizefighter Stanley Ketchel, writes a play with Paul Armstrong, and fixes horse races with a jockey, all the while engaging in New York nightlife. He is like a vaudeville performer keeping an astounding number of plates spinning on the top of poles. He sings of New York,

> Every place you look
> Is an open book,

Every street a new frontier!
If you sizzle, swell.
If you fizzle—well,
Nothing fails for long.
If it doesn't fly, it doesn't,
And it's time to sing another song! (*L* 284)

When, at the end of the song, his wife tosses him out, it is partly because of the rate at which he is spending her money, but also partly from sheer exhaustion: she cannot keep up with his many narratives. This encapsulates his attitude toward life. Don't like prospecting? Buy a saloon. Lose the saloon in a poker game? Marry a rich widow. Widow throws you out? Find some new narrative. In his Boca Raton sales pitch, Wilson puts his own spin on his father's vision of a progressive, constantly improving movement through time when he says that as we go along the journey we are constantly "reinventing ourselves" (91).[53] Rather than follow one road or one life story through time to the inevitable closure of death, Wilson takes multiple roads and lives multiple life stories at the same time, taking a quantum leap from one orbit to another or, when necessary, creating a brand new orbit. His philosophy of reinvention, using exhausted language to create something temporarily new and then moving on to something else, allows him to resist closure and entropy.

That his multiple narratives enliven the world can be seen in the pleasure those people who end up being victimized by them take in them. Ketchel, Armstrong, the imprisoned jockey, even to a certain extent Mrs. Yerkes, all remember their year with Willie fondly. This possibility of enlivening the world accounts for Addison's continually becoming caught up in his brother's schemes—prospecting for gold in the Yukon, designing a mansion for Mrs. Yerkes, becoming the artistic genius behind the Boca Raton scheme—against his better judgment. After the spectacular failure of Boca Raton, in the musical climax of the play, Addison tells Wilson to "Get out of my life, / So I can live it . . ." (*L* 212). But the loss of Wilson from his life is connected to his death: while the brothers sing, Wilson prepares Addison's deathbed and tucks him in it; and when Addison repeats his dying gesture of grasping for something, which we saw at the top of the show, it's now clear that he is reaching for his brother. Wilson is irresponsible, selfish, and maddening, but the narratives he generates and acts on at least temporarily resist the entropic, deathward movement of the American myth in the twentieth century.

Road Show's treatment of the theme of transcending closed systems ends ambiguously. On the one hand, Wilson's multiple, enlivening narratives are only temporary. In the Yukon, in New York, and in Florida, he can keep things bouncing only so long. The sound effect of the giant crash that signals the end of the land boom also marks the falling and smashing of Wilson's many spinning plates. On the other hand, in the return to the show's frame, the brothers find themselves in some kind of heavenly afterlife—they have beaten death. Death, it turns out, is not an end—narrative closure, the stoppage of time, the completion of structure—but a beginning, another chance for reinvention, a starting point for infinite possibilities. When Wilson asks, "where do you think guys like us go after they die?," Addison responds, "I don't think they go anywhere. They just keep going . . ." (99). At this point, the road to eternity appears before them, and Wilson proclaims that it is "The greatest opportunity of all!" (99). It is a road that never ends, toward a frontier that never closes, offering infinite possibilities for reinvention and spinning narratives. This is the opposite of the entropy of a closed system. *Road Show* suggests that postmodernism as an alternative to the totalized narratives of the American mythos may not be as exhausted as it appears. In its insistence on multifarious narratives putting multiple worldviews in dialogue, it still offers the possibility for surprise and a way out of a closed system.

Sondheim's career traces a path from the apex and decline of Rodgers and Hammerstein–style realism through a movement toward the postmodern through the dominance of postmodernism to the beginnings of discontent with the postmodern and yearnings for something beyond. In the next chapter, I survey how some of his contemporaries' works engage the spirit and techniques of postmodernism and how some recent musicals by a new generation of composers, lyricists, and librettists have sought to move through the web of self-referring discourse to a reconnection with the real outside of language.

Five

Move On

Having examined the musicals of Stephen Sondheim and his collaborators through the lens of postmodernism, I return now to the broader picture of the musical theater at the end of the twentieth century and beginning of the twenty-first. To start, I want to emphasize three things that I am *not* arguing. First, I am not arguing that as each of these three, perhaps four, aesthetics of the musical theater came along, the door was slammed on previous aesthetics. The Rodgers and Hammerstein musical did not bury the musical comedy nor did the postmodern musical bury the Rodgers and Hammerstein musical. The twenty-first century has seen examples of all three aesthetics on Broadway.

The second thing I am not arguing is that the narrative I have composed to place over my chronological presentation of the musicals Sondheim has written with his collaborators is inevitable, definitive, or totalizing. The foregoing analyses have surely taught us that from a postmodern point of view, narratives are structures brought to phenomena to organize them and give them meaning. Narratives bring with them their own content and, in a way, their own conclusions toward which the events they narrate will be driven. Every set of events can support at least two, probably many more, narratives. Thus the story I have argued for here, the story of Sondheim's career as a bridge spanning the Rodgers and Hammerstein era and the postmodern era, as well as the burgeoning aesthetic of the new century, is to me a helpful one because it places his work in a larger cultural and aesthetic context and gives us interpretive strategies for approaching his work that I hope are revealing. I am aware that other narratives—other ways of organizing his career and other conclusions to draw from it—are possible, and I think this is a good thing. As we saw in our discussion of Bakhtin, the more narratives we have competing to persuade us, the richer the resulting dialogues and the more likely that participants in the dialogue will be inspired to find their own ways of understanding. The third thing I am not arguing is that the musicals by Sondheim and his collaborators are unique in being manifestations of what I have called the *postmodern aesthetic*. They are, in my opinion, the smartest, richest, and most rewarding ones, but there are other playwrights, lyricists, composers, directors, and choreographers who over the past fifty years produced musicals that demonstrate many of the aesthetic characteristics I have examined here and, concomitantly, explored the same kinds of themes concerning the problems of knowing the world, defining the self, and reproducing or resisting ideology. This is not to say that these other musicals were directly influenced by what Sondheim and his collaborators were doing. Rather, these shows were immersed in and responding to the postmodern zeitgeist in the way that many artists in many genres—serious and popular—were.

It is beyond the scope of this study to offer a comprehensive review of the postmodern musical theater, but I will offer a brief survey of some of the musicals that operate in ways and explore ideas similar to Sondheim's. There were a number of shows that, to varying degrees of seriousness, experimented with self-referentiality of form. That is, they self-consciously set their stories in forms other than the realistic narrative so as to provide an analogue or metaphor for their subject and to emphasize the performative nature of their stories and characters. *Pippin* (1972) foregrounds the musical-comedy form as a way of tracing its title character's search for a meaningful life. The Leading Player and his company of actors are certain that the search is doomed to failure because they have completely bought into the life-is-show-business metaphor: everything is an act; there is only a void behind the makeup and scenery. Pippin surprises them by finding that meaning, modest and contingent though it may be, can be found through love of another. *Chicago* (1975) employs the vaudeville form to tell the story of two murderesses who turn their notoriety into show-business success. Ensemble members announce the musical numbers, which are then performed presentationally. More cynical than *Pippin,* this show offers no redemption to the life-is-show-business metaphor. *Your Arms Too Short to Box with God* (1976) uses the form of a black revival meeting to engage and re-present the Gospel according to Matthew. *Barnum* (1980) takes the form of a circus, complete with ringmaster, to tell the story of showman P. T. Barnum and his more reserved, pragmatic wife. The main conflict of the play is between Barnum's flash and humbug and Mrs. Barnum's practicality, but the play's form stacks the evening very much in the former's favor. The second act of *A Day in Hollywood/A Night in the Ukraine* (1980) uses the form of a Marx Brothers movie to treat Anton Chekhov's story "The Bear," the disjunction between form and content providing much of the humor. *Nine* (1982) uses the form of a film to explore the psychological background of a director suffering from writer's block—he cannot create a satisfactory narrative for his next film or for his life. *Grind* (1985) uses the form of burlesque to turn its Depression-era burlesque-house setting into a microcosm of American racial and gender injustice. *The Mystery of Edwin Drood* (1985) uses a music-hall form and setting to layer performance on top of performance and confuse notions of a stable identity. Near the end, the audience votes to determine the solution to Charles Dickens's unfinished mystery, thus unsettling epistemological expectations for a stable, totalized narrative.

Another set of shows was purposely plotless, using something akin to the revue form in order to collapse plot-dictated distinctions in time, place, and character and to explore an idea or theme from a variety of angles. This focus on primarily presenting an idea, with plot and characters secondary, if they were there at all, was labeled by some reviewers as the *concept musical.*[1] *Godspell* (1971) overlays the Gospel according to Matthew with a series of songs and skits so as to reimagine the story of Jesus for the age of the counterculture. *Ain't Supposed to Die a Natural Death* (1971) and *Don't Bother Me, I Can't Cope* (1972) both employ the revue form to explore the urban black experience. *A Chorus Line* (1975) uses an audition for a Broadway-musical ensemble as a setting to explore the inner lives of dancers. *Runaways* (1978) uses the revue form to examine children who, for various reasons, have run away from home. *Working* (1978) studies labor in contemporary America: who does it, why they do it, and what forms it takes. *Is There Life after High School?* (1982) looks back at high school from a variety of adults' perspectives to discover the ways that experience has shaped their grown-up lives.

Another set of musicals challenged the conventions of narrative structure by breaking down boundaries between narrator and narration, between the outer life and inner life of characters, and between what is supposed to be fiction and what is supposed to be reality. *I Love My Wife* (1977) brought its small band from the pit to the stage, where the musicians (besides playing their instruments) acted as characters inside the story and narrators and commentators outside the story. *They're Playing Our Song* (1979) is essentially a two-character musical, but each character is supported by three actors representing his or her internal voices and thus fragmenting the coherent self each character tries to present to the world. *City of Angels* (1989) tells two stories: one about a hard-boiled-mystery novelist who is writing a screenplay based on one of his books; the other about the detective in the screenplay that is being written. As the play goes on, the boundary between the real-life frame and the fictional screenplay becomes fuzzy and then breaks down completely. By the end, instead of the novelist creating and controlling the world of the detective, the detective is controlling events in the so-called real world. *Kiss of the Spider Woman* (1993) is set in the prison of a repressive South American country. A Marxist rebel learns from his homosexual cellmate how to escape from the pain of the moment into fantasies inspired by movie musicals. The movies, however, have a life of their own: their star, Aurora, who in her role of the Spider Woman symbolizes death, plots to ensnare both men.

While many shows, most successfully *1776* (1969), found their subject matter in actual history, some musicals were historical while simultaneously being about how history is narratized and the power it has to shape our knowledge of our nation and our sense of identity. *Hallelujah, Baby!* (1967) sets three African American characters who never age against changing American history from the turn of the century to the mid-1960s. This reversal—we usually see a fairly stable social setting while characters change—allowed the play to foreground the ways in which social dynamics, including economic depression and war, create the conditions that define the possibilities for identity. The play shows us the characters struggling against or submitting to the limitations of these possibilities and sometimes struggling against each other as they seek a human and humane way to be. Similarly, *1600 Pennsylvania Avenue* (1976), with Leonard Bernstein's last score for Broadway, uses the White House as its setting and a metaphor and traces American history from its first president to the beginning of the twentieth century, looking at history through the frame of racial division: the presidents and their wives on the one side and the White House's black servants on the other. All the presidents, wives, and servants are played by the same four actors, lending a sense of continuity to the problem of race relations while social conditions arranged them in different permutations. The various historical scenes are set in the context of a play rehearsal, foregrounding the theatricality of the evening and serving as a metaphor for our nation's history as a series of attempts to get things right. *Evita* (1979) offers a complex presentation of the construction of history through the frames of two antagonists, both historical figures. On the one hand, the play presents the story of Eva Perón through her own attempts at mythmaking. On the other hand, the Argentine-born Communist guerrilla Che Guevara provides a constant, skeptical commentary questioning Eva's motives and actions, but he is also bewildered by the popular appeal of the myth and almost seduced by it. The play leaves us wondering where, if anywhere, the truth of Eva, the truth of history, lies.

As we saw in the preceding three chapters, the aesthetic of postmodernism, by challenging the limits of the realist aesthetic, including its rigid reliance on a narrative construction of reality and its celebration of an autonomous, ideologically neutral individual, offered new possibilities for how meaning can be conjured, especially in its liberating meaning from the restrictions of totalized systems and recognizing the value of nontotalized, ambiguous, contingent meaning. We saw how it helps us understand the person as a subject constructed within a social process of power relations and ideological reproduction. We saw how it insists on the mediated nature of experience, that our knowledge of ourselves and our world is layered by a variety of discourse systems. We also saw the concern that, by the 1990s, many of the aesthetic features of postmodernism were themselves becoming formulaic. More important, we saw how Sondheim's most recent musicals addressed a broader cultural sense that postmodernism's self-referentiality and intertwining language systems had reached a point of crisis. His musicals, in their form, style, and content, began to express a desire to work through the freeplay of language to say real things about a world we all more or less share. These more recent aspects of the postmodern musical have been manifested in the musical theater of the 1990s and twenty-first century, with some shows acknowledging the trap of discourse and representation and seeking a way to the real.

One sign of the routinization of the postmodern aesthetic is the frequency with which postmodern techniques, especially self-referentiality, are employed for easy laughs. In *The Producers* (2001), when Ulla makes the girl-shy Leo Bloom nervous, she breaks the fourth wall, asking why he walks so far down stage right. Later, in the song "Betrayed," jailed Max Bialystock summarizes the show's action, even sitting silently for a few moments to mark the intermission. *Spamalot* (2005) relies on self-referentiality more centrally for its humor. In "The Song That Goes like This," Sir Galahad and the Lady of the Lake mock the contemporary Broadway-pop love duet, singing not of each other but of the song itself, especially its seemingly never-ending key changes. In "The Diva's Lament," the Lady of the Lake complains about her diminished role in the second act. By the end of the show, the search for the Holy Grail has been transformed into the scramble for a hit musical. *[title of show]* (2006, Off Broadway; revised for Broadway 2008) takes self-referentiality even further: it is a show about the writing of the show we're seeing. The actors, two of whom, Hunter Bell and Jeff Bowen, wrote the show, play themselves as characters in the past writing the show and as characters in the present telling us about their writing the show. The musical is full of jokes for theatrical insiders (announcing an impending key change in the opening number; voice messages left by such stars as Kerry Butler, Marin Mazzie, and Emily Skinner; a reference to actress Mary Stout being hit by a runaway hot-dog cart) and jokes recognizing the artificiality of the proceedings. In all of these cases the self-referentiality works humorously but not with the defamiliarization postmodern theater strives to achieve. In fact, it's the very familiarity of this breaking of the fourth wall that makes it such an easy way to get a laugh.

Connected to and at times overlapping with this use of self-referentiality for easy laughs is the use of awareness of form to mock the form, what one might call the self-loathing musical. This kind of musical generates laughs by basically calling attention to the silliness of the musical form: the overused showbiz conventions of song and dance; the absurdity of

people breaking into song; the supposed inappropriateness of the musical form for treating certain kinds of content. The most successful of this
kind of musical is *Urinetown* (2001). Set in a not-too-distant future, when
water has become so scarce that people must pay a fee to pee, *Urinetown*
explores issues of social justice, resource management, the failure of revolution, and the operations of power. It also, however, explores itself as a
musical play and the failures of the form, primarily through the narration
of Officer Lockstock and his conversations with Little Sally, an urchin.
Early on, Sally encourages Lockstock to explain to the audience the water
shortage:

> LOCKSTOCK: Everything in its time, Little Sally. You're too young to
> understand it now, but nothing can kill a show like too much exposi-
> tion.
> LITTLE SALLY: How about bad subject matter?
> LOCKSTOCK: Well—
> LITTLE SALLY: Or a bad title, even? That could kill a show pretty
> good.[2]

The self-loathing musical is a twenty-first-century version of 1950s shows
like *Little Mary Sunshine* and *The Boyfriend,* which mocked a previous
generation's musical conventions, knowing the audience would be familiar enough with the conventions to get the joke. That the postmodern
musical's conventions can be similarly mocked confirms that its form,
once so startling, has become formulaic.

Audience familiarity with the heightened attention to form has not
only reduced this postmodern technique to the conventional, it also can
have something of a reactionary effect. In providing a frame for the narrative, many recent musicals, instead of drawing attention to the artificiality
of the proceedings as the Sondheim-Prince musicals of the 1970s did,
end up offering an aesthetic justification for the characters breaking into
song, as in their own way the Rodgers and Hammerstein musicals did. For
example, *Catch Me If You Can* (2011) begins with the capture of elusive
con man Frank Abagnale Jr., then takes the audience into his imagination
as he presents his life story in the form of a 1960s TV special. During the
preshow for *Once* (2012), audience members are welcomed onstage to the

working Irish pub while the cast members perform a variety of traditional songs. As showtime approaches, the patrons are ushered to their seats, the lights dim, and an unnamed guy with a guitar begins singing and performing his story of the Czech girl who restored his faith in his music and himself. In both cases, the frame creates a context in which characters performing songs and dances seems "natural."

This is not to say that the musical's consideration of its own form must be clichéd; several shows of the early twenty-first century made startling use of form. Some musicals brought popular contemporary music to bear on historical subjects. The power of *Spring Awakening* (2006) comes from the juxtaposition of the puritanical constraints put on its late nineteenth-century German adolescent characters and the sexual exuberance of the contemporary rock music with which they express themselves. Similarly, *Bloody Bloody Andrew Jackson* tells the story of the seventh president, especially his relations with and ultimate displacement of the Native Americans, with an emo-inflected rock score, which makes the story resonate with such contemporary issues as concentrated power, the dangers of populism, and the war on terror. *Here Lies Love* (2013) juxtaposes the story of Imelda and Ferdinand Marcos with its immersive staging in a 1970s-era dance club. *If/Then* (2014) begins with a quotidian moment when its protagonist makes a choice and then follows and interweaves the two strikingly different life stories that result. *Hamilton* (2015) uses multiracial casting and a rap-infused score to defamiliarize the history of America's founding fathers.

Other musicals made use of the history of the musical-theater form to develop their ideas. *Grey Gardens,* based on Albert and David Maysles's documentary about Jacqueline Kennedy's eccentric aunt and cousin, Edith Bouvier Beale and "Little" Edie Beale, places its two acts in two different historical moments and two different musical-theater aesthetics. Act 1, in which Edith sabotages Edie's engagement to Joseph Kennedy Jr., takes place in 1941, and its style—from narration to song style and placement to choreography to realistic set design—recalls the just-pre–Rodgers and Hammerstein musicals of the time. Act 2, which shows elderly Edith and middle-aged Edie trapped in their run-down, overgrown East Hampton mansion, takes place in 1973, and its style—essentially narrativeless and surreal in look and sound—suggests the postmodern musicals of the time, especially *Follies*. Interestingly, neither act is presented parodically; the audience is not invited to laugh at the conventions of either time period. Rather, each style makes possible the story each act wants to tell.

The Drowsy Chaperone (2006) places a fictional 1920s musical comedy, set in a fancy country home and involving a Broadway star who plans to give up show business to marry the heir to an oil fortune, within a contemporary frame wherein a nameless man in a New York City apartment plays for the audience his treasured LP cast recording of the 1920s musical *The Drowsy Chaperone* and talks us through its background and plot. His commentary on the 1920s musical points up the clichés, the stock characters, the narrative non sequiturs, but not so much mockingly as lovingly. In the end, the community represented by the older musical, with its climactic multiple marriages, contrasts sharply with the isolation and loneliness of the contemporary scene, where the narrator is deprived of both connections with others and an identity.

The Scottsboro Boys (2010) uses the minstrel-show form to tell the story of nine black men who were accused of raping two white women in 1931 Alabama. Their blatantly unfair trial became a cause célèbre for northern liberal groups. The minstrel-show form raises issues of representation: how the means of representation mediate between an event and our understanding of the event. In this case, representation as an ideological process is emphasized by the minstrel show's history as an entertainment performed by white actors in blackface, parodying and perpetuating black stereotypes of speech, behavior, and character.[3] Although in the opening number one of the performers asks if they can perform the *true* story this time, the show's form, with its riot of representation—each character performing multiple roles, black and white, male and female; the lies that ensnare the accused men; the real issues of race that the minstrel-show form masks—works against the revealing of any truth. While one character gives up his chance for a pardon because he refuses to give a false confession, the others, in a shocking visual moment, perform the finale in blackface: whatever historical truth lies in the heart of the Scottsboro Boys' story has been lost as they and their story have become entertainment, feeding white society's preconceptions of them as either sexually voracious predators or virtuous martyrs.

The Scottsboro Boys, with its story of the truth buried beneath shifting layers of representation, provides a good transition to a final set of
recent musicals, musicals that join *Passion, The Frogs,* and *Road Show*
in acknowledging but trying to work past the dead end of self-referring
discourse to reference some version of a shared social world outside of
the constructs of narrative and language. These musicals offer examples
of how some of the composers, lyricists, librettists, and directors have
engaged the challenges of the post-postmodern world and contributed
to developing a new aesthetic for the musical theater.

Parade (1998), based on a historic incident, tells the story of Leo Frank,
Brooklyn-born Jew transplanted to Atlanta, who in 1913 was accused of
raping and murdering Mary Phagan, a young girl who worked in his pen-
cil factory. A media circus, political intrigue, and inept legal representation convicted Frank, but, after two years of appeals, the governor in a
politically courageous act commuted his death sentence. However, the
commutation inspired a mob to drag Frank from his jail cell and lynch
him. The play's title refers to its organizing formal conceit: the Confeder-
ate Memorial Day parade, which is part of a process by which the post-
bellum South has generated and reified a myth about itself as a pure,
beautiful, free, and honorable land that has been conquered and degraded
by outsiders. Leo is doomed because his story is so easily cast in terms of
the myth; he is the ravaging Northerner who has destroyed a symbol of
the South's purity. He is thus caught up in larger discourses—the press,
history, religion—that end up dictating his identity. As in *The Scottsboro
Boys,* the truth is lost under layers of ideologically charged discourse, but,
critically, both plays insist on there being a truth—the innocence of their
characters—beyond the language being used to construct it. The multiple
discourses, far from offering the liberation the postmodern heyday promised, here serve as conduits for bringing ideology to bear on its subjects.

Floyd Collins (1996), also based on an actual incident, focuses on its
title character, a spelunker, who, in early 1925, became trapped in a cave
in rural Kentucky. While numerous rescue attempts failed, Floyd's story
grew to be the center of a media frenzy and something of a macabre carnival as newsmen, tourists, salesmen, and hucksters descended on the
site of the cave. As the carnival spun off into a life of its own, Floyd died.
The first section of the play is a long soliloquy for Floyd as he squeezes

through an underground passage and finds the Great Sand Cave. The cave offers a suggestion of the numinous, the ineffable: Floyd experiences it, but cannot know it directly. At first, being in the cave is a religious moment for Floyd, but, after a moment, he signs his name on the dirt floor, claiming ownership of the space and textualizing it. Then thoughts of the numinous disappear as he imagines commercializing the space. Ironically, what Floyd plans to do to the cave is done to him after he becomes trapped: he is textualized and commercialized and subsequently lost. This process of textualization and commercialization disguises the thing that has created the attention and excitement: the very real possibility that Floyd will die. As we saw in our discussion of *Passion,* death is a thing, like the numinous cave, that cannot be represented. At the end of the play, all hope of rescue gone, Floyd reflects on the contact with the ineffable he had flirted with when he first found the cave and about the nature of death, acknowledging that what he wants to know lies beyond the ability of any human systems of knowledge to contain. *Floyd Collins* presents characters and a society trapped in degraded, pettily commercial discourses, trapped every bit as much as Floyd is trapped in his underground passage. The language presented here, far from opening up possibilities for new ways to know and to be, both limits everyone's potential for life and closes off the possibility for the experience of other realities, other worlds.

A Man of No Importance (2002) is set in 1964 Dublin and concerns Alfie Byrne, a bus conductor who sublimates his repressed homosexual desire for his driver into a passion for art, especially the work of Oscar Wilde. Like Charles in *Evening Primrose,* Alfie sees art as something that transcends real life, existing separate from and unsullied by everyday human concerns. As this faith in transcendent art begins to break down, he realizes that his life has been a multilayered performance, from his poetry readings on the bus to the parts he plays in everyday life: brother, bus conductor, good pal, and observant Catholic—an ordinary, unimportant man—his desires complicating every one of these roles. He ends the play seeing the need to immerse himself in the world, rather than try to escape it, order it, and make it safe through art.

Rent (1996), set in the late 1980s, Lower East Side world of a number of young, out-of-the-mainstream artists, offers a different take on art in the postmodern era. Unlike Alfie Byrne, the artists in *Rent* are under no illusion that art transcends the real or provides an escape from society. Their lives and their art are complicated by a variety of social pressures, manifested in the play by AIDS, drug abuse, homelessness, gentrification, and outrageous income inequality. This play's basic question is: How can artists create art in the Baudrillardian hyperreality the United States has become? They strive for an art that is creation ex nihilo rather than the rearrangement of existing images, narratives, discourses, and language. We see, however, that the characters cannot create the breaking-through art they want because they are too caught up in petty personal distractions—egos, defensiveness, judgments, selfishness—that prevent them from really communicating with each other much less with a broader audience. As the play reaches its climax, Angel, with his example of self-lessness, and Mimi, the weak character others take advantage of, inspire artistic and personal breakthroughs for blocked artists Roger and Mark. Roger is finally able to write his song, "Your Eyes," when he recognizes his identification and interconnection with Mimi. Mark, inspired by Angel's immersion in life, in the moment, and in others' good, completes his film, which, it turns out, is the play we have been watching all along.

See What I Wanna See (2005), two one-act musicals by Michael John LaChiusa, develops many of the same themes connected with the transition from postmodernism, yet, as the first musical to deal directly with a specifically post-9/11 America, it addresses the loss of faith in the real and the need for some kind of definite truth with more urgency than the other fin-de-siècle musicals we have discussed. The act 2 "Gloryday" is narrated by a priest who has lost his faith after the destruction of the World Trade Center. Unable to console the many people who turn to him in the wake of the disaster, he decides to show them that the consolation, absolution, and faith they seek from him are lies, so he posts notices that on a certain date, at a certain time, Christ will rise from the Central Park pond. In a city full of people needy for something to believe in, the lie has a ready audience and metastasizes. The priest has fallen into postmodern despair. He concludes that there is no God, no transcendent intelligence who, as creator and guardian, assures us that, even when life seems chaotic, there is an order, a purpose, a meaning to life. Further, he questions any kind of transcendent signified, any center that grounds systems of reference or systems of signification to a definite reality, something, in other words, that makes real the connection between word and object, between image and referent. On the appointed day, while a tornado scatters the gathered throngs, the priest indeed sees Christ rise from the pond, though he is the only one who does. His Aunt Monica, a onetime atheist whose cancer has motivated a turn to the spiritual, missed the miracle too, but when the priest tells her what he saw and asks if she believes him, she replies, "If you say so, baby. Why not?"[4] This, as it turns out, is the closest to truth we can come: our knowledge systems and discourses are incapable of containing, representing, or communicating the transcendent.

The postmodern musical of Stephen Sondheim, his collaborators, and his contemporaries, then, has taken two general forms in the twenty-first century. The first is represented by the acceptance and casual use of the now-familiar conventions of postmodernism, usually divorced from the intellectual depth or aesthetic and social subversion these conventions originally implied. The second is represented by the confrontation with the intellectual legacy of postmodernism, the desire to redeem discourse and gain access to a real beyond language. A few months before his *See What I Wanna See* opened at the Public Theater, Michael John LaChiusa published an article titled "The Great Gray Way," in which he assessed the state of the Broadway musical and candidly criticized many successful shows. His complaint about the majority of Broadway musicals, most of them reproducing on stage popular movies or weaving a plot of some kind around a series of already popular songs, is that they operate out of a degraded or mindless popular postmodernism, although he does not use that term. The term he uses is *faux-musical,* which he draws from Plato's idea of a simulacra: a "'copy of a copy,' a fake that seems more real than the real thing."[5] (We might also think of Baudrillard's hyperreality.) He explains,

> All sense of invention and craft is abandoned in favor of delivering what the audience thinks a musical should deliver. Everyone involved, from the usher to the stage manager to the producer to the landlord to the critic, is satisfied. There is no challenge, no confrontation, no art—and everyone sighs with relief. [. . .]

No aesthetic is involved in creating the *faux*-musical, and it's pointless to disparage the effort or claim that they prove the American Musical is dead. The best of them are exacting copies; they fool the eye and ear to perfection. [. . .]

Instead of choreography, there is dancing. Instead of crafted songwriting, there is tune-positioning. *Faux*-musicals are mechanical; they have to be. For expectations to be met, there can be no room for risk, derring-do or innovation.[6]

Those Broadway musicals that do challenge, that do take risks, and that do aspire to art invariably originate at some nonprofit theater venue, just as all of Sondheim's musicals over the past thirty years have and just as the last five musicals discussed in this chapter have. One might extrapolate from this that there are two kinds of musicals: the faux-musical that dominates Broadway; and the artistically ambitious musical that resides in the nonprofit sector.

Of course, there is nothing new about the two kinds of musicals— one claiming to be nothing but entertainment, the other more serious. The season after *Sweeney Todd* dominated the Tony Awards, one of the big commercial hits was *Sugar Babies,* an unembarrassed love letter to burlesque. Still, when *Oklahoma!* changed the musical theater in 1943, it was a huge success and inspired other musicals to follow in the path it had broken to the point that for better than twenty years, the Rodgers and Hammerstein–style musical dominated Broadway. However, when Sondheim, his collaborators, and his contemporaries pushed the musical in the direction of the postmodern, investors, reviewers, and audiences were not always ready to follow.

It may be useful to consider that, in addition to there being two kinds of musicals, there are two kinds of audiences. Hans Robert Jauss offers a helpful concept: the horizon of expectations. He argues that at any given historical and cultural moment, there is a horizon of expectations, a field marked off by the rough boundaries of the rules and conventions for how audiences expect a work in a given genre to operate. Formula works rely completely on the expected rules and conventions and so can satisfy, but rarely surprise, can be financially successful, but rarely advance the art form. More aesthetically serious works try in various ways to break the rules and defy the conventions and thus surprise their audiences and advance the art form. These kinds of works of art stretch the horizon of expectations in such a way that audiences can move with them. New horizons are created, and other works of art take on the task of stretching them further.[7] To connect this back to LaChiusa's argument, what he calls faux-musicals are those that seek, given the economic conditions under which Broadway musicals are produced, to perfectly meet the audience's horizon of expectations, to send the audience home satisfied, happy, and loaded down with T-shirts, mugs, and souvenir booklets. The faux-musical is mindlessly postmodern, an image of an image, and it is essentially a product. The artistically serious musical seeks to surprise, challenge, and unsettle the audience by playing with the rules and confounding expectations. As Sondheim says, "To me, the theatre is about [. . .] surprise."[8] This is not to say that such a show does not entertain, but there are ideas behind the entertainment. We can remember Sondheim's often-quoted statement of his and his collaborators' goal for *Company*: "We wanted a show where the audience would sit for two hours screaming their heads off with laughter and then go home and not be able to sleep."[9] But, while it is not impossible that such a show could be successful on Broadway, the audience for it is to a great extent different from the audience for the faux-musical and considerably smaller. In a rather despairing 2000 interview with Frank Rich, Sondheim assessed the state of Broadway: "The audience that is there is not an audience who would either like or respond to the kind of stuff I write."[10]

Stephen Sondheim, more than any other composer, lyricist, or playwright, has stretched the horizon of expectations for the musical theater and in the process not only created a new kind of musical but also a new kind of audience for musicals. He has challenged expectations for subject matter, for form and style, for the sophistication of themes, and for the complexity of the development of themes. His work, I have argued, spans the aesthetic development of the musical theater of the past fifty years, moving from the Rodgers and Hammerstein aesthetic to the postmodern musical and beyond. His legacy, beyond the brilliant plays he and his collaborators have given us, plays that continue to surprise, delight, and challenge, is a double one. One part is the next generation of musical-theater artists he has inspired and in some cases personally mentored, artists who have taken up his project of expanding the horizon of expectations. The other part is the audience he has developed, audiences who are attracted to unusual subject matter, who want to go to the theater and not know what to expect, who want to be challenged by complex music and language and ideas, who want to be surprised, who want to be moved, who want to learn. As a member of this audience, I say, give us more to see.

NOTES

Preface

1. Sondheim, qtd. in Bryer and Davison, *Art of the American Musical*, 205.

2. Among these excellent works are Geoffrey Block's *Enchanted Evenings*, John Bush Jones's *Our Musicals, Ourselves*, Bruce Kirle's *Unfinished Show Business*, Raymond Knapp's *The American Musical and the Formation of National Identity* and *The American Musical and the Performance of Personal Identity*, Scott McMillin's *The Musical as Drama*, and especially Larry Stempel's *Showtime*.

3. Sondheim, qtd. in "Tony Awards," 4.

Chapter 1

1. On this claim of language mediating and constructing reality, see Hassan, *Postmodern Turn*, esp. 92–94; Foucault, *Order of Things*; and McHale, *Postmodernist Fiction*, esp. ch. 1.

2. This connects as well to what Brecht called *epic theater*. See Brecht, "Street Scene: A Basic Model for an Epic Theatre."

3. See Barth, "Literature of Exhaustion," and Russell, "Context of the Concept," for discussions of postmodern self-referentiality.

4. Barthes, "Death of the Author," 146–47. For a more detailed introduction to the idea of intertextuality, see Porter, "Intertextuality and the Discourse Community."

5. For the construction of the subject through discourse, see Belsey, "Constructing the Subject."

6. For a discussion of this ideological process, see Althusser, "Ideology and Ideological State Apparatuses." I return to Althusser's ideas in ch. 2.

7. For a more precise definition of the ideological function of performativity, see Butler, *Bodies That Matter*, 241. Knapp, *American Musical and the Performance of Personal Identity*, as his title suggests, links performance and identity in a survey of stage and film musicals. See esp. his ch. 5 and 205–8.

8. For discussions of this merger of the revue (under which general term I am including such specific genres as the minstrel show, the extravaganza, the panto-

mime, burlesque, and vaudeville) with the operetta, see Engel, *American Musical Theater*, ch. 2 and 3, and Knapp, *American Musical and the Formation of National Identity*, ch. 2 and 3. Miller, *Strike Up the Band*, 14–15, argues that anti-German sentiment during World War I lessened the popularity of operettas and increased the demand for American music and thus contributed to the rise of the musical comedy. Also, see Stempel, *Showtime*, 4–5, on narrative and generic distinctions in the musical theater.

9. Stempel, *Showtime*, 222; Knapp, *American Musical and the Formation of National Identity*, 89; Swain, *Broadway Musical*, 19.

10. Kerr, qtd. in Stempel, *Showtime*, 224.

11. Sondheim, *Finishing the Hat*, xxvii.

12. Miller, *Strike Up the Band*, 10.

13. McMillin, *Musical as Drama*, writes that the refrain of a song can serve the same intertextual purpose: a refrain "is an historian of its occurrences, and if it alludes to words from some other poem or song, it calls that poem or song into play as well" (110). Similarly, Block, *Enchanted Evenings*, writes that the waltz "as far back as Franz Lehár's *The Merry Widow* and Johann Strauss Jr.'s *Die Fledermaus* had come to represent the language of love for American as well as European audiences" (36).

14. Rodgers, qtd. in Secrest, *Somewhere for Me*, 27–28.

15. Mordden, *One More Kiss*, 48.

16. Woodruff, *Necessity of Theater*, 18.

17. Kirle, *Unfinished Show Business*, 50.

18. Calderazzo, "Most Intense," citing research in cognitive science, calls this double awareness "conceptual blending": "the idea of conceptual blending binds what we often think of as two separate worlds (the 'pretend' world of the characters and the 'real' world of the actors and spectators)" (25). Knapp, *American Musical and the Formation of National Identity*, 12, calls this same phenomenon "dual attention." McMillin, *Musical as Drama*, argues that in the musical theater there is always a distinction between the characters as they exist in the book and as they exist in song and dance, a distinction particularly marked in the musical comedy (15). Kirle, *Unfinished Show Business*, goes further in arguing that the musical-comedy stars were in essence cocreators of their shows. He interprets the introduction of integration into the musical as a passing of the authority of the show from the performer to the authors; see his ch. 2 and 3.

Notes

19. See McMillin, *Musical as Drama*, 102–14, on the distinction between what he calls "diegetic" and "out-of-the-blue" numbers.

20. See Wilk, *OK!*, and Carter, *Oklahoma!*, for background on the creation of *Oklahoma!*

21. When Al Jolson walked out of *Hold On to Your Hats* (1940), claiming illness, the show closed until the producers brought a lawsuit to force him to return to the show; see Bryer and Davison, *Art of the American Musical*, 119–22. Stempel, *Showtime*, notes that in the musical-comedy era, producers usually signed stars before hiring writers, who were then expected to tailor the material to the stars' strengths (225). Also see Stempel on *Oklahoma!*'s innovations (300–312).

22. McMillin, *Musical as Drama*, 3–4, connects the articulation of the Rodgers and Hammerstein aesthetic with the prevailing literary theory of new criticism and its valorization of organic unity in the arts.

23. Hammerstein, *Lyrics*, 19.

24. Sondheim, qtd. in Carnelia, "In Conversation with Stephen Sondheim," 15.

25. Engel, *Words with Music*, 39–40. McMillin, *Musical as Drama*, takes a different approach. He argues that the songs rarely advance the plot or characterization separately from the book. Rather, the songs offer a second order of time—a time based in repetition as opposed to book time, which is based in narrative cause and effect—in which plot and characterization can be developed in a different mode; see his ch. 1.

26. Lane, qtd. in Bryer and Davison, *Art of the American Musical*, 121.

27. Kirle, *Unfinished Show Business*, 76–85, discusses the introduction of realism as a style first into the American drama in the 1920s and then gradually into the musical theater, primarily through the work of Hammerstein. He sees realism as concerned with the presentation of the characters' psychology and not, as I am here, as concerned primarily with a transparency of style.

28. Engel argues that a play's musical moments create a "super-real world"; see *American Musical Theater*, 83–89. McMillin, *Musical as Drama*, 59, argues that the introduction of song and dance into a realistic book calls for a double suspension of disbelief.

29. Stempel, *Showtime*, 307.

30. *Love Life*, with its story tracing a married couple through 150 years of American history punctuated by vaudeville turns, anticipates such later shows as *Halleluiah, Baby!*, *1600 Pennsylvania Avenue*, and *Chicago*.

31. Bergreen, *As Thousands Cheer*, 450.

32. See Swain, *Broadway Musical*, 106–7, on the "rush of composers and writers to conform to the new standard after *Oklahoma!*," especially the serious ballets.

33. Bordman, *American Musical Theatre*, agrees: "At a time when tightly knit librettos were often propping up disappointing, unmelodic, or pretentious scores, the book for *Hair* represented a startling reversion to an older approach to musical theatre" (658).

34. Many histories of the Broadway musical take as a premise that the Rodgers and Hammerstein form was the pinnacle toward which the history of the musical theater was struggling and so see these aesthetic rebellions of the late 1960s as disappointing regressions. See, for example, Ewen, *New Complete Book of the American Musical Theater*, Engel, *American Musical Theater*, and Bordman, *American Musical Theatre*. In *Words with Music*, Engel discusses *Man of La Mancha*, *Cabaret*, and *Sweet Charity* (1966) in his ch. 11, titled "Failures." In *One More Kiss*, Mordden studies 1970s musicals as representing variously the last gasp of and the degeneration of the golden age of Broadway musicals. Singer takes a similarly elegiac approach in *Ever After*. Miller, *Strike Up the Band*, refreshingly, argues that in the 1960s, "the art form entered its most exciting, most daring, most thrilling time in decades" (98). Adler, "Sung and the Said," connects the "freer forms" of these 1960s musicals to parallel developments in nonrepresentational drama; to be fair, he is also skeptical about the extent to which Rodgers and Hammerstein–style realism established a fourth wall (see 38–39). In *Musical as Drama*, McMillin argues against the aesthetic of integration, saying that the musical's dramatic power lies in difference, primarily the difference between the book and the numbers. In place of the concept of integration, he offers coherence as a principle that holds the various elements of a musical together; see his ch. 1 and 182 and 208–9.

35. *Assassins*, Sondheim and Weidman, 96, 98.

36. For studies of Sondheim's life and career, see Secrest, *Stephen Sondheim: A Life*; Zadan, *Sondheim & Co.*; Gottfried, *Sondheim*; and Citron, *Sondheim and Lloyd Webber*. Also, see Sondheim, *Finishing the Hat* and *Look, I Made a Hat*; while mainly collections and commentary on his lyrics, these volumes are also something of a career-focused autobiography.

37. For detailed discussions of Sondheim's work on these apprentice shows, see Banfield, *Sondheim's Broadway Musicals*, 15–25, and Swayne, *How Sondheim Found His Sound*, ch. 4.

38. Rich, "Conversations with Sondheim," 41. For Sondheim's reflections on *Saturday Night*, see *Finishing the Hat*, ch. 1.

39. Laurents, *Original Story*, 363.

40. This 1965 collaboration was famously troubled: Sondheim was unhappy writing lyrics only; Rodgers resented Sondheim and feuded with him and Laurents; British director John Dexter offended everyone; leading lady Elizabeth Allen was insecure and unsympathetic. The original production had a modestly successful 220-performance run but has been infrequently revived. In the late 1990s Laurents and Sondheim returned to the play, and their revised version was presented at the George Street Playhouse in 2000 and at the Pasadena Playhouse in 2001. The latter production was recorded. For background on the Broadway production, see Zadan, *Sondheim & Co.*, ch. 10, and Sondheim, *Finishing the Hat*, ch. 6.

41. Chapin, "Magical, Mystical Miracle."

42. Sondheim, qtd. in Zadan, *Sondheim & Co.*, 100.

43. Sondheim, qtd. in Secrest, *Somewhere for Me*, 371.

44. *Do I Hear a Waltz?*, Rodgers, Sondheim, and Laurents, 63.

45. Laurents, *Original Story*, 215.

46. See Shklovsky, *Theory of Prose*, ch. 1 on the defamiliarizing power of art, which the translator renders as *estrangement*.

Chapter 2

1. See Wells, *"West Side Story,"* for a comprehensive account of the musical's genesis and production, a musicological study of Bernstein's score, discussions of the sociological contexts for the musical, and an argument about the musical's reception. For background, also see Zadan, *Sondheim & Co.*, ch. 2, and Sondheim, *Finishing the Hat*, ch. 2.

2. Laurents, *Original Story*, 348.

3. For Sondheim's critique, see his essay "Theater Lyrics," 76, 83–86, and *Finishing the Hat*, ch. 2. On the other hand, Harold Prince, *West Side Story*'s coproducer, defends the way the lyrics and Laurents's dialogue create a unified, stylized language for the characters; see "Interview: Harold Prince." After years of criticizing his lyrics for "I Feel Pretty," Sondheim finally got them out of the show in the 2009 Broadway revival for which that song as well as "A Boy Like That" and the Sharks' section of the "Tonight" quintet were translated into Spanish by Lin-Manuel Miranda. Sondheim says that he did not insist on a rigidly accurate translation: "The idea of the song is so simple. [. . .] I was only concerned that Lin observe the rhyme schemes"; Sondheim, qtd. in Cohen, "Same City, New Story," 6.

4. Bernstein, qtd. in Gussow, "'West Side Story,'" 5.

5. See Lyotard's introduction to *Postmodern Condition*.

6. See Foucault, *History of Sexuality*, 92–102.

7. See Althusser, "Ideology and Ideological State Apparatuses," and Belsey, "Constructing the Subject."

8. See Gates, *Signifying Monkey*, ch. 2.

9. *West Side Story*, Laurents, Bernstein, and Sondheim, 143; hereafter cited parenthetically.

10. This legendary original production starred Ethel Merman, in the last role she would originate on Broadway, Sandra Church, and Jack Klugman. For background on *Gypsy*, see Zadan, *Sondheim & Co.*, ch. 4, and Sondheim, *Finishing the Hat*, ch. 3.

11. *Gypsy*, Laurents, Sondheim, and Styne, 16; hereafter cited parenthetically.

12. More than forty years after *Gypsy*, Sondheim returned to the image of the closed-off frontier in *Road Show*.

13. See Baudrillard, "Precession of the Simulacra," esp. 342–47.

14. Lee, *Gypsy*, 20; for more biographical background, see Quinn, *Mama Rose's Turn*.

15. In *Saturday Night* the socially ambitious protagonist Gene expresses similar contempt for "some people" in his first number, "Class."

16. Lee, *Gypsy*, 231.

17. Knapp, *American Musical and the Performance of Personal Identity*, examines the way in which the play shows that "achieving a strong personal identity is a matter of performance" (221). See especially 215–28.

18. Laurents writes, "Rose wouldn't change and she doesn't; she goes right back to doing it all for herself all over again"; see *Original Story*, 394.

19. For background on *Forum*, see Zadan, *Sondheim & Co.*, ch. 6, and Sondheim, *Finishing the Hat*, ch. 4.

20. Sondheim and Shevelove, qtd. in Zadan, *Sondheim & Co.*, 68. Gelbart suggests that this characterization of the score may be oversimplified. He points out that "Love, I Hear" and "Free" are both book songs in the traditional sense. See Bandler's interview with Gelbart, "What Collaboration Is About," 26.

21. The only fully staged production of the play I have seen was at the Berkshire Theatre Festival in 1980, starring George Hearn and Mary Louise Wilson. For background on *Anyone Can Whistle*, see Zadan, *Sondheim & Co.*, ch. 8, and Sondheim, *Finishing the Hat*, ch. 5.

Notes

22. *Anyone Can Whistle,* Laurents and Sondheim, 3; hereafter cited parenthetically.

23. See Sondheim, *Finishing the Hat,* 345, on how "the chorus sings separate thoughts until Hapgood molds them into a group of like-minded people, the unison lyrics illustrating their loss of individuality."

24. Sondheim, qtd. in Zadan, *Sondheim & Co.,* 83. Pastiche, which Sondheim also makes significant use of in *Follies, Pacific Overtures,* and *Assassins,* connects to the self-referentiality of postmodern musical theater. Gottfried, *Sondheim,* offers an interesting description: "Pastiche does not merely evoke a period but comments on it. Even when the tone is nostalgic and affectionate, there is mockery in the air and a sense of dissembling, a crooked smile on a covered heart. While the words are the character's, the musical comment is the composer's" (79–80). Gottfried, however, does not approve of pastiche because of its self-consciousness, the way it breaches the fourth wall.

25. Sondheim, qtd. in Zadan, *Sondheim & Co.,* 88.

26. For background on *Company,* see Zadan, *Sondheim & Co.,* ch. 12, and Sondheim, *Finishing the Hat,* ch. 7.

27. See Lyotard, *Postmodern Condition;* Bauman, *Modernity and Ambivalence,* especially ch. 7; and White, *Content of the Form.*

28. Foucault, *Order of Things,* 217–21. Writing at around the same time but from a different philosophical approach, Kermode, *Sense of an Ending,* similarly argues that narrative provides a sense-making structure to time-in-process. Like Foucault, he argues that the anticipation of an imagined end allows us to see a completed structure where there might only be incidents. He writes, "Men in the middest [in the middle of things] make considerable imaginative investments in coherent patterns which, by the provision of an end, make possible a satisfying consonance with the origins and with the middle" (17).

29. See White, *Content of the Form,* ch. 2, esp. 42–44.

30. See Bauman, *Modernity and Ambivalence,* ch. 7.

31. See Hutcheon, *Poetics of Postmodernism,* 6–7, 13.

32. Sondheim, qtd. in Lipton, "Stephen Sondheim: The Art of the Musical," 269. In another interview, Sondheim says, "What's innovative about *Company* is it blends two traditional forms for the first time: the revue and the book show. It's a revue, but it tells a story. Doesn't have a plot, but it has a story"; "Interview: Stephen Sondheim."

33. Sondheim, qtd. in Secrest, *Stephen Sondheim,* 192.

Notes

34. Gordon, *Art Isn't Easy*, offers a similar take on the play's structure: "Unlike the traditional hero, Robert does not journey forward. The audience can perceive the cumulative effect of his experiences but never has the sense of inevitable progression and growth that would suggest the gradual enlightenment of a hero" (42).

35. *Company*, Sondheim and Furth, 55; hereafter cited parenthetically. This 1996 edition is a revision of the original 1970 script based on changes made for two 1995 productions, one by the Donmar Warehouse in London, the other by the Roundabout Theatre Company Off Broadway, and this is the version of the play currently licensed for performance.

36. John Olson, in "*Company*—25 Years Later," disagrees, arguing that the continuing relevance of the play's themes allows for a contemporary setting. Banfield, *Sondheim's Broadway Musicals*, thinks the play has to take place in 1970, but he considers this a flaw (160–63).

37. As Knapp, *American Musical and the Performance of Personal Identity*, puts it, "The specific problems of *Company*'s couples, and of Bobby's inability (or reluctance) to commit, may easily be understood as representing a set of issues especially relevant to the 'silent generation' of urban professionals, born between 1924 and 1945, who were too old for the counterculture" (294).

38. Discussing the use of reprises in musicals, Sondheim says, "*Company* was a show where we could have used reprises, because it was about a fellow who stayed exactly the same"; Sondheim, qtd. in Zadan, *Sondheim & Co.*, 234.

39. Olson argues that Robert is "a *risk-aversive* person. We never see him initiate contact with his friends or acquaintances. [. . .] Most often, he appears merely to react to the actions of others"; see "*Company*—25 Years Later," 64.

40. In "Theater Lyrics," 92–97, and *Finishing the Hat*, 193–96, Sondheim discusses the four songs that were proposed as Robert's final number: "Multitudes of Amy"; "Marry Me a Little"; "Happily Ever After"; and "Being Alive." See also Banfield, *Sondheim's Broadway Musicals*, for a comparative discussion of these four songs (166–73).

Chapter 3

1. For discussions of Prince's career, see Prince's autobiography, *Contradictions*; Hirsch, *Harold Prince and the American Musical Theater*; and Ilson, *Harold Prince: From "Pajama Game" to "Phantom of the Opera."*

2. *Follies* (1971), Goldman and Sondheim, 53; hereafter cited parenthetically. The authors revisited and revised *Follies* several times over the subsequent decades. In

Notes

September 1985 the New York Philharmonic presented a concert version of the show with an all-star cast; the score was presented complete, but much of the book was reduced to narration. In 1987 Cameron Mackintosh produced the London premiere of the show for which Goldman made a number of revisions and Sondheim wrote several new songs; in addition, the show was split into two acts (on Broadway it had been intermissionless), and the order of the songs was altered. (See James Fisher's assessment of the London revisions in "Nixon's America and *Follies*," 81–82.) Sondheim was reluctant to revise the show so significantly, was unhappy with the results, and has insisted that this version not be produced again (see Horowitz, *Sondheim on Music*, 123). In 1998 the Papermill Playhouse, a regional theater in New Jersey, produced a major revival, and in 2001 the Roundabout Theatre Company produced the first Broadway revival. Both these productions used a further revised book by Goldman, who died in 1998. This script was published in 2001. In 2007 a concert version was presented as part of the Encores! revival series at the City Center in New York, and a second Broadway revival, starring Bernadette Peters and directed by Eric Schaeffer, played a limited engagement in the second half of 2011. The upshot of Goldman's revisions was to move the play from its original surreal style to something more realistic. I will be referring to the 1971 script both because I prefer it to the subsequent versions and because I want to examine the play in the context of postmodern thought in the 1970s. For a fascinating behind-the-scenes look at the rehearsal period, out-of-town tryout, and Broadway opening of the original *Follies*, see Chapin, *Everything Was Possible*. See also Zadan, *Sondheim & Co.*, ch. 14, and Sondheim, *Finishing the Hat*, ch. 8.

3. "Interview: Stephen Sondheim."

4. Harvard undergraduate Frank Rich, reviewing the Boston tryout for the *Crimson*, saw the good-bye but missed the possibilities for the future of the form. He wrote, "There is no getting around the fact that a large part of the chilling fascination of *Follies* is that its creators are in essence presenting their own funeral" (Rich, qtd. in Chapin, *Everything Was Possible*, 194).

5. See Pascal, *Design and Truth in Autobiography*, 1–20, on the narrating subject's standpoint as a "condition of autobiography" (10). A standpoint from which to organize and interpret is necessary before any narrative can be made from life events. For Pascal, autobiographies are always the story of the creation of the narrating self: "they tell of the realization of an urgent personal potentiality" (112). Gusdorf, in "Conditions and Limits of Autobiography," also argues that autobiography is not so much a study of the past as "a work of personal justification" (39).

253

Notes

6. Gusdorf, "Conditions and Limits of Autobiography," argues that the sequence of life events only appears to govern a life story's organization: "The illusion begins from the moment that the narrative *confers a meaning* on the event which, when it actually occurred, no doubt had several meanings or perhaps none. This postulating of a meaning dictates the choice of the facts to be retained and of the details to bring out or to dismiss according to the demands of the preconceived intelligibility" (42).

7. See Renza, "Veto of the Imagination," on the subject-object dichotomy in autobiography and the problematic personal pronoun.

8. Kierkegaard, *Papers and Journals*, 161.

9. In the first production of *Follies* I ever saw, at the Off-Broadway Equity Library Theatre in 1976, the actress playing Sally (Lori Ann Saunders) emphasized her metal instability throughout, and her insanity was front and center during "Losing My Mind."

10. Sondheim, qtd. in Zadan, *Sondheim & Co.*, 157.

11. Sondheim has identified the models for some of his pastiches: see Zadan, *Sondheim & Co.*, 147, and Sondheim, *Finishing the Hat*, ch. 8.

12. Prince, *Contradictions*, 183.

13. *A Little Night Music* was one of Sondheim's most successful shows in its original production, winning six Tony Awards and running for 601 performances. For background, see Zadan, *Sondheim & Co.*, ch. 18, and Sondheim, *Finishing the Hat*, ch. 9.

14. See Puccio, "Enchantment on the Manicured Lawns," for a discussion of the Armfeldt estate as a Shakespearean green world "where characters come to greater self-knowledge, where submerged emotions surface, and where lovers ultimately discover, or rediscover, one another" (136).

15. *A Little Night Music*, Sondheim and Wheeler, 30; hereafter cited parenthetically.

16. Tunick, "Introduction," 3.

17. In the 2009 revival, designer David Farley set the action among mirrored walls, the reflections emphasizing the characters' bifurcated sense of identity.

18. See Puccio, "Sondheim 101: *A Little Night Music*," 7, on the role of the Liebeslieders as observing commentators, both inside and outside the action, and as reminders of the self-referential theatricality of the play. Gordon, *Art Isn't Easy*, makes a similar point (127). Fraser, "Revisiting Greece," 230–34, argues that the Liebesliebers keep the audience emotionally distanced from the characters.

19. Knapp, *American Musical and the Performance of Personal Identity*, argues

that the play's surreal treatment of time connects to the characters' search for narrative-based identity: "Always, the show looks forward or back, rooted in its moment, imprisoned by its characters' seeming inability to find their way to a coherent
link between past and future" (57).

20. For background, see Zadan, *Sondheim & Co.*, ch. 20, and Sondheim, *Finishing the Hat*, ch. 11.

21. For a good conventional history of the opening of Japan, see Feifer, *Breaking
Open Japan*.

22. *Pacific Overtures*, Sondheim and Weidman, 134; hereafter cited parenthetically.

23. Sondheim talks about the inspiration for this stage moment coming during a
visit to Japan when he saw "a Japanese woman in an obi buying Chanel in a department store" (Sondheim, qtd. in Horowitz, *Sondheim on Music*, 156).

24. See White, *Content of the Form*, 14, 20.

25. This assumption about the makeup of the audience is less true for subsequent
productions. *Pacific Overtures* has been surprisingly popular in Japan. The original
Broadway production was filmed for Japanese television. In 2000 the New National
Theatre in Tokyo produced the Japanese premiere of the play, directed by Amon
Miyamoto. When the Roundabout Theatre Company produced a Broadway revival,
directed by Miyamoto, in 2004, sponsors included the Japan Foundation, Canon
USA, the Mitsui USA Foundation, Toyota, and Japan Airlines.

26. Knapp, *American Musical and the Formation of National Identity*, writes,
"American musicals play to American audiences, who will be acutely aware of anything that challenges their notions of what or who America is or stands for, or of
its place in the world. If Americans see representatives of other lands and cultures
on the musical stage, they will see them in relation to some sense of who *they* are
as Americans" (103). *Pacific Overtures* purposely unsettles these audience assumptions.

27. Sondheim, on the 1976 television documentary program *Anatomy of a Song*.

28. Sondheim, qtd. in Zadan, *Sondheim & Co.*, 210. In his interview with Craig
Carnelia, Sondheim suggests that this approach was unspoken during the process
of writing and articulated only after the play was completed. See Carnelia, "In Conversation with Stephen Sondheim," 18.

29. Bhabha, "Of Mimicry and Man," 361, Bhabha's italics.

30. Sondheim defines *pastiche* differently, as "fond imitations," which do not
"comment on the work or the style being imitated"; see *Finishing the Hat*, 200.

31. Using Sondheim's manuscripts, Banfield, in *Sondheim's Broadway Musicals*, analyzes the composition of "A Bowler Hat" (63–76).

32. Sondheim, *Finishing the Hat*, 327. Knapp, *American Musical and the Formation of National Identity*, explains that the authors create "two versions of 'reduced' English, one reduced for poetic effect, the other to indicate a more crass sensibility so as to turn the tables on typical American portrayals of foreigners" (272).

33. Pratt, *Imperial Eyes*, 6, 7.

34. Sondheim, qtd. in Horowitz, *Sondheim on Music*, 39.

35. Sondheim, qtd. in Zadan, *Sondheim & Co.*, 211.

36. Banfield, *Sondheim's Broadway Musicals*, 251–53.

37. For background, see Zadan, *Sondheim & Co.*, ch. 22, and Sondheim, *Finishing the Hat*, ch. 12.

38. Sondheim says, "When I started it, there was no Hugh Wheeler; there was just me and the Christopher Bond text. Then I realized, Christopher Bond's entire play was thirty-five pages long in acting form, and I was only up to page three—or something like that—and the show was twenty minutes long. The point was, it was going to turn out to be the *Ring* if I didn't cut it down. And I got panicky. I wish I hadn't—I wish I'd stuck to my guns and just done it myself, but I couldn't. [. . .] And I'm very glad, because [Wheeler] made some changes that are very important and very good for the show" (Sondheim, qtd. in Horowitz, *Sondheim on Music*, 148–49).

39. Sondheim, "Larger Than Life," 12.

40. "Interview: Harold Prince."

41. Sondheim, "Larger Than Life," 11.

42. Prince, qtd. in Zadan, *Sondheim & Co.*, 245.

43. Sondheim, "Larger Than Life," 3.

44. See Sondheim, *Finishing the Hat*, 333–34, on the importance of this first line.

45. This storytelling aspect of the play was given a different twist in director John Doyle's 2005 Broadway revival: here the story was told by the inmates of an asylum to which, apparently, Toby had been committed after the events of the play.

46. Anthony shares the young Sweeney's naïveté: early in act 2, despite his previous run-in with the Beadle, Anthony turns to him for help in rescuing Johanna from Fogg's Asylum.

47. *Sweeney Todd*, Sondheim and Wheeler, 10; hereafter cited parenthetically.

48. Mack, "Introduction," notes the tendency in nineteenth-century accounts of Todd's story to create a background that accounts for the barber's villainy: "Sweeney Todd had not been *born* a villain, the story of his 'life' looks to reassure us, he was

himself a *victim* of a society that was guilty of treating an entire class of people as little more than a disposable source of cheap labour—of treating them as objects rather than as individuals" (xx).

49. Žižek, *Plague of Fantasies*, 39.

50. Sondheim, qtd. in Gottfried, *Sondheim*, 133.

51. In the 1989 Broadway revival, Beth Fowler played Mrs. Lovett as essentially lovesick, which not only was markedly different from Angela Lansbury's performance but also, for this viewer anyway, lost much of the significance of Mrs. Lovett as amoral entrepreneur.

52. In the film version of *Sweeney Todd*, the "By the Sea" sequence, a fantasy showing what life at the seaside would be like for the unholy family of Sweeney, Lovett, and Toby, is the only part played for laughs. Mechler, "Mrs. Lovett's Meat Pies," argues that this sequence emphasizes that once one commits vengeance, he lives outside the bounds of normal society and can never reenter.

53. In the film version, after Anthony rescues Johanna and brings her to Sweeney's barbershop, Johanna undercuts Anthony's confidence that they have achieved a safe, happy ending when she skeptically asks, "Safe? So we run away and then all our dreams come true?"

54. Sondheim calls melodrama "the obverse side of farce" ("Larger Than Life," 4), and in this sense, Sweeney finding himself in the wrong story, along with many of the other characters similarly imagining themselves in the wrong story—the Judge in a story of a recalcitrant bride, Anthony in a love story, Johanna in a story of escape—connects to the characters in *Forum*, who, as we saw in chapter 2, each imagines himself or herself in a different story.

55. Sondheim, qtd. in Secrest, *Stephen Sondheim*, 56. Sondheim worked as a gofer on *Allegro*, his first professional theatrical experience.

56. Sondheim, *Finishing the Hat*, 421. See Milner, "'Let the Pupil Show the Master,'" for a comparison of *Allegro* and *Merrily We Roll Along* set in the context of the Sondheim-Hammerstein relationship.

57. I heard Sondheim, in a 1994 question-and-answer session at New York's Museum of Television and Radio, explain that observing Hammerstein's disappointment at the failure of *Allegro* made him wary of being too experimental and ambitious. Working on *West Side Story* with Leonard Bernstein later helped give him the confidence to aim high and succeed or fail spectacularly.

58. Sondheim, qtd. in Secrest, *Stephen Sondheim*, 53–54.

59. For more on the Broadway *Merrily We Roll Along*'s problems, see "Interview:

Notes

Harold Prince"; Zadan, *Sondheim & Co.,* ch. 24; and Sondheim, *Finishing the Hat,* ch. 13.

60. For discussions of the show's revisions, see Stoddart, "Visions and Re-Visions," Buchman, "'Growing Pains,'" and Sondheim, *Finishing the Hat,* ch. 13.

61. *Merrily We Roll Along,* Sondheim and Furth, 26; hereafter cited parenthetically.

62. Sinatra recorded the song for his 1981 album *She Shot Me Down,* which was released before the cast recording. Carly Simon also recorded a song from the show, "Not a Day Goes By," for her album *Torch,* before the show had opened.

63. Sondheim, qtd. in Zadan, *Sondheim & Co.,* 270.

Chapter 4

1. Chapin, *Everything Was Possible,* 9; Zadan, *Sondheim & Co.,* 185.

2. Prince, *Contradictions,* 179.

3. Zadan, *Sondheim & Co.,* 298–99; see also Zadan's ch. 26 for the genesis of *Sunday in the Park with George,* and also Sondheim, *Look, I Made a Hat,* ch. 1.

4. Sondheim, *Look, I Made a Hat,* 6.

5. *Sunday in the Park with George,* Sondheim and Lapine, 160; hereafter cited parenthetically.

6. In the Horowitz interviews, Sondheim talks about the paint Seurat used for *Sunday Afternoon,* on the advice of his friend Pissarro, paint that shimmered but that also began to fade quickly. Horowitz, *Sondheim on Music,* 95.

7. See Greenblatt, "Resonance and Wonder," for the argument that modernism tried to separate art from its historic contexts so as to see it as autonomously functioning and universally meaningful rather than as intertwined with a multiplicity of discourses, artistic and nonartistic.

8. Sondheim, *Look, I Made a Hat,* 21.

9. For more background, see Zadan, *Sondheim & Co.,* ch. 28, and Sondheim, *Look, I Made a Hat,* ch. 2.

10. *Into the Woods,* Sondheim and Lapine, 3; hereafter cited parenthetically.

11. See Zadan, *Sondheim & Co.,* 338, for Lapine on Bettelheim. In his book, Bettelheim argues that the brutality of fairy tales in their earliest versions (not the sanitized Disney versions) serves important psychological functions for children, essentially preparing them for the awful things that can happen in their lives—the loss of their parents, for example—and assuring them that they can endure and

prosper. Sondheim has more recently said that Bettelheim was not as significant an influence on the play as Jung (see Lipton, "Stephen Sondheim: The Art of the Musical," 275; Menton, "Maternity, Madness, and Art in the Theater of Stephen Sondheim," 76 n. 8; and Sondheim, *Look, I Made a Hat*, 58).

12. See Lacan, *Ecrits*, ch. 1. MacKenzie, *Theatre of the Real*, presents a sophisticated Lacanian reading of Sondheim's work; see esp. ch. 4.

13. While creating the play, the authors tried to find a way to indicate that the Narrator was the Baker's son grown to adulthood. Having heard the story as a child, he was now passing the story on to the audience, the entire play being this passing on. When Lapine and Sondheim could not find a way to make this work, they moved to the idea of having the Narrator killed by the Giant, the change being made during the Broadway previews. See Zadan, *Sondheim & Co.*, 343–44. The 2012 Delacorte Theater production cast a little boy as the Narrator, who, we come to understand, is the Baker's son.

14. Bishop, "Preface," vii.

15. Rich, "Cast of Killers Made in America," B1.

16. For background on the genesis of *Assassins*, see Sondheim, *Look, I Made a Hat*, ch. 3.

17. Sondheim and Weidman, qtd. in "*Assassins* Postpones Broadway Debut."

18. Including Rich, who credited the changed, post-9/11 world for his new response rather than admitting his own 1991 critical shortcomings (Rich, "At Last, 9/11 Has Its Own Musical").

19. This production made several revisions to the 1991 script. Most significant is a new song, first added in the London production, "Something Just Broke," sung by ordinary citizens across several decades as they respond to the news of the death of a president and inserted just after the JFK assassination. Also, fitting with Mantello's vision of the show and scenic designer Robert Brill's set, the flashy but seedy understructure of a roller coaster, the play takes place in a surreal amusement park, and the shooting-gallery Proprietor becomes something of a master of ceremonies for the entire show. He serves as a foil for the Balladeer, representing, the dark, money-grubbing side of the American Dream as opposed to the Balladeer's optimistic articulation, and, as such, much of the assassins' parts of "Another National Anthem" are reassigned to him. Connected with this, at the end of "Another National Anthem," the Balladeer, instead of being driven off the stage by the assassins, is transformed into Lee Harvey Oswald. These revisions have, in my opinion, some

virtues and some drawbacks; however, for my purposes here, I will use the 1991 script, plus "Something Just Broke," since that combination is the version of the show that is currently licensed for performance.

20. For discussions of symbolic convergence theory, see Bormann, *Communication Theory* and *Force of Fantasy*.

21. For more on heteroglossia, see Bakhtin, *Dialogic Imagination*. Although they do not use this terminology, Puccio and Stoddart, "'It Takes Two,'" also argue that Sondheim's songs "construct a musical space where two narrative or expressive voices meet" (122).

22. *Assassins*, Sondheim and Weidman, 6; hereafter cited parenthetically.

23. Clarke demonstrates that this fame-lost interpretation of Booth's motives has held currency with many historians, especially the influential Stanley Kimmel in his *The Mad Booths of Maryland* (1940) (see Clarke, *American Assassins*, 19–20). Clarke's study seems to have been an important source for Weidman and Sondheim as they wrote *Assassins*: many of the details Clarke mentions in his portraits of the assassins appear in the dialogue and lyrics. Also, Clarke maintains that Booth killed himself (as the character does in the play) contrary to most historians, who report that he was shot by a Union soldier.

24. Weidman, qtd. in Bishop, "Preface," x–xi.

25. For the styles Sondheim was pastiching, see John Pike's interview with *Assassins* orchestrator Michael Starobin, "Michael Starobin: A New Dimension for *Assassins*."

26. For more on this folk tradition, see Lomax, *Folk Songs of North America*, 264–66; and Davis, *Folk Songs of Virginia*, 262–63.

27. "Mister MacKinley," in Lomax, *Folk Songs of North America*, 274–75; "Charles Guiteau," in Lomax, *Folk Songs of North America*, 273–74.

28. Lomax, *Folk Songs of North America*, 265.

29. Rich, "Cast of Killers Made in America," B4.

30. An English translation of *Fosca* by Lawrence Venuti was published with the title *Passion* in 1994, just after the musical opened on Broadway.

31. For more background on *Passion*, see Sondheim, *Look, I Made a Hat*, ch. 4.

32. For more on this, see McLaughlin, "Post-Postmodern Discontent."

33. The original production of *Passion* eschewed song titles, even in the *Playbill*, presumably to emphasize the integrated flow of the play, but titles were appended for the cast recording and the published sheet music, and, for clarity's sake, I use them here.

34. *Passion,* Sondheim and Lapine, 6–7; hereafter cited parenthetically.

35. Sondheim, *Look, I Made a Hat,* 177.

36. Parry, "Fosca's Female Gaze," argues that the audience's discomfort with *Passion* arises from its gender reversals, Giorgio being passive, gazed upon, and acted upon, and Fosca aggressively and manipulatively pursuing the object of her affection. Also see Miller, *Deconstructing Harold Hill,* 101–5, on Fosca as manipulator.

37. See Breu, *Insistence of the Material,* 17.

38. See Sondheim's account of the original and Broadway productions of *The Frogs* in *Finishing the Hat,* ch. 10.

39. All dialogue quoted from *The Frogs* is from the Broadway cast recording and from my notes from viewing the show at the Vivian Beaumont Theater and at the Division of Theatre on Film and Tape of the New York Public Library for the Performing Arts.

40. See Sondheim's explanation of these elements, *Finishing the Hat,* 289, 293, 295, 297, 298, 300.

41. See Wallace, "*E Unibus Pluram,*" and McCaffery, "Interview with David Foster Wallace."

42. Sondheim, *Look, I Made a Hat,* 243–44.

43. For a brief history of the transition from *Wise Guys* to *Bounce,* see Jones, "Sondheim's Journey to 'Bounce,'" 1, 9. For Sondheim's take on the long road from *Wise Guys* to *Road Show,* see *Look, I Made a Hat,* ch. 5.

44. Johnston, *Legendary Mizners,* 3.

45. Sondheim, *Look, I Made a Hat,* 179.

46. See Seebohm, *Boca Rococo,* for an argument of Addison's importance as an architect. For a survey of Addison's work, see *Florida Architecture of Addison Mizner.*

47. Sondheim, *Look, I Made a Hat,* 185.

48. *Road Show,* Sondheim and Weidman, 98; hereafter cited parenthetically.

49. Johnston, *Legendary Mizners,* 4–5.

50. Ibid., 25–26, 54–60.

51. Ibid., ch. 14. A half mile of the highway was actually built.

52. In *Wise Guys,* the 1999 workshop of the musical, the final scene before the return to the afterlife frame showed a verbally exhausted Wilson unable to recall any of his famous quips for a young newspaperman and, when asked if he has a comment about the death of his brother, responding with a simple "no."

53. In *Bounce,* the 2003 Chicago and Washington, DC, version of the show,

when Addison resists Wilson's plan for the Boca Raton project, saying he already has everything he wants, Wilson replies, "Then it's time to want something else" (Sondheim, *Look, I Made a Hat,* 264).

Chapter 5

1. See Swayne's helpful appendix sorting through the ways the term *concept musical* has been used in *How Sondheim Found His Sound,* 257–59; see also Stempel, *Showtime,* 517–22.

2. Kotis and Hollmann, *Urinetown,* 10.

3. After the Civil War, some black performers started minstrel troupes, wearing blackface and performing the stereotypes (see Stempel, *Showtime,* 57–60).

4. LaChiusa, *See What I Wanna See,* 62.

5. LaChiusa, "Great Gray Way," 33.

6. Ibid.

7. See Jauss, "Literary History."

8. Sondheim, qtd. in Secrest, *Stephen Sondheim,* 355.

9. Sondheim, qtd. in Zadan, *Sondheim & Co.,* 119.

10. Sondheim, qtd. in Rich, "Conversations with Sondheim," 42.

WORKS CITED

Primary Sources: Stephen Sondheim Musicals

Anyone Can Whistle. By Arthur Laurents and Stephen Sondheim. 1964. New York: Leon Amiel, 1976.

Assassins. By Stephen Sondheim and John Weidman. New York: Theatre Communications Group, 1991.

Company. By Stephen Sondheim and George Furth. 1970. New York: Theatre Communications Group, 1996.

Do I Hear a Waltz? By Richard Rodgers, Stephen Sondheim, and Arthur Laurents. 1965. New York: Random House, 1966.

Follies. By James Goldman and Stephen Sondheim. New York: Random House, 1971.

Gypsy. By Arthur Laurents, Stephen Sondheim, and Jule Styne. 1959. New York: Theatre Communications Group, 1994.

Into the Woods. By Stephen Sondheim and James Lapine. 1987. New York: Theatre Communications Group, 1989.

A Little Night Music. By Stephen Sondheim and Hugh Wheeler. 1973. New York: Applause, 1991.

Merrily We Roll Along. By Stephen Sondheim and George Furth. [Final version.] New York: Music Theatre International, 1994.

Pacific Overtures. By Stephen Sondheim and John Weidman. 1976. New York: Dodd, Mead, 1977.

Passion. By Stephen Sondheim and James Lapine. New York: Theatre Communications Group, 1994.

Road Show. By Stephen Sondheim and John Weidman. 2008. New York: Theatre Communications Group, 2009.

Sunday in the Park with George. By Stephen Sondheim and James Lapine. New York: Dodd, Mead, 1986.

Sweeney Todd, the Demon Barber of Fleet Street. By Stephen Sondheim and Hugh Wheeler. New York: Dodd, Mead, 1979.

Sweeney Todd, the Demon Barber of Fleet Street. Dir. Tim Burton. Perf. Johnny

Works Cited

Depp, Helena Bonham Carter, and Alan Rickman. DreamWorks and Warner Bros., 2007.

West Side Story. By Arthur Laurents, Leonard Bernstein, and Stephen Sondheim. 1957. New York: Random House, 1958.

Secondary Sources

Adler, Thomas. "The Sung and the Said: Literary Value in the Musical Dramas of Stephen Sondheim." *Reading Stephen Sondheim: A Collection of Critical Essays*. Ed. Sandor Goodhart. New York: Garland, 2000. 37–60.

Althusser, Louis. "Ideology and Ideological State Apparatuses (Notes towards an Investigation)." *Lenin and Philosophy and Other Essays*. Trans. Ben Brewster. London: NLB, 1971. 121–73.

"Anatomy of a Song." *Camera Three*. CBS. 28 March 1976. Television.

"*Assassins* Postpones Broadway Debut." *Playbill*, 13 September 2001. *Playbill On Line*. http://www.playbill.com.

Bakhtin, M. M. *The Dialogic Imagination: Four Essays*. Ed. Michael Holquist. Trans. Caryl Emerson and Michael Holquist. Austin, TX: University of Austin Press, 1981.

Bandler, Michael J. "What Collaboration Is About: Larry Gelbart Reminisces about Co-Writing the Book for *Forum*." *Sondheim Review* 16, no. 1 (Fall 2009): 25–27, 49.

Banfield, Stephen. *Sondheim's Broadway Musicals*. Ann Arbor: University of Michigan Press, 1993.

Barth, John. "The Literature of Exhaustion." *Atlantic Monthly*, August 1967, 29–34.

Barthes, Roland. "The Death of the Author." *Image Music Text*. Ed. and trans. Stephen Heath. New York: Hill and Wang, 1977. 142–48.

Baudrillard, Jean. "The Precession of Simulacra." *A Postmodern Reader*. Ed. Jospeh Natoli and Linda Hutcheon. Albany: State University of New York Press, 1993. 342–75.

Bauman, Zygmunt. *Modernity and Ambivalence*. Ithaca, NY: Cornell University Press, 1991.

Belsey, Catherine. "Constructing the Subject: Deconstructing the Text." *Feminist Criticism and Social Change: Sex, Class, and Race in Literature and Culture*. Ed. Judith Newton and Deborah Rosenfelt. New York: Methuen, 1985. 45–64.

Bergreen, Laurence. *As Thousands Cheer: The Life of Irving Berlin*. New York: Viking, 1990.

Works Cited

Bettleheim, Bruno. *The Uses of Enchantment: The Meaning and Importance of Fairy Tales.* 1976. New York: Vintage, 2010.

Bhabha, Homi. "Of Mimicry and Man: The Ambivalence of Colonial Discourse." 1983. *Modern Literary Theory: A Reader.* Ed. Philip Rice and Patricia Waugh. 3rd ed. London: Arnold, 1996. 360–67.

Bishop, André. "Preface." *Assassins.* By Stephen Sondheim and John Weidman. New York: Theatre Communications Group, 1991. vii–xi.

Block, Geoffrey. *Enchanted Evenings: The Broadway Musical from "Show Boat" to Sondheim and Lloyd Webber.* 2nd ed. New York: Oxford University Press, 2009.

Bordman, Gerald. *American Musical Theatre: A Chronicle.* New York: Oxford University Press, 1978.

Bormann, Ernest G. *Communication Theory.* New York: Holt, Rinehart and Winston, 1980.

———. *The Force of Fantasy: Restoring the American Dream.* Carbondale: Southern Illinois University Press, 1985.

Brecht, Bertolt. "The Street Scene: A Basic Model for an Epic Theatre." Trans. John Willett. *The Theory of the Modern Stage: An Introduction to Modern Theatre and Drama.* Ed. Eric Bentley. Rev. ed. New York: Penguin, 1976. 85–96.

Breu, Christopher. *Insistence of the Material: Literature in the Age of Biopolitics.* Minneapolis: University of Minnesota Press, 2014.

Bryer, Jackson R., and Richard A. Davison. *The Art of the American Musical: Conversations with the Creators.* New Brunswick, NJ: Rutgers University Press, 2005.

Buchman, Andrew. "'Growing Pains': Revising *Merrily We Roll Along.*" *The Oxford Handbook of Sondheim Studies.* Ed. Robert Gordon. New York: Oxford University Press, 2014. 117–32.

Butler, Judith. *Bodies That Matter: On the Discursive Limits of "Sex."* New York: Routledge, 1993.

Calderazzo, Diana. "The Most Intense: Why Audiences Respond to John Doyle's *Sweeney Todd* Revival." *Sondheim Review* 14, no. 1 (Fall 2007): 24–26.

Carnelia, Craig. "In Conversation with Stephen Sondheim." *Sondheim Review* 15, no. 1 (Fall 2008): 15–20.

Carter, Tim. *Oklahoma! The Making of an American Musical.* New Haven, CT: Yale University Press, 2007.

Chapin, Ted. *Everything Was Possible: The Birth of the Musical "Follies."* New York: Knopf, 2003.

Works Cited

Chapin, Theodore S. "A Magical, Mystical Miracle." Liner notes. *Do I Hear a Waltz?* Music by Richard Rodgers, lyrics by Stephen Sondheim, book by Arthur Laurents. Perf. Alyson Reed, Anthony Crivello, Carol Lawrence. Cat. no. 302062126, Fynsworth Alley, 2001.

Citron, Stephen. *Sondheim and Lloyd Webber: The New Musical.* New York: Oxford University Press, 2001.

Clarke, James W. *American Assassins: The Darker Side of Politics.* Rev. ed. Princeton, NJ: Princeton University Press, 1992.

Cohen, Patricia. "Same City, New Story." *New York Times,* Arts and Leisure. 15 March 2009, 1, 6.

Davis, Arthur Kyle, Jr. *Folk Songs of Virginia: A Descriptive Index and Classification.* 1949. New York: AMS Press, 1965.

Engel, Lehman. *The American Musical Theater.* New York: Collier, 1975.

———. *Words with Music.* New York: Macmillan, 1972.

Ewen, David. *New Complete Book of the American Musical Theater.* New York: Holt, Rinehart and Winston, 1970.

Feifer, George. *Breaking Open Japan: Commodore Perry, Lord Abe, and American Imperialism in 1853.* New York: Smithsonian/HarperCollins, 2006.

Fisher, James. "Nixon's America and *Follies*: Reappraising a Musical Theater Classic." *Stephen Sondheim: A Casebook.* Ed. Joanne Gordon. New York: Garland, 1997. 69–84.

Florida Architecture of Addison Mizner. 1928. New York: Dover, 1992.

Foucault, Michel. *The History of Sexuality.* Vol. 1. *An Introduction.* 1976. Trans. Robert Hurley. New York: Vintage, 1990.

———. *The Order of Things: An Archeology of the Human Sciences.* 1970. New York: Vintage, 1994.

Fraser, Barbara Means. "Revisiting Greece: The Sondheim Chorus." *Stephen Sondheim: A Casebook.* Ed. Joanne Gordon. New York: Garland, 1997. 223–48.

Gates, Henry Louis, Jr. *The Signifying Monkey: A Theory of Afro-American Literary Criticism.* New York: Oxford University Press, 1988.

Goodhart, Sandor, ed. *Reading Stephen Sondheim: A Collection of Critical Essays.* New York: Garland, 2000.

Gordon, Joanne. *Art Isn't Easy: The Achievement of Stephen Sondheim.* Carbondale: Southern Illinois University Press, 1990.

———, ed. *Stephen Sondheim: A Casebook.* New York: Garland, 1997.

Works Cited

Gordon, Robert, ed. *The Oxford Handbook of Sondheim Studies*. New York: Oxford University Press, 2014.

Gottfried, Martin. *Sondheim*. New York: Harry N. Abrams, 1993.

Greenblatt, Stephen. "Resonance and Wonder." 1990. *Modern Literary Theory: A Reader*. Ed. Philip Rice and Patricia Waugh. 3rd ed. London: Arnold, 1996. 305–24.

Gusdorf, Georges. "Conditions and Limits of Autobiography." Trans. James Olney. *Autobiography: Essays Theoretical and Critical*. Ed. James Olney. Princeton, NJ: Princeton University Press, 1980. 28–48.

Gussow, Mel. "'West Side Story': The Beginnings of Something Great." *New York Times*, 21 October 1990, sec. 2, 5.

Hammerstein, Oscar, II. *Lyrics*. New York. Simon and Schuster, 1949.

Hassan, Ihab. *The Postmodern Turn: Essays in Postmodern Theory and Culture*. Columbus: Ohio State University Press, 1987.

Hirsch, Foster. *Harold Prince and the American Musical Theater*. Cambridge: Cambridge University Press, 1989.

Horowitz, Mark Eden. *Sondheim on Music: Minor Details and Major Decisions*. 2nd ed. Lanham, MD: Scarecrow Press, 2010.

Hutcheon, Linda. *A Poetics of Postmodernism: History, Theory, Fiction*. New York: Routledge, 1988.

Ilson, Carol. *Harold Prince: From "Pajama Game" to "Phantom of the Opera."* Ann Arbor: UMI Research Press, 1989.

"Interview: Harold Prince." *Academy of Achievement*. 22 June 2007. www.achievement.org.

"Interview: Stephen Sondheim." *Academy of Achievement*. 5 July 2005. www.achievement.org.

Jauss, Hans Robert. "Literary History as a Challenge to Literary Theory." *New Literary History* 2 (1967): 11–19.

Johnston, Alva. *The Legendary Mizners*. 1953. New York: Farrar, Straus, and Giroux, 1986.

Jones, Chris. "Sondheim's Journey to 'Bounce.'" *Chicago Tribune*, 22 June 2003, sec. 7, 1, 9.

Jones, John Bush. *Our Musicals, Ourselves: A Social History of the American Musical Theatre*. Hanover, NH: Brandeis University Press, 2003.

Kermode, Frank. *The Sense of an Ending: Studies in the Theory of Fiction*. 1967. New York: Oxford University Press, 2000.

Works Cited

Kierkegaard, Søren. *Papers and Journals: A Selection*. Ed. and trans. Alastair Hannay. London: Penguin, 1996.

Kirle, Bruce. *Unfinished Show Business: Broadway Musicals as Works in Progress*. Carbondale: Southern Illinois University Press, 2005.

Knapp, Raymond. *The American Musical and the Formation of National Identity*. Princeton, NJ: Princeton University Press, 2005.

———. *The American Musical and the Performance of Personal Identity*. Princeton, NJ: Princeton University Press, 2006.

Kotis, Greg, and Mark Hollmann. *Urinetown*. New York: Faber and Faber, 2003.

Lacan, Jacques. *Ecrits: A Selection*. Trans. Alan Sheridan. New York: Norton, 1977.

LaChiusa, Michael John. "The Great Gray Way: Is the Prognosis Negative for the Broadway Musical?" *Opera News*, August 2005, 30–35.

———. *See What I Wanna See*. New York: Dramatists Play Service, 2007.

Laurents, Arthur. *Original Story by Arthur Laurents: A Memoir of Broadway and Hollywood*. New York: Knopf, 2000.

Lee, Gypsy Rose. *Gypsy: A Memoir*. 1957. Berkeley, CA: Frog, 1999.

Lipton, James. "Stephen Sondheim: The Art of the Musical." *The Paris Review Interviews, IV*. Ed. Philip Gourevitch. New York: Picador, 2009. 259–78.

Lomax, Alan. *The Folk Songs of North America in the English Language*. Garden City, NY: Doubleday, 1960.

Lyotard, Jean-François. *The Postmodern Condition: A Report on Knowledge*. Trans. Geoff Bennington and Brian Massumi. Minneapolis: University of Minnesota Press, 1984.

Mack, Robert L. "Introduction." *Sweeney Todd: The Demon Barber of Fleet Street*. Ed. Robert L. Mack. New York: Oxford University Press, 2007. vii–xxviii.

MacKenzie, Gina Masucci. *The Theatre of the Real: Yeats, Beckett, and Sondheim*. Columbus: Ohio State University Press, 2008.

McCaffery, Larry. "An Interview with David Foster Wallace." *Review of Contemporary Fiction* 13, no. 2 (1993): 127–50.

McHale, Brian. *Postmodernist Fiction*. 1987. London: Routledge, 1989.

McLaughlin, Robert L. "Post-Postmodern Discontent: Contemporary Fiction and the Social World." *Fiction's Present: Situating Narrative Innovation*. Ed. R. M. Berry and Jeffrey R. Di Leo. Albany: State University of New York Press, 2008. 101–17.

McMillin, Scott. *The Musical as Drama: A Study of the Principles and Conven-

Works Cited

tions behind Musical Shows from Kern to Sondheim. Princeton, NJ: Princeton University Press, 2006.

Mechler, Mary. "Mrs. Lovett's Meat Pies: Tracing Revenge Tragedy from Renaissance to Modern Day." Joint Conference of the National Popular Culture Association and American Culture Association. New Orleans Marriott, New Orleans. 9 April 2009.

Menton, Allen W. "Maternity, Madness, and Art in the Theater of Stephen Sondheim." *Reading Stephen Sondheim: A Collection of Critical Essays.* Ed. Sandor Goodhart. New York: Garland, 2000. 61–76.

Miller, Scott. *Deconstructing Harold Hill: An Insider's Guide to Musical Theatre.* Portsmouth, NH: Heinemann, 2000.

———. *Strike Up the Band: A New History of the Musical Theatre.* Portsmouth, NH: Heinemann, 2007.

Milner, Andrew. "'Let the Pupil Show the Master': Stephen Sondheim and Oscar Hammerstein II." *Stephen Sondheim: A Casebook.* Ed. Joanne Gordon. New York: Garland, 1997. 153–69.

Mordden, Ethan. *One More Kiss: The Broadway Musical in the 1970s.* New York: Palgrave Macmillan, 2003.

Olson, John. "*Company*—25 Years Later." *Stephen Sondheim: A Casebook.* Ed. Joanne Gordon. New York: Garland, 1997. 47–67.

Parry, Sally E. "Fosca's Female Gaze." *Sondheim Review* 17, no. 4 (Summer 2011): 34–36.

Pascal, Roy. *Design and Truth in Autobiography.* Cambridge, MA: Harvard University Press, 1960.

Pike, John. "Michael Starobin: A New Dimension for *Assassins*." *Show Music* (Fall 1991): 13–17.

Porter, James E. "Intertextuality and the Discourse Community." *Rhetoric Review* 5, no. 1 (1986): 34–47.

Pratt, Mary Louise. *Imperial Eyes: Travel Writing and Transculturation.* London: Routledge, 1992.

Prince, Hal. *Contradictions: Notes on Twenty-Six Years in the Theater.* New York: Dodd, Mead, 1974.

Puccio, Paul. "Enchantment on the Manicured Lawns: The Shakespearean 'Green World' in *A Little Night Music*." *Reading Stephen Sondheim: A Collection of Critical Essays.* Ed. Sandor Goodhart. New York: Garland, 2000. 133–69.

Works Cited

———. "Sondheim 101: *A Little Night Music.*" *Sondheim Review* 15, no. 1 (Fall 2008): 6–9.

———, and Scott F. Stoddart. "'It Takes Two': A Duet on Duets in *Follies* and *Sweeney Todd.*" *Reading Stephen Sondheim: A Collection of Critical Essays.* Ed. Sandor Goodhart. New York: Garland, 2000. 121–29.

Quinn, Carolyn. *Mama Rose's Turn: The True Story of America's Most Notorious Stage Mother.* Jackson: University Press of Mississippi, 2013.

Renza, Louis A. "The Veto of the Imagination: A Theory of Autobiography." *New Literary History* 9 (1977): 1–26.

Rich, Frank. "At Last, 9/11 Has Its Own Musical." Review of *Assassins*, by Stephen Sondheim and John Weidman. *New York Times,* 2 May 2004, sec. 2, 1, 14.

———. "A Cast of Killers Made in America Sings Sondheim." Review of *Assassins*, by Stephen Sondheim and John Weidman. *New York Times,* 28 January 1991, B1, B4.

———. "Conversations with Sondheim." *New York Times Magazine,* 12 March 2000, 38–43, 60–61, 88–89.

Russell, Charles. "The Context of the Concept." *Bucknell Review: Romanticism, Modernism, Postmodernism.* Ed. Harry R. Garvin. Lewisburg, PA: Bucknell University Press, 1980. 181–93.

Secrest, Meryle. *Somewhere for Me: A Biography of Richard Rodgers.* New York: Knopf, 2001.

———. *Stephen Sondheim: A Life.* New York: Knopf, 1998.

Seebohm, Caroline. *Boca Rococo: How Addison Mizner Invented Florida's Gold Coast.* New York: Clarkson Potter, 2001.

Shklovsky, Viktor. *Theory of Prose.* 1929. Trans. Benjamin Sher. Elmwood Park, IL: Dalkey Archive Press, 1991.

Singer, Barry. *Ever After: The Last Years of the Musical Theater and Beyond.* New York: Applause, 2004.

Sondheim, Stephen. *Finishing the Hat: Collected Lyrics (1954–1981) with Attendant Comments, Principles, Heresies, Grudges, Whines and Anecdotes.* New York: Knopf, 2010.

———. "Larger Than Life: Reflections on Melodrama and *Sweeney Todd.*" *Melodrama.* Ed. Daniel Gerould. New York: New York Literary Forum, 1980. 3–14.

———. *Look, I Made a Hat: Collected Lyrics (1981–2011) with Attendant Comments, Amplifications, Dogmas, Harangues, Digressions, Anecdotes and Miscellany.* New York: Knopf, 2011.

Works Cited

——. "Theater Lyrics." *Playwrights, Lyricists, Composers on Theater.* Ed. Otis L. Guernsey Jr. New York: Dodd, Mead, 1974. 61–97.

Stempel, Larry. *Showtime: A History of the Broadway Musical Theater.* New York: Norton, 2010.

Stoddart, S. F. "Visions and Re-Visions: The Postmodern Challenge of *Merrily We Roll Along." Reading Stephen Sondheim: A Collection of Critical Essays.* Ed. Sandor Goodhart. New York: Garland, 2000. 187–98.

Swain, Joseph P. *The Broadway Musical: A Critical and Musical Survey.* 2nd ed. Lanham, MD: Scarecrow Press, 2002.

Swayne, Steve. *How Sondheim Found His Sound.* Ann Arbor: University of Michigan Press, 2005.

Tarchetti, I. U. *Passion.* 1869. Trans. Lawrence Venuti. San Francisco: Mercury House, 1994.

"Tony Awards." *Sondheim Review* 15, no. 2 (Winter 2008): 4.

Tunick, Jonathan. "Introduction." *A Little Night Music.* By Stephen Sondheim and Hugh Wheeler. New York: Applause, 1991. 1–11.

Wallace, David Foster. "*E Unibus Pluram*: Television and U.S. Fiction." *A Supposedly Fun Thing I'll Never Do Again: Essays and Arguments.* Boston: Little, Brown, 1997. 21–82.

Wells, Elizabeth A. *"West Side Story": Cultural Perspectives on an American Musical.* Lanham, MD: Scarecrow Press, 2011.

White, Hayden. *The Content of the Form: Narrative, Discourse, and Historical Representation.* Baltimore: Johns Hopkins University Press, 1987.

Wilk, Max. *OK! The Story of "Oklahoma!"* New York: Applause, 2002.

Woodruff, Paul. *The Necessity of Theater: The Art of Watching and Being Watched.* New York: Oxford University Press, 2008.

Zadan, Craig. *Sondheim & Co.* 2nd ed., updated. New York: Perennial, 1989.

Žižek, Slavoj. *The Plague of Fantasies.* London: Verso, 1997.

PERMISSIONS

Extracts from pp. 25–38, ch. 2, "Sondheim and Postmodernism" by Robert McLaughlin from *The Oxford Handbook of Sondheim Studies*, edited by Robert Gordon (2014), are courtesy of Oxford University Press.

Sections of chapters 3 and 4 were originally published in the *Sondheim Review* and are reprinted here with permission of the editor.

Permissions

ANOTHER HUNDRED PEOPLE
Written by Stephen Sondheim
Used by permission of Herald Square Music, Inc., on behalf of Range Road Music,
Inc., Jerry Leiber Music, Silver Seahorse Music LLC, Rilting Music, Inc., and
Burthen Music Company, Inc.

Another National Anthem
from ASSASSINS
Words and Music by Stephen Sondheim
© 1991 RILTING MUSIC, INC.
All Rights Administered by WB MUSIC CORP.
All Rights Reserved Used by Permission
Reprinted with Permission of Hal Leonard Corporation

Any Moment—Part I
from INTO THE WOODS
Words and Music by Stephen Sondheim
© 1988 RILTING MUSIC, INC.
All Rights Administered by WB MUSIC CORP.
All Rights Reserved Used by Permission
Reprinted with Permission of Hal Leonard Corporation

The Ballad of Booth (Part I)
from ASSASSINS
Words and Music by Stephen Sondheim
© 1991 RILTING MUSIC, INC.
All Rights Administered by WB MUSIC CORP.
All Rights Reserved Used by Permission
Reprinted with Permission of Hal Leonard Corporation

The Ballad of Czolgosz (Part I)
from ASSASSINS
Words and Music by Stephen Sondheim
© 1990 RILTING MUSIC, INC.
All Rights Administered by WB MUSIC CORP.

Permissions

Permissions

BEING ALIVE
Written by Stephen Sondheim
Used by permission of Herald Square Music, Inc., on behalf of Range Road Music,
Inc., Jerry Leiber Music, Silver Seahorse Music LLC, Rilting Music, Inc., and
Burthen Music Company, Inc.

The Blob
from MERRILY WE ROLL ALONG
Words and Music by Stephen Sondheim
© 1981 RILTING MUSIC, INC.
All Rights Administered by WB MUSIC CORP.
All Rights Reserved Used by Permission
Reprinted with Permission of Hal Leonard Corporation

A Bowler Hat
from PACIFIC OVERTURES
Words and Music by Stephen Sondheim
© 1975 (Renewed) RILTING MUSIC, INC.
All Rights Administered by WB MUSIC CORP.
All Rights Reserved Used by Permission
Reprinted with Permission of Hal Leonard Corporation

Children and Art
from SUNDAY IN THE PARK WITH GEORGE
Words and Music by Stephen Sondheim
© 1984 RILTING MUSIC, INC.
All Rights Administered by WB MUSIC CORP.
All Rights Reserved Used by Permission
Reprinted with Permission of Hal Leonard Corporation

Children Will Listen
from INTO THE WOODS
Words and Music by Stephen Sondheim
© 1988 RILTING MUSIC, INC.
All Rights Administered by WB MUSIC CORP.

Permissions

278

Permissions

Leonard Bernstein Music Publishing Company LLC, publisher. Boosey & Hawkes, agent for rental.
International copyright secured.
Reprinted by permission.

Get Out/Go
from ROAD SHOW
Words and Music by Stephen Sondheim
© 2003 RILTING MUSIC, INC.
All Rights Administered by WB MUSIC CORP.
All Rights Reserved Used by Permission
Reprinted with Permission of Hal Leonard Corporation

Giants in the Sky
from INTO THE WOODS
Words and Music by Stephen Sondheim
© 1988 RILTING MUSIC, INC.
All Rights Administered by WB MUSIC CORP.
All Rights Reserved Used by Permission
Reprinted with Permission of Hal Leonard Corporation

God, That's Good!
from SWEENEY TODD
Words and Music by Stephen Sondheim
© 1978 RILTING MUSIC, INC.
All Rights Administered by WB MUSIC CORP.
All Rights Reserved Used by Permission
Reprinted with Permission of Hal Leonard Corporation

Good Thing Going
from MERRILY WE ROLL ALONG
Words and Music by Stephen Sondheim
© 1981 RILTING MUSIC, INC.
All Rights Administered by WB MUSIC CORP.
All Rights Reserved Used by Permission
Reprinted with Permission of Hal Leonard Corporation

Permissions

Happiness
from PASSION
Words and Music by Stephen Sondheim
© 1994 RILTING MUSIC, INC.
All Rights Administered by WB MUSIC CORP.
All Rights Reserved Used by Permission
Reprinted with Permission of Hal Leonard Corporation

HAVE I GOT A GIRL FOR YOU
Written by Stephen Sondheim
Used by permission of Herald Square Music, Inc., on behalf of Range Road Music, Inc., Jerry Leiber Music, Silver Seahorse Music LLC, Rilting Music, Inc., and Burthen Music Company, Inc.

How I Saved Roosevelt
from ASSASSINS
Words and Music by Stephen Sondheim
© 1990 RILTING MUSIC, INC.
All Rights Administered by WB MUSIC CORP.
All Rights Reserved Used by Permission
Reprinted with Permission of Hal Leonard Corporation

Hymn to Dionysos (Reprise)
from THE FROGS
Words and Music by Stephen Sondheim
© 1974 (Renewed) RILTING MUSIC, INC.
All Rights Administered by WB MUSIC CORP.
All Rights Reserved Used by Permission
Reprinted with Permission of Hal Leonard Corporation

IF MOMMA WAS MARRIED (from "Gypsy")
Lyrics by STEPHEN SONDHEIM
Music by JULE STYNE
© 1959 (Renewed) STRATFORD MUSIC CORPORATION and WILLIAMSON MUSIC CO.

Permissions

Words and Music by Stephen Sondheim
© 1984 RILTING MUSIC, INC.
All Rights Administered by WB MUSIC CORP.
All Rights Reserved Used by Permission
Reprinted with Permission of Hal Leonard Corporation

It's in Your Hands Now
from ROAD SHOW
Words and Music by Stephen Sondheim
© 2003 RILTING MUSIC, INC.
All Rights Administered by WB MUSIC CORP.
All Rights Reserved Used by Permission
Reprinted with Permission of Hal Leonard Corporation

It's Only a Play
from THE FROGS
Words and Music by Stephen Sondheim
© 1974 (Renewed) RILTING MUSIC, INC.
All Rights Administered by WB MUSIC CORP.
All Rights Reserved Used by Permission
Reprinted with Permission of Hal Leonard Corporation

I Wish I Could Forget You
from PASSION
Words and Music by Stephen Sondheim
© 1994 RILTING MUSIC, INC.
All Rights Administered by WB MUSIC CORP.
All Rights Reserved Used by Permission
Reprinted with Permission of Hal Leonard Corporation

Jet Song (from *West Side Story*) by Leonard Bernstein and Stephen Sondheim
© 1956, 1957, 1958, 1959 by Amberson Holdings LLC and Stephen Sondheim.
Copyright renewed.
Leonard Bernstein Music Publishing Company LLC, publisher. Boosey &
Hawkes, agent for rental.

Permissions

Johanna
from SWEENEY TODD
Words and Music by Stephen Sondheim
© 1978 RILTING MUSIC, INC.
All Rights Administered by WB MUSIC CORP.
All Rights Reserved Used by Permission
Reprinted with Permission of Hal Leonard Corporation

Johanna (Judge's version)
from SWEENEY TODD
Words and Music by Stephen Sondheim
© 1978 RILTING MUSIC, INC.
All Rights Administered by WB MUSIC CORP.
All Rights Reserved Used by Permission
Reprinted with Permission of Hal Leonard Corporation

Just Another Love Story
from PASSION
Words and Music by Stephen Sondheim
© 1994 RILTING MUSIC, INC.
All Rights Administered by WB MUSIC CORP.
All Rights Reserved Used by Permission
Reprinted with Permission of Hal Leonard Corporation

Kiss Me
from SWEENEY TODD
Words and Music by Stephen Sondheim
© 1978 RILTING MUSIC, INC.
All Rights Administered by WB MUSIC CORP.
All Rights Reserved Used by Permission
Reprinted with Permission of Hal Leonard Corporation

Permissions

Permissions

THE STORY OF LUCY AND JESSIE
Written by Stephen Sondheim
Used by permission of Herald Square Music, Inc., on behalf of Range Road Music, Inc., Jerry Leiber Music, Silver Seahorse Music LLC, Rilting Music, Inc., and Burthen Music Company, Inc.

Sunday
from SUNDAY IN THE PARK WITH GEORGE
Words and Music by Stephen Sondheim
© 1984 RILTING MUSIC, INC.
All Rights Administered by WB MUSIC CORP.
All Rights Reserved Used by Permission
Reprinted with Permission of Hal Leonard Corporation

That Was a Year
from ROAD SHOW
Words and Music by Stephen Sondheim
© 2009 RILTING MUSIC, INC.
All Rights Administered by WB MUSIC CORP.
All Rights Reserved Used by Permission
Reprinted with Permission of Hal Leonard Corporation

THERE WON'T BE TRUMPETS (from "Anyone Can Whistle")
Words and Music by STEPHEN SONDHEIM
© 1964 (Renewed) BURTHEN MUSIC COMPANY, INC.
All Rights Administered by CHAPPELL & CO., INC.
All Rights Reserved

Tonight (from *West Side Story*) by Leonard Bernstein and Stephen Sondheim
© 1956, 1957, 1958, 1959 by Amberson Holdings LLC and Stephen Sondheim.
Copyright renewed.
Leonard Bernstein Music Publishing Company LLC, publisher. Boosey & Hawkes, agent for rental.
International copyright secured.
Reprinted by permission.

Permissions

INDEX

Index

"Fear No More," 214

Feifer, George, 255n21

Fiddler on the Roof, viii, 18, 65

Field, Ron, 136

Fields, Dorothy, 14

Fields, Herbert, 14

"Final Instructions to the Audience,"
218–19

Finian's Rainbow, 14

"Finishing the Hat," 162, 164

Fisher, James, 252n2

"Flashback," 203–5

Floyd Collins, 237–38

Follies, 3–4, 22, 50, 79–100, 101, 104,
105, 107, 109, 112, 120, 138, 139,
146, 148, 149, 151, 165, 184, 192, 212,
220, 236, 251n24, 252n2, 253n4,
254n9

Ford, Gerald, 190, 191

Fosse, 7

Foster, Jodie, 190

Foucault, Michel, 30–31, 66, 85, 148,
212, 245n1, 250n6, 251n28

Fowler, Beth, 257n51

"Franklin Shepard, Inc.," 141, 145

Frogs, The, 213–19, 220, 237,
261nn38–39

"Frogs, The," 215

Fromme, "Squeaky," 191, 194, 197

Front Porch in Flatbush, 17

Fuller, Larry, 136

Funny Girl, 62

*Funny Thing Happened on the Way to
the Forum, A,* 18, 50–52, 65, 78, 79,
213, 250n19, 257n54

Furth, George, ix; *Company,* 65,
67–78; *Merrily We Roll Along,*
134–46

"Game, The," 225

"Garden Sequence," 203

Garfield, James, 190, 194

Gates, Henry Louis, Jr., 31

"Gee, Officer Krupke," 31, 32, 33, 36

Gelbart, Larry, ix, 18, 50–52, 250n20

George M!, 15

George White's Scandals, 7

Gershwin, George, 10

Gershwin, Ira, 10

"Get Out," 226

"Giants in the Sky," 170, 172, 176

Gilbert and Sullivan, 119

Godspell, 230

"God, That's Good!," 129–30

"God-Why-Don't-You-Love-Me Blues,
The," 90, 98

Goldman, Emma, 194

Goldman, James, ix, 3, 22, 80, 134,
252n2; *Follies,* 79–100, 252n2

"Good Thing Going," 142–43, 144

Gordon, Joanne, xi, 252n34, 254n18

Gottfried, Martin, 248n36, 251n24

Great Depression, 23, 46, 97, 230, 231

"Green Finch and Linnet Bird," 126

Greenblatt, Stephen, 258n7

Grey Gardens, 235–36

Griffin, Gary, 18

Grind, 230

"Growing Up," 144–45

Guiteau, Charles, 190, 191, 192, 194,
197, 199

"Gun Song," 190, 192

Gusdorf, Georges, 253n5, 254n6

Gypsy, 18, 41–50, 65, 78, 88, 90, 96, 101,
185, 220, 222, 223

Hair, 16, 248n33

Hallelujah, Baby!, 231, 247n30

Hamilton, 235

Hammerstein, Oscar, II, x, 10–14, 17,
29, 68, 134–35, 247n27, 257nn56–57

Index

CPSIA information can be obtained
at www.ICGtesting.com
Printed in the USA
BVHW030236081221
623496BV00006B/380

9